FROM
CONCEPT TO
COMMERCIALIZATION

A STRATEGIC APPROACH
FOR BRINGING EVERYDAY
IDEAS TO MARKET

DICK J. LIOU
WWW.TINKERMINDS.COM

ISBN: 978-1-4662-1610-5
ISBN-10:   1466216107

Printed in the United States of America

Disclaimer

This publication is designed to provide an understanding of the process behind taking a concept to commercialization. It in no way guarantees any financial success or profitability.

While websites have been referenced as accurately as possible, the author cannot assume any responsibility for errors, or for changes that occur after the publication. Likewise the author has no control over the web contents of any third-party mentioned in this publication and cannot assume any responsibility for them thereof.

An estimated 1 out of 30,000,000 ideas are likely to become commercially profitable.

According to the SBA, there were 627,200 new businesses, 595,600 business closures, and 43,546 bankruptcies in 2008.

Seven out of 10 new employer firms survive at least two years, and about half survive five years.

How will **YOU** bring your idea to market successfully?

Acknowledgements

I would like to express my deepest gratitude to:

My wife, whose selfless love and acts made everything possible to achieve.

My children, who inspired the AeroBloks invention and grew with us every step of the way, for their love, understanding, and for being an integral part of the entire journey.

Our parents, for their incredible support in everyway possible.

Our family members (especially **Rick**, **Wei and Tim**), for being a part of the early process that helped shape the company.

Additionally, to our dear friends who have made a tremendous difference in the editing of this book and/or in our lives during the AeroBloks venture.

Sal Di Cecca, my wise friend whose constant encouragement and insights were instrumental in shaping the organization and writing style of this book.

Steve Ng, whose excellent executive coaching skills and acute business insights have challenged me to produce a more practical suite of intellectual products than I could have done so by myself.

Emily Chuo, for helping me with final reviews of this book and providing a fresh perspective.

The Mitchell family (especially Jen and Jack), for their friendship, help, and being the stars of our product showcases.

Bill Bradlee, for being a great mentor and counselor, and for his enduring friendship before, during, and after the venture.

Rosemarie Woods, for being a wonderful friend who provided wisdom and tremendous help in launching the business venture.

Dr. Keith Asarkof, DDS, not only for volunteering to be our first customer (a daring act) but also for his generosity, support, and encouragement.

Dr. Bill Trevens, DC, for his ongoing encouragement and healing hands that provided us with good health to tackle the gruesome workload.

CONTENTS

FROM
CONCEPT TO
COMMERCIALIZATION

Introduction

Anyone who has ever flirted with bringing an idea to market eventually arrives at the same question… how?

It is a well known fact that the odds of success are astronomically stacked against new ventures. There are various estimates on the odds of turning an everyday idea into a profitable venture. One viable estimate puts it at about 1 in 30 million[1].

If you are starting out with just an idea, what will it take to actually become successful?

A STRATEGIC APPROACH

Taking a leisurely walk in the park should be spontaneous and most likely as a result of a free-flowing idea. Taking a man to the moon for a walk, on the other hand, took a systematic and disciplined approach based on strategic planning. No one in their right mind would nonchalantly jump into a highly risky situation without considering all the critical factors and then some more. Why then do so many people risk their hard-earned money, time, career, and possibly future quality of life without taking a strategic approach?

Individual circumstances differ, but I believe in general that it is a lethal combination of naïveté and the lack of information that is the main culprit. Missing information from how to start to what it takes, and what it's like to go through the purest form of entrepreneurialship are just some of the reasons.

People who choose to bring their ideas to market might discover that there is not a single source of answers but an array of highly disorganized information out there. This is because commercializing an idea is a very involved, complex, and challenging task that few people have mastered.

The key to optimizing your chances of success lies largely in your ability to stay realistic, focused, and disciplined. Such traits are necessary to tackle the myriad of challenges of an entrepreneurial commercialization path. The right step to begin

---

[1] See calculation in Chapter 1 – Commercial Viability Overview… Is Your Concept a Good Investment?

with is business strategy formulation. It is a subject I hold a deep reverence for because of its impacts on the odds of business survival and success. The business strategy discipline not only deserves but requires a separate volume to describe in detail and to do it justice. For this reason I will only touch lightly upon the essence of the strategic approach as it relates to the concept commercialization process.

If this sounds too intimidating, you should not be concerned. Each one of us already takes on some degree of strategic approach in various aspects of our lives. For example, planning an extended vacation already involves thinking ahead and making preparations with details so we can reap the experience that we would like to have.

In its bare essence, the strategic formulation approach begins with envisioning the end state, or goal, that you have for an idea. The goal is divided into components that can be tackled separately or concurrently. If you had envisioned building your dream house, for instance, such a vision would have been broken down into actionable items such as excavation, landscaping, frame building, interior design, and HVAC system installation, etc.

The action items are then grouped by functions and then arranged and prioritized according to a logical and practical sequence. Within the same example, you would excavate the grounds for a foundation and landscaping concurrently but lay the carpets only after you have built interior walls.

Armed with the details of what needs to be done, when, and how, your next step would be to develop contingency plans that ask and answer the various what-if scenarios. In the concept commercialization process this would include competitive analysis, marketing and industry analysis scenarios, for example.

How you then implement will naturally be based on choices made from all this groundwork. The decision at this point becomes strategic.

Finally, as the last component of a strategic approach, any project one takes on will require continuous monitoring and course adjustments. This is no different than what went on behind the scenes of the first rocket launch to the moon. Mission control had to have constant monitoring and course adjustments to ensure that the goal of putting a man on the moon would be realized.

Transforming a mere idea into a profitable venture can be just as complicated and requires just as much strategic thinking behind the scenes. This might explain the astronomical rates of failure experienced by the average aspiring entrepreneur or inventor who does not take on such disciplined approach.

As you can see the process can be complicated and not as light-hearted as some other books on bringing an idea to market would suggest. There will be several components of this approach we will identify and dissect to help you get on the right track and stay on it.

INVENTIONS, IDEAS & COMMERCIALIZATION

For clarifications, an everyday idea can be a household product invention (e.g. can opener), a unique service-based business model (e.g. Zipcar®), or a technology breakthrough/scientific discovery (e.g. solar cell/genetic mapping) that could be deployed as a product or a service.

Regardless of the type of classification, all of them share at least two commonalities. First, they are all created by people for the benefit of people. Second, if they are to be publicly available, as opposed to being a springboard for further research and development, then they must go through the commercialization process.

The first characteristic dictates that an understanding of human behavior and motivation factors are necessary. The second requires an understanding of business creation and management knowledge, process, and tools. Together they will help generate profit.

Therefore an understanding of the concept to commercialization process is a fundamental step in continued innovation of all sorts. It is a required knowledge for anyone involved in the entrepreneurial movement intended to create a better economy, more direct and indirect commercial activities and jobs, and hopes for a better future for everyone.

HOW MY BACKGROUND CONTRIBUTES TO THIS WRITING

Several years ago I came up with what I thought was a great idea that met a universal need of parents with young kids. The idea was to create a lifesize construction play system that could be easily built, recombined, and stored all without hassle. After some preliminary research I decided to pursue the idea further. We named it AeroBloks.

I set up Tinker Minds Inc. to manufacture and market the AeroBloks product lines. Both the concept and the company were created from scratch; everything originated from a simple idea and evolved into complete product lines and a fully operational business infrastructure respectively. There were lessons as well as many steps and missteps learned along the way. Some of these will be used as examples throughout the book to help illustrate the various business guidelines.

In time I was able to distribute the AeroBloks product lines domestically via top tier catalogs, online, and brick & mortar resellers in the educational, occupational therapy, and specialty toy segments. Likewise I placed AeroBloks with distributors in Canada and UK, which led to sales in other countries as far as New Zealand. The market reception for this product was overwhelmingly positive at its debut tradeshow. I collected over four inches of business cards from distributors and resellers worldwide wanting to do business with us from that tradeshow alone.

Our team built every aspect of our business infrastructure from scratch, bootstrapping style. At one point the total revenue potential was near $6M for this children's inflatable construction play system. All this achievement masked the tremendous amount of work behind the scenes fighting against brutal rising costs. At every phase of the business the combined cost of goods rose astronomically. By the time I made the business decision to close the operation the cost had increased by 456%[2]. This was a "hell of a ride" from a concept to commercialization perspective. Yet, looking back, it was an experience that trumped anything else we've done and taught us lessons and wisdom that no money can buy.

My earlier professional experiences included launching and running a small service-based business from scratch. I also played a pivotal role in a highly profitable startup group within a $1B corporation. Collectively I know enough to share the following insights with you.

When it comes to bringing your newfound idea to market…

1. There is a fine line between dreams & nightmares, and between risk taking & recklessness. Crossing that line may not always be intentional; sometimes it happens by accident or by forces beyond one's control.

2. Coming up with an idea is relatively easy compared to figuring out how to bring it to market and make money from it.

3. Not all ideas are worth pursuing. You need to very carefully evaluate an idea's profit potential before taking concerted efforts.

4. In this information age, the challenge is in the organization of information, not the acquisition of information, which will play a pivotal role in your venture.

5. No matter how smart you are or how good your idea is, you will need other people.

6. An experienced voice is like a compass; knowledge of the landscape is like a map. You need both to navigate the hidden dangers. If you don't have both, you need at least one and a lot of persistence, not to mention luck.

---

[2] To view the AeroBloks venture's developmental history please visit www.tinkerminds.com

THE PURPOSE OF THIS BOOK

It takes an evolutionary process to transform a pure concept to a marketable physical product or service. Evolution takes time, there's simply no argument there. A process requires many steps. Each step involves a sequence of activities that are interdependently linked to another. When multiple processes are combined they form a system that delivers the desired function predictably.

Examples of systems surround us. A watch is a system of inter-related gears, springs, and display mechanism. A car is a system of components and their parts. The human body is the most intricate system that is made up of subsystems like circulatory, respiratory, digestive, and so on. Each subsystem performs a particular function. Altogether they produce the overall functions of telling time, providing transportation, and maintaining life respectively.

In a nutshell the purpose of this book is to create a concept to commercialization (C2C) system to help an independent inventor or aspiring entrepreneur beat the odds when the right idea comes along. The system is necessarily formed strategically from the highest level to the minutest details.

How you go about starting the process matters tremendously. This book does not tell you everything you need to know on the subject. You still need to acquire specific information on any topic you need more information on separately. Meanwhile you should use the tools here to help you organize your thoughts and your plan of attack.

Over the recent years the amount of written work on entrepreneurialship has exploded. This is both good and bad news. It has become easier to learn from others' experiences and at the same time be drowned in regurgitated material and background noise. The Internet is a goldmine for information. Business management text books offer tools and techniques. Invention management publications provide coverage on a wide array of topics. Most of these are useful information but they leave the serious aspiring entrepreneur at a loss on exactly how to proceed. Something is amiss and that's what I intend to fill with this book.

I have designed the book to be a primarily strategic process-driven tool. The business knowledge contained here is nothing new; a first year MBA student would easily recognize some of the business subjects and tools. Some of my insights may coincide with those derived by someone else who has gone through similar in-the-trench experiences and drew the same conclusions. However the system that lays out the entire scope, creates a step-by-step blueprint, generates an evaluation list, spawns questions and answers to them, leads to a substantiated Go/No Go decision, and covers the company building and business growing concerns process is entirely original and critically needed by anyone thinking about bringing a product or service to market.

I should mention that this book is not for the faint of heart, the impatient, the channel-surfers among us, or those looking to read for entertainment. The subjects dive deeply into the processes and any underlying rationale so that you will manage the tools with expertise and your venture with confidence.

By reading this book you will benefit from the lessons I learned including:

- ◈ What I did right in retrospect
- ◈ How to avoid some common mistakes
- ◈ What I wish I knew when I first started
- ◈ What works really well and can be repeated for other products
- ◈ How to systematically tackle the process of commercializing an invention

COMPONENTS OF THE C2C SYSTEM

This concept to commercialization (C2C) system works well regardless of whether a concept is intended for a product invention, a product-based company, a service company, or a product-based service company.

The system contains five components which are interlinked within a common go-to-market strategy. They are:

1. **Players** – Understanding the arena in which your invention or venture will operate within is of the utmost importance. Knowing who is involved, when, where, and why will help you navigate your way around.

2. **Blueprint** – Lays out a phased, step-by-step approach that includes conceptual, marketing, operational, and financial management activities needed from beginning to profitability.

3. **Evaluation Questions** – Provide a checklist designed to weed out unprofitable ideas early on and enhance the quality of the ideas that pass the stringent criteria.

4. **Business Insights** – Lessons learned from the trenches that mostly identify hidden truths often missing from business text books. They correspond to the evaluation questions.

5. **Framework** – A tracking and monitoring tool for managing various aspects of a business creation process over time.

If you look closely you will see the strategic approach pattern behind the formation of each subcomponent of the C2C system. These components are like sections of a puzzle while the end vision is like a completed image. Action items within the components are like the puzzle pieces that integrate into a whole. Together this system allows you to take a strategic approach to beating the astronomical odds even as the components themselves have been formed using the same approach.

HOW THIS BOOK IS ORGANIZED

To help you relate to the knowledge and insights discussed in this book I will provide practical examples based on a real life product commercialization experience as well as a simulated concept development process. You will be able to appreciate the importance of certain marketing principles with illustrated flowcharts, tables, and figures. I will also provide numerical examples to explain the financial aspects in an easy to understand style.

The materials will be covered in five major parts. Additional supporting materials are contained mostly in the appendix. A listing of entrepreneurial resources is also available at the end of the book. By the time you finished reading this book and completed the evaluation exercise of a concept you will be leaps and bounds ahead of the typical inventor or aspiring entrepreneur in your understanding and readiness to take on this incredible risky yet potentially rewarding path.

The five parts are:

1. **Part One** explores typical situations that an inventor or entrepreneur might experience. It has high level questions and practical evaluation criteria that someone with a new concept will find familiar and useful (**Chapter 1**).

2. **Part Two** examines the fundamental building blocks, or the foundations of a commercialization infrastructure. Specifically it asks and answers the two most important questions, namely who's involved and what's involved. The "who's involved?" question is answered in the ecosystem (**Chapter 2**) while the "what's involved?" is described in the blueprint building process (**Chapter 3**).

3. **Part Three** digs into the nuts and bolts of a concept's commercialization viability evaluation. It includes detailed discussions on the preparation work (**Chapter 4**), the marketing and sales aspects (**Chapter 5**), the business operational aspects (**Chapter 6**), and finally the financial aspects (**Chapter 7**). Each of these chapters provides business insights that correspond to the 120 evaluation questions listed in **Appendix 4**.

4. **Part Four** takes a commanding view of the entire system by introducing a progress monitoring framework (**Chapter 8**) and ten of the most important business insights to apply in the commercialization process (**Chapter 9**).

5. **Part Five** refocuses the lens back on the inventor or aspiring entrepreneur. It asks self-introspection questions designed to help with evaluating different options of product or idea commercialization (**Chapter 10**).

At the end of each chapter is also a list of action items that an aspiring entrepreneur should take. These questions help with recapturing the vast amount of information contained within the book and turn them into actionable tasks.

WHO THIS BOOK IS WRITTEN FOR

You will find this book very useful if you are a(n):

- Aspiring entrepreneur who is intending on building a product or service business and needs to understand the business creation process.

- Inventor who is serious about commercializing an invention by licensing, but has no idea how a concept becomes a product.

- Entrepreneurial program student looking for real life insights not covered by conventional text books or startup books.

- Professor of entrepreneurial studies looking to supplement your curriculum with a first person account of an entrepreneurial experience.

- University researcher contemplating on how to commercialize your scientific discovery or technological breakthrough.

- New product introduction professional looking to supplement your current evaluation system.

This book is ideally read by someone who has some familiarity with business management concepts, particularly in the marketing and sales arenas. Regardless, the content can be understood by a non-business person as well. Although in this case I would recommend that a business person gets involved in the commercialization assessment process to get the most out of this book.

Although I use mostly material from a consumer product to illustrate, the business principles are universally applicable to most new ventures. The fact is that more similarities than differences exist in the processes behind product, product-based service, or purely service-based ventures than most people realize.

If you are a first time entrepreneur with a product invention you will be able to emulate more from the examples. If you are an aspiring entrepreneur dwelling on a service business model you will similarly find the thought process and the elements used to build a company just as relevant.

REAL LIFE IMPLICATIONS

Beyond describing the steps and the logical sequence that tie the processes together, this writing reveals something that often only experience can divulge; namely the interrelatedness of every step to one another in a business, no matter what size the business entity is.

For instance, let's say you need to come up with a retail package design. This task seems to be something that can be resolved easily by hiring an expert designer. Not so. You will need to incorporate cost, function, positioning, compliance, liability, and pricing considerations onto the design. Any change in scope in a subcomponent will invariably propagate across the entire project. A change in the number of retail packages that can fit inside a master carton will impact its allocated cost, and possibly force price changes, thereby affecting the positioning strategy and so on.

It takes years of business experiences to understand how this entire system is put together and which levers pull which other ones. It also takes actual field experiences to master the management of these seemingly unrelated business issues. In some ways this hidden essence is as significant as, if not more than, the visible processes, tables, and figures.

The real value of this book boils down to five points:

1. It brings **clarity** to a subject that is highly complex and often muddled with noises and confusions from too much information.

2. It presents a **system** for tackling a highly complex and often convoluted process that few people have mastered.

3. It gives you **efficiency** in eliminating ideas with a low probability of success early on and enables you to be more confident of the ones you decide to pursue further.

4. It provides hard-earned business **insights** from the trenches dispersed across all the pages so you can avoid the same mistakes.

5. It highlights the fact that every aspect of the commercialization and business venturing process is intimately **linked** with the others. No decisions should be made in a vacuum but that a central strategy spawns separate strategies to ensure a coherent business operation.

If there is one thing that I consistently learned, it is that knowledge is power. Lack of knowledge is a weakness; it is one that could prove costly in many ways.

My intent for this intellectual product is to arm you with such knowledge so you will make informed decisions instead of being forced into a seat-of-the-pants reactionary mode. My "tuition bill" for such knowledge exceeded several hundred thousand dollars. Let's hope yours does not.

The figure on the following page provides an overview of the entire C2C system whose components will be described in detail in the rest of the book.

Starting with an idea, you will be able to take a step-wise approach using the C2C blueprint as a guide. You will be able to evaluate your concept in great depth using the evaluation questionnaire and the corresponding business insights. You will also be able to monitor and manage your commercialization efforts with a progression monitoring framework to keep you on track and rooted in reality. Finally you will be able to make a rational, well substantiated decision as to whether or not you should pursue a particular concept.

Bringing an Idea to Market...
The BIG Picture

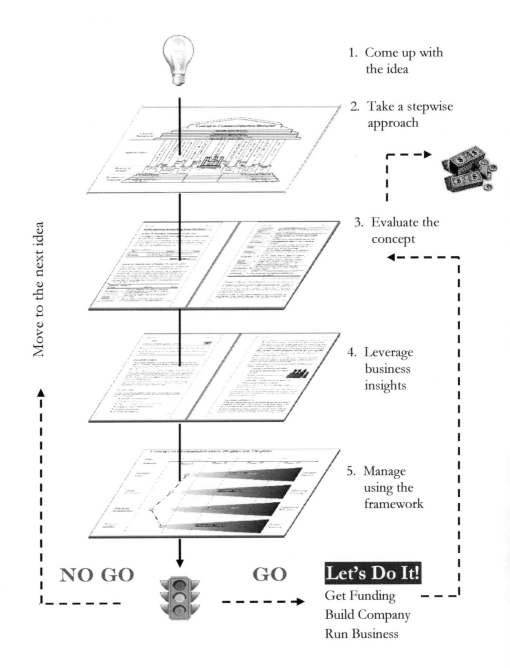

1. Come up with the idea

2. Take a stepwise approach

3. Evaluate the concept

4. Leverage business insights

5. Manage using the framework

Move to the next idea

NO GO   GO   **Let's Do It!**

Get Funding
Build Company
Run Business

Part I

BEATING THE ODDS!

"The odds of hitting your target go up dramatically when you aim at it."

Mal Pancoast

Chapter 1

Commercial Viability Overview... Is Your Concept a Good Investment?

99.8% fail. Only 3,000 patents out of 1.5 million patents are commercially viable.

"In truth, odds are stacked astronomically against inventors, and no marketing outfit can change them. There are around 1.5 million patents in effect and in force in this country, and of those, maybe 3,000 are commercially viable."

Richard Maulsby, director of the Office of Public Affairs for the U.S. Patent & Trademark Office[3]

Do you think your idea can beat the odds? How will you know?

To answer this "loaded" question diligently, we will need to cover an extensive number of topics. They will help identify things you need to consider with any idea that you think has commercial applications. They serve as a precursor to the detailed explorations in Chapters 4 through 7, including references to the evaluation questionnaire in Appendix 4.

The topics are:

1. **The euphoric moment**

2. **The odds of success**

---

[3] Invention Statistics | Invention Data http://www.inventionstatistics.com/Innovation_Risk_Taking_Inventors.html

3. **Idea vs. concept vs. innovation**

4. **What you need to realize about your first invention**

5. **Is it for you or your pocket book?**

6. **What 3-headed superhero is needed?**

7. **What does concept evaluation involve?**

8. **I have an idea [that I rejected]**

9. **Attributes: the good, the bad, and the ugly**

10. **Why all the fuss?**

11. **Concept evaluation vs. commercial viability assessment**

12. **Organization of the commercial viability assessment chapters**

1.1 THE EUPHORIC MOMENT

Even though I continue to experience it, each time the rush of adrenaline and the possibilities can make my heart pound faster and faster. I'm referring to the feeling you get at the moment when you realize that you have come up with an absolutely fantastic product idea or a business idea that is so universally applicable and exciting that you just know will be a huge hit and make you millions of dollars. If you are reading this book chances are you've also experienced it.

So what do you do when you have one of these "aha!" moments? Does anything here sound familiar?

I have a great idea!

How do I protect my creation?

Will it make money?

Should I take the plunge?

Does it already exist?

Where do I start selling my product?

What do others think?

What is my marketing strategy?

How do I make a prototype?

Who can make a functional prototype?

How do I find a manufacturer?

How do I become profitable?

Who can I pitch the plan to?

After I get the funding, what's the next step?

What do I need to make it happen?

What do I start building first?

How do I build the right team?

What marketing activities do I do?

Is there an example of a product idea that got commercialized?

What does the entrepreneurial path look like at a high level?

By now you may have spotted the spastic firing of questions in all directions when in fact there is a natural order that can be applied to them.

Starting is hard not because the tasks are necessarily difficult but because there are so many ways to reach the goal, making the entire project confusing. There is, however, a process with which an aspiring entrepreneur can take a simple idea, walk it through a complex system, and yet proceed in a simple and logical manner. Obviously there is more than one path to the treasure hunt. What is noteworthy is that the sequence of activities suggested in this commercialization system has been designed to achieve the results both efficiently and effectively.

1.2 THE ODDS OF SUCCESS… ARE YOU PLAYING THE LOTTERY?

For every "great idea" you come up with, there are two questions you need to spend some time thinking about:

1. **What do I do to make my new product or service profitable?**

2. **How can I be sure if my idea is a good one worthy of investment?**

If you were to take what seems like a natural step and begin working on "*what to do*" to make your idea profitable as your first order of business, you may have just made a fatal error.

There is a huge difference between the two questions. One asks whether something can become profitable and the other assumes profitability and proceeds to make it happen.

A quick online search using terms similar to "statistics on ideas commercialized" will yield all sorts of data on the likelihood of an idea getting patented and becoming commercialized. There isn't a definitive number per se, but in general most ideas don't get patented. Of the patents granted, only 0.2% become commercialized and make money for their inventors. Getting to market is one thing, but becoming profitable on a sustained basis is yet entirely a different story. Again the numbers stagger, but the general finding is approximately 95% of new businesses also fail within 5 years.

Let us do a little arithmetic using common assumptions[4]:

1 in 3000 ideas become a patentable product

3000 out of 1.5 million patents issued are commercially viable

5% of commercialized products survive beyond 5 years to become profitable

$$\frac{1 \text{ patent}}{3000 \text{ ideas}} \quad X \quad \frac{3000 \text{ commercialized}}{1.5M \text{ patents}} \quad X \quad \frac{5 \text{ profitable}}{100 \text{ commercialized}} \quad = \quad \frac{15,000 \text{ profitable}}{450,000,000,000 \text{ ideas}}$$

That's **3.33 out of 100 million** ideas become profitable. Or put it another way, 1 out of 30 million ideas becomes commercially profitable. Does this feel like playing a slot machine to you?

The number seems incredible and astronomical to be real. Yet statistics generally don't lie. What is important to recognize is that ideas abound, but a winner is extremely rare. Our culture emphasizes on the winner and so we hear success stories but don't hear the failures that surround them as often. Any experienced entrepreneur will attest that even the best idea in the world is not a guarantee without meticulous planning and execution, and requires more than a dash of good luck to becoming profitable.

What this means in practicality is that even though you should focus on the end goal of profitability, your primary objective should be to kill any unsound idea as early as possible. Because when you do this, you actually get to the winning idea much sooner.

Behind each idea is a person with hopes and dreams; one who truly believes his or her concept has the potential to make it big. It can be heart-breaking at times to see someone getting the thumbs down after all the work he or she has done but I believe the greater sin is not to prevent a bad idea from moving forward. Truth can feel devastating in the short term but falsehood can mislead a person to financial ruins that last a very long time.

---

[4] Invention Statistics | Invention Data http://www.inventionstatistics.com/Innovation_Risk_Taking_Inventors.html

1.3 IDEA VS. CONCEPT VS. INNOVATION

To fully appreciate the purpose of commercial viability assessment, it is necessary to understand how a product or service comes to be.

An **idea** begins as a thought. Thoughts are fleeting; they come and go as quickly as the next moment in time. But ideas are those thoughts that linger on and get refined because they serve a purpose. An exciting idea is a thought greatly amplified to capture one's imagination and attention. But in the end, that's all there is to it. If not followed through, eventually it dissipates just like any other thought. Hence many people will tell you that ideas are worthless by themselves.

This is where a **concept** comes in. Concepts are ideas further refined. To conceptualize something is to visualize its physical manifestation of an otherwise mass-less thought. A concept is of much more value simply because it contains much more substance than a mere idea. A concept can be described, analyzed, pondered, modified, and eventually represented by some modeling. Yet a concept is not truly physical in the sense that it exists for all to see and use as with things in the physical world.

An **innovation or invention**, on the other hand, is a concept that takes on much more physical presence and meaningful objective. To innovate typically means to come up with better, newer, improved versions of the existing. To invent means creating something unique that was previously non-existing even if the process involved improving something existing. The two terminologies are different but intersect and are often used interchangeably in our daily lives.

In its essence, an invention is part of an innovative process which contains many steps. Both an invention and an innovation need modeling to help illustrate the difference from the "old" and implications of the "new." They represent when an idea has evolved to a stage where commercial viability assessments can be most accurate. Yet, arriving at this stage costs much time and money. The concept evaluation process contained in this book has been designed primarily for assessing the profitability potential of an invention. Nevertheless the spirit of the questions is easily transferrable to evaluating innovative processes such as those that spawn new business services.

1.4 WHAT YOU NEED TO REALIZE ABOUT YOUR FIRST INVENTION

Most newbie inventors tend to begin a conversation with an expression that essentially says "I've got the world's biggest secret, and I'm going to be very successful."

It is both cute and sad to see this again and again. It is cute for the innocence that is typically seen in a child with a secret and excitement; sad because the innocence will eventually be replaced with (most times) failure or a weathered look.

The biggest worry they have is someone else stealing their "secret" and so their primary concern is how to patent their invention, as if the very act will ensure their success. Very wrong indeed. The right way to start on the path of evaluation is by <u>describing</u> <u>what</u> <u>problems</u> <u>they</u> <u>are</u> <u>trying</u> <u>to</u> <u>solve</u> as specifically as possible.

For instance, putting in a new mailbox post requires a lot of work. It is both tedious and expensive. The conventional solution is to dig a big hole, pour concrete, mix with gravel and water, set the post, and wait for it to dry. There is yet another issue; the newly set post could also be accidentally damaged by cars backing up or by teenagers cruising at night and swinging bats against mailboxes for fun.

So the problem statement actually contains two parts. Solving one is good, solving both is superior.

As it turns out, someone came up with a mounting bracket that allows for the mounting of a standard 4" x 4" post by pounding the sharp end of the bracket into the ground. The post is then screwed onto the mounting bracket. This solves the first problem nicely.

To solve the second problem, one solution is to make a post flexible by having a spring at its base. This is what I have installed at my house for a little over 15 years, which probably saved my mailbox from mischievous teens looking for fun without any regard for others' properties. My neighbors' mailboxes did not fare as well over the years.

I have not seen a combination of the two solutions for mailbox installation yet, but it would be a superior product if sold at similar prices to existing post-mounting methods.

As for protecting your solution, you should keep in mind that after the problem is clearly stated, and before a novel solution is described, a nondisclosure agreement should be signed so as to protect your idea from being stolen. The truth is, most people are not in discussions to steal ideas. That's because the amount of work and investment to transform the idea into reality is not easy, and risking legal disputes is not worth it. The fear that most first-time inventors (and entrepreneurs alike) have with their precious ideas getting stolen from a conversation is mostly understandable but unfounded. Most idea thefts happen at tradeshows where a working prototype has been developed and the kinks have been worked out.

The next question you need to ask is whether the problem you're solving is yours alone or everyone else's problem. In so many words, what is the potential size of the market and sales revenue?

Mailbox installation is a fairly common problem so the market size can be considerable. Mounting a wind chime between two trees you have in the backyard in a particular configuration, for instance, is not a common problem, regardless of how brilliant your solution is.

Once you identify the specific problems, created a solution for it, and determined whether it's worthy to commercialize (market size), the next question is how the product will get to the store shelf. Aside from the obvious manufacturing process, who will then distribute, promote, and place a product in a visible retail space (think local hardware store or national chains such as Walmart)? This is perhaps the most crucial of all questions. After all, if you solved the world's hunger problem but no one knows about it, you haven't really solved anything.

Financial questions naturally rise, and the retail price must be comparable to existing similar products or be reasonable and at par with value or customer expectations. What cost level will then allow you to sell at these price ranges and still net you a healthy profit margin and income?

It is only beyond exploring these initial questions and with satisfactory answers that you should then move forward to exploring the other aspects of commercializing your invention.

1.5 IS IT FOR YOU OR YOUR POCKET BOOK?

What makes a good commercializable product or service? Or, to be more specific, what is the difference between a good product vs. a product that has a high probability of commercial success?

Yes, there is a big difference between the two. Let us answer this question by looking at the way that most first time inventors or entrepreneurs view their ideas.

When someone presents their ideas to others for the first time, they tend to say things like:

> "My idea is a…" or "My idea is to…"
>
> "It is used to (perform certain function)…"
>
> "It will sell because of its ease of use, safety feature, comfort, etc."

All these are attributes of a good product, one that obviously the inventor or idea originator firmly believes in. They are product or service functionality, feature, and benefit oriented. The problem is, this type of description tends to justify why the creator would buy or use his own creation, which is hardly a guarantee of whether others would see the idea in the same light.

On the other hand, descriptions that center on the attributes of commercially successful products and business models tend to sound like:

> "The design has been made with the fewest parts possible at the cheapest cost…"

> "The production quality is highly consistent…"

> "The product has mass-market appeal and applicability…"

> "The profit margin is better than industry standard…"

> "The breakeven point is… and return on investment on this opportunity is…"

This second set of sample declarations describe why someone else besides the inventor or aspiring entrepreneur would pay for the new idea or service. They are much more business oriented.

The answer to the question "What makes a good commercializable product?" is therefore the same answer as to the question 'What makes good business sense?" instead of "What makes a good product?"

This is not to say the latter is unimportant, but when the focus is on commercialization, the business-oriented evaluation criteria take priority.

To address commercialization potential, each new idea must be measured against its consumer appeal, manufacturing feasibility, patentability, functionality, durability, production cost, marketability, market characteristic and dynamics, resource requirement, macro and micro economic conditions that might have a direct impact on the idea, etc., just to name a few top-level concerns.

The diagram below illustrates this two-part filtration process:

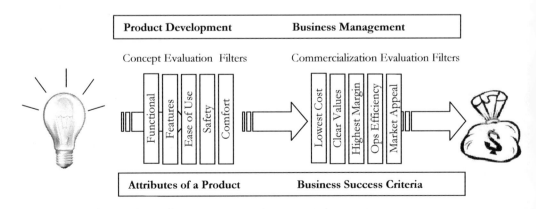

An effective evaluation process requires both parts. An easy way to remember is:

Attributes of products + Business concerns = Commercial viability

It would be a mistake to omit either of these parts and their filters when evaluating a concept's commercial viability. A concept evaluation session is far from complete if it focuses only on the product development aspects. There are simply too many unknowns and variables that can influence the outcome of an idea gone commercialized. Unfortunately this is the part most familiar to inventors and idea generators. Chances are, most people will approach others they know and ask for comments. This is a good first step as long as they do not rely on such informal and shallow feedback before deciding to launch a business from the idea.

We have all seen an otherwise excellent invention or business concept gone bust, and equally shocked by essentially useless, short term fads that have made their creators millions.

The important thing is that even as no guarantees can be given to good ideas, bad ideas can at least be sniffed out early to avoid financial disasters. Drawing an example from real life, no one is guaranteed to reach the summit of the world's highest peak even with years of training and preparation; bad weather can prevent the goal from ever getting reached. But experience will help to identify  those without proper training or preparation before they commit to a path destined for devastation.

I once met an inventor who absolutely insisted that his idea was going to make it big. When asked about whether he had help evaluating his "invention," the answer was a strong "No, and I don't need help. I know my invention will make it big." Needless to say it was a fruitless discussion. All I can hope is that he did not spent too much time and money on a disastrous path; his "invention" was no more than a different iteration of a foot stool which had a cumbersome assembly process and provided very little value to anyone other than apparently himself.

> The most popular products and services are free. The most profitable business has the lowest cost or subsidized revenue from someone other than the consumers. Successful companies have both popularity and profitability. How does your innovation fare?

1.6 WHAT 3-HEADED SUPERHERO IS NEEDED?

There are three distinct roles needed to transform a mere concept to a profitable venture. Each one has a different set of skills from the others. It is very rare to find someone who has the experiences of all three in his or her background.

The inventor. This person is the creator of an idea which has merits to allow it to be commercialized. The type of work is typically creative and discovery.

Entrepreneurs and venture capitalists (VCs). This role involves examining a concept closely and involves activities from analysis, planning, to implementation. This is the commercialization team that takes an idea and gives it physical form and infrastructures including people and other resources.

Professional product lifecycle management (PLM) and business managers. This team takes an infant venture and manages every aspect of its business to profitability.

Inventor + Commercialization Team + PLM Professionals

An effective concept commercial viability evaluation leverages proven business management principles to assess whether an idea has the potential to reach its market profitability. This level of evaluation requires years of professional experiences and a keen business sense. The most experienced evaluators can sometimes do a great job simply by listening to the idea description coupled with their understanding of the particular industry. Others may need to see prototypes or modeling of business service flowcharts before recommending whether to commercialize the concept or not.

Short of such expertise, an inventor or aspiring entrepreneur's best chance is to understand what is involved in the evaluation process and take heed and extreme care in being objective and critical of his or her own idea.

An inventor who does not heed this advice risks going down a futile path even as he surrounds himself with invention books and marketing books. While following all the recommended steps from such books, he would inadvertently progress closer and closer to disaster without even realizing it. Similarly an entrepreneur who imitates others' "success stories" or "success formulas" will find herself in hot waters if she doesn't make sure that her idea is not flawed at the onset. The concepts may differ in such cases but the outcomes are similarly doomed.

It may help to think about the commercialization process as loosely analogous to the lifecycle of a chicken. The egg represents the foundation phase where an idea is born. The incubation represents the planning and strategy phase where ideas are brewed and cared for. Hatching the egg so a chick comes out is synonymous to the implementation phase where something of life and movement is established. The nurturing of a young chick until adulthood when it becomes productive is similar to what business managers do for a young venture. But the first question that must be answered before any of such activities take place is...*is the egg even fertilized?* Are you wasting time and resources trying to hatch an egg that has no potential for life?

1.7 WHAT DOES CONCEPT EVALUATION INVOLVE?

Ideally evaluation should be done with as little expenditures as possible; therefore it makes most sense to evaluate something at the concept stage where sufficient vision and understanding exist without having spent too much resource.

This is not to say that an idea or invention cannot be evaluated in the same way; the issue is trade-off.

Evaluating just an idea results in high uncertainty. Evaluating an invention costs more money than may be justifiable (if the invention was obviously not profitable to begin with). Nevertheless these terms are used interchangeably and appear throughout the evaluation process. It is done so to demonstrate that the process can be used anywhere from the idea to the product/service development process as long as you are aware of the tradeoffs.

Finally, although the questions are geared more towards product inventions, the process can be used for a new business model, a new technology, or a scientific discovery that results in either a product or a service.

At a high level both evaluation and commercialization processes involve these components:

      * Innovation Description

        * Comparative Research

          * Concept Development

            * Prototype and Modeling

              * Validation & Refinement

* Target Market Analysis

* Marketing Strategy

* Distribution & Sales Strategy

* Intellectual Property Management

* Resources Acquisition & Management

* Business Infrastructure & Processes

* Financial Analysis

* Funding & Ownership

* Product Lifecycle Management

When you first ask for feedback on your idea, the exchange is probably quite casual and quick. What is the value of this type of exchange? It depends on the quality of feedback. You should be aware that your own description matters tremendously; how much information you can describe in a short burst has a lot to do with what you get back as feedback. But in general you will want to gauge your time based on the type of feedback and the background/experience level of the person you talk to. As the duration increases so does the process evolve from a pure concept evaluation to a commercial viability assessment:

Duration of Evaluation	Type of Feedback
1-Minute Evaluation	Casual feedback
15-Minute Evaluation	Exploratory at best
1-Hour Evaluation	Whether the concept is worthy of pursuing
1-Day Evaluation	Investor/VC level investment feedback

Good and useful feedbacks will measure your concept against a set of proven attributes. For example, attributes of a good...

	Proven Attributes
Product	Quality, durability, ease of use, safety, versatility, storage convenience, power consumption, works as advertised, low maintenance, consumable parts and accessories, light weight for lowered shipping cost, repeat sales, add-on sales from modularity, does not cause other problems, etc.

Service	Reliability, consistency, meets needs, good response, availability, readiness, preparedness, capable, inexpensive, etc.
Employee	Skilled, loyal, low training cost, self-motivated, shares common goals, team player, etc.
Vendor	Reliable, reasonable price, good reputation, solid product or service, responsive, communicates well, etc.
Manufacturer	Low production cost, high quality, dependable, well maintained facility, good response rate, etc.
Distributor	Brand power, good locations, established customer base, reasonable terms, collaborates instead of dictates, etc.
Operations	Scalable for cost efficiency, predictable, low maintenance, in alignment with overall growth strategy, etc.

When you receive feedback you should keep the following in mind … the value of anything in commerce is measured by how much money someone is willing to pay you for it. If people tell you it's a great idea but won't pay you for it, then it's just empty flattery. If you believe the idea is fantastic but no one is willing to pay anything for it, then it may still be fantastic but only to you, for you, and by you alone.

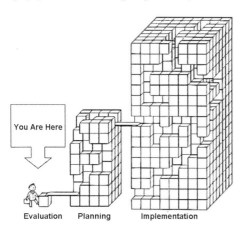

You Are Here

Evaluation   Planning   Implementation

Even as your end goal is to make money, profitability is the end result of many steps and hard work preceding it. There are hundreds of steps and thousands of questions you will need to go through in order to continue on track. All together, these steps and questions make up an extensive evaluation process that uncovers real life issues as you assess your own progression. In the process you are also building the baseline upon which you will decide whether to continue with your idea or not.

1.8 I HAVE AN IDEA [THAT I REJECTED]

The process and criteria used to evaluate concepts did not come out of thin air; rather, they have been painfully thought about and organized into a collection and built into a process that I also follow.

Beyond the AeroBloks venture, I have had many more ideas that I thought were pretty good, at least at the moment. In all cases I have either rejected them or deferred for more refinement. Let me share some of the rationale here so as to make it clearer why the criteria make much sense:

Idea #1 - Replacement String Winder

It is a line-winding device that helps with winding electric string trimmer lines onto the spools quickly, precisely, and effortlessly.

Anyone who has tried to manually wind the trimming lines onto an empty spool can relate to the pain of winding it tightly and precisely so it would not get caught when dispensed. It takes time and effort to do this mundane work, time away from a precious weekend afternoon when every extra minute of yard work is a no-no.

The Design: I successfully created a spool that has a mounting just like film projectors where the replacement line spool would spin and the original equipment manufacturer's (OEM) spool would catch and spin simultaneously. There is even a guide to help align the string. Winding is almost effortless.

The Decision: Reject.

Rationale: This is a bona fide problem for people who use string trimmers. The design works well, and requires mostly plastic parts which means low cost and reasonable profit margins. The issue is with marketing. Not only does it have a narrow niche of consumers, but getting to them requires hardware distribution channels which I do not have. Working with a manufacturer of string trimmers is a possibility if it were to be bundled as an add-on device. Yet the killer factor was that I bought an automatic-feeding trimmer for about the same price, which makes this idea pretty much either obsolete or even more limited in terms of demand.

Idea #2 - Improved Mosquito Net Shirts

It is a shirt that is weaved with mosquito net material while having soft foam-like material sewn between the two layers. This gives the added height that prevents the mosquito's proboscis from reaching the skin.

Part of the "joy" of working in the yard in the evening is trying to fight these almost invisible pests that carry West Nile disease. Invariably I would lose and still get bitten despite having worn the anti-mosquito net shirts sold in the market place. This is because the net sticks to the skin and does not prevent mosquitoes from having their dinner on me when I remain stationary at one spot too long.

The Design: I created a design that calls for a double-layering of the net so that there is a space of at least 0.25" between the skin and the surface where mosquitoes land. Laying out the pattern so the two layers remain fairly constantly apart was the most difficult aspect.

The Decision: Reject.

Rationale: This is a bona fide problem for people who must be in the presence of disease carrying mosquitoes. It would even be useful in a dengue fever infested area. However, the decision to reject has to do with the market size which is small. Most people (at least in developed countries) would probably not be seen with one of these modified shirts when taking an evening stroll. It would take a miracle or a genius to make a fashion statement out of it. There is a very low likelihood that I could ever get international distributor to carry the amount required to make it consistently profitable (read: make a living out of it). Therefore as a fulltime device or a part time loyalty-only invention, it would cost too much time and return very little.

Idea #3 - Converter Kit for Backpacked Leaf Blowers

Anyone who has to rake leaves would appreciate a leaf blower. The person who has too many trees would appreciate having two blowers during the foliage season. Using two simultaneously saves having to redirect the wind and allows for stirring up wet leaves while blowing them to the intended direction. This method literally saves three times (not twice) as much time and effort.

The Design: I was able to create a frame that can be worn as a backpack. The frame also has quick releases that secure two blowers, whether electric or gas based. The device worked extremely well for me and I was able to shave off much time by using two leaf blowers simultaneously.

The Decision: Reject.

Rationale: The device solved a real need, worked extremely well, but only for people who already have or are willing to purchase two blowers. Not many people have yards lined with huge trees. Even less are people who use two blowers simultaneously. It could be sold as an add-on by manufacturers of leaf blowers to entice more sales. However, it is just as easy for them to bypass my design and create one with the same purpose and even customized to their blowers. Furthermore, it would be easier still to split the nozzle into two on any existing machine even though the power is then halved. Apparently someone else also thought of the same idea and had created backpacked blowers for the professionals. Changing the hose to a split output is cheap. There is insufficient reason to do this even as I will continue to use it myself.

There are at least 10 other ideas that I rejected or deferred based on the commercialization assessment criteria. In all cases it was a matter of knowing the criteria, what makes them practical in the real market, and a willingness to recognize it and move on. Are they opportunity losses? Not necessary. I believe the process saved me from losing my time, money, and other resources.

1.9 ATTRIBUTES: THE GOOD, THE BAD, AND THE UGLY

In contrast to the attributes of a good product/service/business, I have also a **list of undesirable traits that should put any idea to rest**. They are:

* Limited market sizes

    * Limited usefulness

      * Outdated methods

        * Cost too much to produce

          * Price is too high

            * No distribution channel

              * Don't have the necessary skills, knowledge, money, time

                * No lasting value

                  * Barrier to entry too low; knock-offs too easy

                * Short shelf life

                  * Too difficult to manufacture

                    * Infrastructure is not there

                      * Existing products good enough

                    * Too much liability

Notice that I freely share these three ideas fully even as they have not been commercialized or protected. This is because it takes so much more to bring each to market and make it profitable. This is just a reminder that you are better off if you focus on finding a tested concept instead of dwelling on an idea that may not be "fertilized."

Concept evaluation is done on several dimensions. It is important to keep all of them in mind when looking at something that you believe has profit potential. You should start with this baseline of thinking…

Dimension	Consider
Idea	good/bad aspects
Physical	function, safety, looks & feel, testing
Market	size, location, reachable?
Operation	logistics planning, can things happen, how?
Financial	money, money, money (the ones you spend and hopefully make)

By now you should have a pretty good idea on what to look for if you were to do a self-evaluation of your ideas. The table below gives a very high level view for this purpose.   Much more detail will be covered in Appendix 4 where 120 evaluation questions will examine the most critical aspects of your concept in concrete terms.

Each aspect below has its corresponding condition(s). For example, a product's function should be needed, the competitive product or substitutes should be inferior, and the design must work, etc.

HIGH LEVEL IDEA SELF-EVALUATION CHECKLIST

ASPECT	CONDITION IS
CONCEPT EXPLORATION	
DESCRIPTION	ACCURATE
FUNCTION	NEEDED
VALUE PROPOSITION	RELEVANT
COMPARATIVE LANDSCAPE	
COMPETITION	INFERIOR
DESIGNING AND PROTOTYPING	
DESIGN	WORKS
PROTOTYPE	DESCRIPTIVE
MATERIAL	LEGAL
QUALITY	CONSISTENT
FEEDBACK, VALIDATION, REFINEMENT	
FEEDBACK	FAVORABLE

☐	IMPROVEMENTS	ON TARGET

MARKET IDENTIFICATION

☐	MARKET	LARGE ENOUGH
☐	CUSTOMER PROFILE	COMPREHENSIVE

MARKETING STRATEGY

☐	PRICE	REASONABLE
☐	PROMOTIONAL EFFORTS	EFFECTIVE
☐	POSITIONING	CORRECT

DISTRIBUTION & SALES APPROACH

☐	DISTRIBUTION CHANNEL	WITHIN REACH
☐	SALES EFFORT	REPEATABLE

SECURING YOUR PATENT, TRADEMARK, COPYRIGHTS

☐	INTELLECTUAL PROPERTY	PROTECTABLE

RESOURCES ASSESSMENT

☐	RESOURCES	COMPLETE

HUMAN RESOURCES

☐	TALENTS AND SKILLS	ACQUIRABLE

BUSINESS INFRASTRUCTURE

☐	INFRASTRUCTURE	DEPENDABLE

BUSINESS OPERATIONS

☐	OPERATIONS	EFFICIENT
☐	CUSTOMER INTERFACE	CAN BE MANAGED WELL

MANUFACTURING & VENDORS

☐	FACTORY	TRUSTWORTHY
☐	SUPPLIERS/SERVICE VENDORS	CAPABLE

LEGAL AND INSURANCE PROTECTION

☐	INSURANCE	SUFFICIENT

DETAILED FINANCIAL ASSESSMENT

☐	COST OF GOODS SOLD	LOW
☐	PROFIT MARGIN	WITHIN INDUSTRY NORM
☐	CAPITAL REQUIREMENT	CAN BE FUNDED
☐	EXIT STRATEGY	REALISTIC
☐	VENTURE	HAS ATTRACTIVE ROI

An Evaluation List "On the Go"

Not everyone has the time to thoroughly evaluate a concept at anytime. Chances are, there is a need to be able to give a quick but solid mental evaluation for every idea that you come across, whether it is your own or someone else's. If you review the material here in depth and practice giving feedback, you will develop such a mental list over time.

Until then, if and when you do come in contact with a new idea, product, or service, you will probably have lots of questions or know that you should have lots of questions but can't think of any at that moment. There is a way that you can quickly sort out this mental checklist of questions.

Just as there are four subcategories (4Ps) under the art of marketing, there are also 4Ps in the concept evaluation process, of which the marketing 4Ps are a subset.

The 4Ps of Concept Evaluation

PRODUCT addresses a concept that is or not yet a product or service and all its attributes

PEOPLE examines the management behind the proposed idea and the people it will serve

PROSPECT looks at the potential of the idea including marketing considerations and analyses

PROFIT focuses on the financial aspects including business operations and cost structures

You will find a "to-go" go-to list in Appendix 1 that you can carry with you for quick evaluations. The questions are categorized by the 4Ps of concept evaluation in a common sense sequence. You should be able to dig up a lot of information on a new idea simply by asking those questions.

1.10 WHY ALL THE FUSS?

The only way to truly know if your idea is a good one is to test it out in the real market. However, reaching that point takes time and lots of money. I know this first hand because we found our answer only after doing the first tradeshow. A better way would be to simulate the commercialization process and assess the risk and readiness without actually taking the risk.

Just as first year medical students are always taught to "Do No Harm," when you are contemplating on bringing something to the public market, you must also heed this advice, not only for the general public but also for yourself, because there are serious financial consequences.

I have seen ideas proposed by "inventors" that should be immediately dismissed. They are extremely dangerous and ill-conceived. A lot of times ideas of this sort come from combining different functionalities into a single device. I am not at liberty to disclose them in detail but imagine what would happen if someone combines a stationary object that requires stability with an exercising function that creates movement and motion! The stationary object needed to be stationary because of safety reasons. By introducing an exercise function the immobility is now replaced by motion which destabilizes the user. At best the user becomes unsteady and uncomfortable and at worst he gets seriously injured and sues the inventor!

Products that are poorly designed also share common traits such as expensive parts, overly complex design, awkward movements, cumbersome assembly and disassembly, incorrect dimensions (non-anthropometric measurements), toxic raw material, and the list goes on. These products are essentially time bombs waiting to explode and cause either bodily harm or financial ruins. Sometimes the market will correct such mistakes with a lack of buyers when words get out. However it only takes one serious injury to generate product liability suits that could ruin a person for life.

A lesser known danger for first time inventors and entrepreneurs is market timing. This often has to do with technology-based products. Imagine someone trying to improve a computer keyboard while the rest of world has already begun to endorse touch screen as a preferred input method. What will happen to the hundreds of thousand of dollars invested in the entire process and a whole warehouse of unsold "improved" keyboards?

These are some of the reasons why it is necessary to take the time and patience to evaluate your ideas very carefully. The earlier you catch a bad idea the better off you are. Every step further down the wrong path costs exponentially more money and time.

Most first time inventors are preoccupied with knowing how to determine if their ideas will make money. This is relatively easy to answer, just look at the attributes of good products and services presented earlier.

Seasoned entrepreneurs will tell you that the real question should be "How do I make sure I don't lose my shirt over my invention?"

This is the reason why so much attention has been devoted to helping newbie inventors and aspiring entrepreneurs understand the process and what is at stake in this book.

Even if an inventor has no intentions of taking the idea to commercialization by himself, it would help to understand what is required from A to Z so that the license fee or royalty percentage makes sense. Often times companies refuse to deal with individual inventors because the latter is considered too greedy, and for good reasons.

Understanding the amount of work and risks involved in the entire process regardless of who does what helps everyone at the table to be more reasonable, which is all we should strive for.

1.11 CONCEPT EVALUATION VS. COMMERCIAL VIABILITY ASSESSMENT

There are existing business services that evaluate concepts, products, or services and may include some preliminary market assessment. In contrast, a worthwhile commercialization viability assessment also includes the execution and management capability aspects.

The reason why most evaluation services shy away from the execution and management capability components is understandable. It is difficult to project the likelihood of success when only a concept is available. However, I find this reasoning insufficient. Experienced business people will tell you that planning is great but implementation is greater. To that I'll add that the human component of business management has the greatest impact.

It might make more sense if you relate this notion to the decision of whether to have a baby or not. If a young couple's goal to have a baby is to ensure that the child will grow up and become a well-balanced and successful individual, then simply having their genetic testing to weed out any preexisting diseases is insufficient. It may guarantee a healthy baby but it does not say anything about his future.

What if the couple were to take into consideration their ability to provide both financial and emotional support by looking at their foreseeable earning power and parenting philosophy? The financial foundation is future oriented but both people presumably are capable of earning income. Their parenting value and style would be consistent with what they project for the child when he grows up. Assessing these future considerations with reasonable projections yields a much better evaluation of whether they can meet their goal for their child than simply looking at the genetic makeup of a baby.

Likewise, to pull off a solid commercial viability assessment we will need to look beyond what is measurable. The entire process basically involves looking at product attributes, underlying infrastructure, and then the required resources (talent and money).

We will identify the ideal states for each of the evaluation criteria. We will also look at potential problems that the concept may run into. Together we will measure the sufficiency of the underlying infrastructure and the management skills needed to achieve the ideal states.

Remember that no matter who ends up commercializing a concept, the process does not change. Even if you fully intend on licensing your concept to a licensee or a product commercialization company, you owe it to yourself to do some due diligence on their capabilities. This evaluation list gives you the tools to do just that.

1.12 ORGANIZATION OF THE COMMERCIAL VIABILITY ASSESSMENT CHAPTERS

Just as you can use a computer purely for word processing, someone else can use the same PC to create amazing multi-media works or programming. In the same way the questions in the next few chapters are designed to probe your thinking and guide your research. What you put in will dictate what you get out.

Ultimately, concept commercialization assessment has much more do to with marketing and sales than with logistics and operations. This is not to diminish the role of the latter as the key to financial success is largely dependent on implementation efforts.

All business components play essential roles in generating profits, but marketing and sales considerations almost always dictate whether to pursue an idea or not, which is the first thing to determine. As such the bulk of the evaluation questions will be on marketing related concerns and relatively fewer on business operations and the other supporting infrastructures.

Conventional wisdom tells us that who you know is often more crucial than what you know. This is absolutely true when it comes to bringing a concept to market. We will devote an entire chapter to isolating the key players whom you must become familiar with if you were to pursue a business venture.

Last but not least, it is crucial that you know how best to organize your thoughts and approaches. The next few chapters have been assembled to help you mentally categorize information and knowledge based on this necessity.

Chapter 2 describes the ecosystem of the commercialization process. What this means is that you will develop a brief understanding of the who's who in the business creation and management arena. **Chapter 3** takes on a step-by-step process in the form of a blueprint. Understanding the different steps allows you to superbly organize your thoughts and approaches.

Chapters 4 and 5 cover the marketing and sales aspects of concept to commercialization evaluation. **Chapter 6** covers the implementation portion which includes various operations systems and their corresponding processes. **Chapter 7** covers the financial aspect of commercial viability evaluation which is the most important part but cannot be fully explored until the legwork is done earlier. Collectively these four chapters serve as a foundation of business knowledge that helps you decipher and respond to the probing questions in **Appendix 4**.

The sequence of the evaluation questions reflects the typical thought process of a new inventor or entrepreneur. On the other hand the topics in the business knowledge chapters (4 to 7) are organized in a progressively evolved fashion. Therefore the sequences do not necessarily match but are cross referenced.

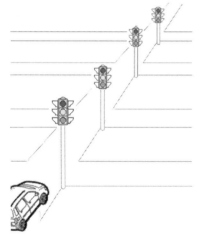

Think of each section in Appendix 4 as a traffic junction. An idea needs to receive green lights at each junction before it proceeds to the next one. A red light stops the flow but can be a life saver later on.

You should begin the concept evaluation process by reading and becoming familiar with the criteria and explanations in Chapters 4 through 7 on a first pass. Afterwards you rate your responses to the evaluation questions by referencing the corresponding topics in those chapters. The rating and scoring methods are explained in Appendix 4. Ideally you should seek out subject matter expertise to help answer the questions, but if not, the systematic and objective approach should be sufficient for self-evaluation.

Finally, in **Chapter 8** you will see a progress tracking and monitoring framework that essentially takes a bird's eye view of the entire process. This framework will allow you to gauge your progress for sanity check along each step of the commercialization blueprint process.

CHAPTER 1 ACTION ITEMS

1. Generate a list of preliminary questions you have about your invention or business idea.

2. Identify the problem your invention or business solution will solve for other people.

3. Describe exactly how your concept solves the problem.

4. Run your idea through the list of undesirable traits. Does it have any of them and if so determine if you can overcome them.

5. Run your idea through the high level self-evaluation list. Determine where your idea needs further development.

6. Do a quick assessment of your own capabilities. What skill sets are you missing in terms of bringing your idea from concept to business venturing?

7. Place your focus on the business aspect of your idea and identify how you would convince a group of business people to invest in your idea.

Food for thought:

It takes... **Creativity** to come up with a useful idea

Knowledge to build a company

Experience to run a business

And collectively they culminate in...

Seasoned Judgment to assess an opportunity

Part II

FOUNDATIONS OF A DIFFERENT WORLD

"If you have built castles in the air, your work need not be lost; that is where they should be. Now put the foundations under them."

Henry David Thoreau

Question:
How many people does it take to turn on the light bulb?

Answer:
Just one, but at least 50 others to make it visible.

Chapter 2

Who's Who in the Commerce Loop?

Are you ready to meet and transact with hundreds of strangers? In this chapter we will identify the pool of players involved in taking a concept to the market place, and ultimately landing it with the consumer in the form of a finished product. The bulk of this material will address the 5Ws of each role, leaving the "How" questions to be answered in subsequent chapters.

The "How" questions will examine the players' paradigm in terms of their objectives, their constraints, how they relate to you and how they interact with you as a potential vendor/customer. For now let's identify them and place them in easy to understand categories so you can manage them strategically.

PEOPLE WHO CAN IMPACT YOUR VENTURE

There are roughly three levels of impact that people you interact with in business can have on you and your venture.

Given that the basis of business transaction is the transfer of money for the exchange of goods and services, it should come as no surprise that people who can influence whether money flows in your direction should garner your most attention. In terms of negotiation power, they tend to have more over you. This is the group that is typically associated with sales and revenue generation.

The next group of people may be mission critical for your ongoing business management. These would be the marketing promotional experts, lawyers, accountants, and other professionals you depend on to run your business. It is a good practice to have a contingency plan when dealing with this group.

The last group is essentially vendors, suppliers, and service providers who are necessary for your continued business operations. These folks are "replaceable" and you should have alternatives lined up if and when they "misbehave."

THE CONCEPT COMMERCIALIZATION ECOSYSTEM

How many hands are involved from the time an idea is generated to the time it is consumed as a product? The answer depends on how complicated the product's design is, the complexity of the distribution system, whether there are regulatory factors involved, and how the consumer finds out and acquires it.

Naturally the more complex any of these components, the more people will get involved and the longer it will take. Nevertheless the process resembles a natural ecosystem where there are producers and consumers. A manmade commercialization system introduces an additional layer called distribution, which many of us refer to as the "middleman." As much as we would like to reduce retail prices by whacking the middleman, without this layer of function most goods would not be efficiently distributed across vast amounts of space (distance) and time (storage and preservation).

The diagram on the next page illustrates a representative process that most single product inventor-turned-entrepreneurs go through.

Starting with you as the brainchild behind your product, going in a clock-wise rotation, the major entities where the physical product travels have been encircled. Notice the path eventually leads into the center which is the customer.

Each silhouette represents the person you will most likely interact with directly. Some will interface with secondary players without your involvement. For example, the accountant will interact with the tax regulating entities. Some of them will act as intermediaries where you will then collaborate and work with as the second tier. The manufacturer's rep is a perfect example where he would introduce you to the buyer and guide you throughout the process together.

Activities shown in diagram are coded by line types:

Production Activities	●————————————●
Procurement Activities	●— · — · — · — · — · — · —●
Promotional Activities	●···●
Business Infrastructure	●— — — — — — — — — —●

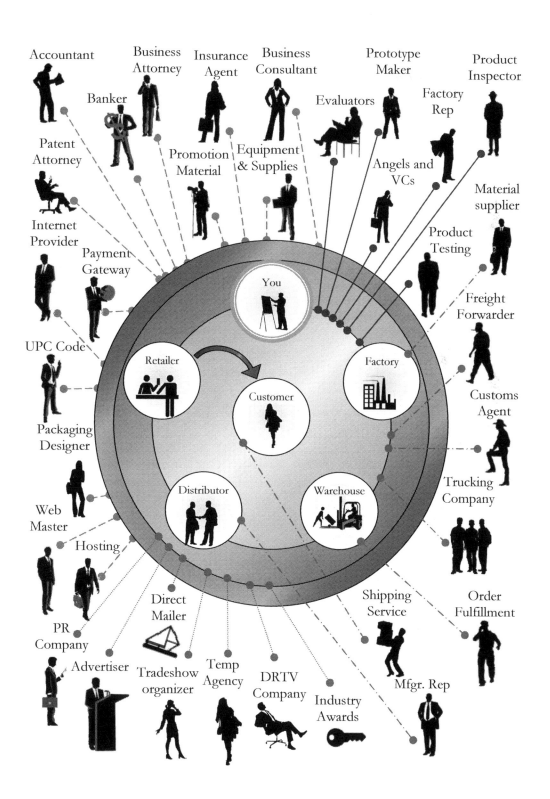

A natural ecosystem is made up of producers and consumers. This system here is no different. However a distinction is made for the consumer of the finished product which is your customer. All other parties tend to play both producer and consumer along the chain as they transact.

Notice that the inner ring represents both production and procurement related activities and people. The next ring outwards represents promotional activities and people involved in them. The outer ring represents infrastructure related activities and players. Where the interaction is directly involved, the line is drawn to the encircled entity. For example, material suppliers typically deal directly with the factory without involving you. However if you have components from multiple raw suppliers or factories then you would need to get involved. Combination products that include cloth, electronics, and plastic are examples of this arrangement.

By tracing through the circle in a step-wise and clock-wise fashion you should be able to identify the individual components and determine your own product's ecosystem. Now that is a lot of phone calls, emails, and handshakes by the time you establish all the links! Be sure to stay highly organized.

THE 5WS OF PLAYERS AND CHARACTERS

In this section we examine each player and briefly describe their role in the overall scope of your venture. This list is not comprehensive as each situation is different. It focuses on the most common types of players a new entrepreneur would most likely interface with. For each role we will be asking the typical 5Ws questions. Feel free to skip any role that you are already familiar with.

- ❖ Who are they?
- ❖ What do they do?
- ❖ When do you engage them?
- ❖ Where do you find them?
- ❖ Why do you need them?

Who: Evaluators

What: These are the folks that hopefully give you straight, honest feedback that prevents you from running full speed ahead down a cliff.

When: As soon as you have an idea that you can clearly describe, with or without a physical prototype, you should begin asking them for feedback. However, please don't waste anyone's valuable time until you've thoroughly convinced yourself that there is true value in your idea and either it is unique or you have an improved version of something that already exists.

Where: Begin by asking your friends and families. Inventor clubs are an excellent resource so long as you make sure non-disclosure agreements are signed. When you become more prepared, try getting acquaintances or your target consumers to serve as your focus group in a more formal setting where you can reasonably demonstrate your product in its intended glory.

Why: They are the first gatekeepers. If you do a thorough and honest job here asking for truth, then you would end up saving a lot of time and money, and possibly a trip to hell. At the same time, if the audience is the same target consumer, then you can also ask for valuable feedback such as acceptable price ranges and where they would buy your product.

Who: Prototype Maker

 What: There are new advances in prototype-making techniques. Professional shops can create prototypes by printing with 3D ink. Part time prototype makers are typically hobbyists and tend to charge less.

When: If your product requires engineering prints or detailed artwork, as soon as you are confident of them you should find a prototype maker to help you make functional demo units. If you can make the prototype out of everyday material then you should do so while refining your idea.

Where: The best place is through referrals from inventor clubs. Alternative online searches will also yield professional shops. Hobbyists are harder to find but you can always tab into different online networks and post questions.

Why: A rough prototype helps others to give you feedback that is more relevant than from just your description or an artwork. A professionally created prototype can be used for formal funding purposes as well as for promotional photo shooting sessions which feed into the promotional literature you will produce. If the prototype is quite close to the final product in looks, feel, and function, you could also use it to present to buyers.

Who: Angels and VCs

 What: Angels invest for various reasons. Typical starting-out entrepreneurs get their funding from friends and families. VCs are professional money managers in the sense that their job is to grow money for their investors and themselves.

When: If you follow along the commercialization blueprint, you will have gathered sufficient business information and strategies to assemble a business plan. You should seek them out when you are certain that your business plan is realistic and you are ready to take the next step and defend your vision and strategy.

Where: Venture Capitalists are business people. They are looking for investments no different than stocks or bonds that will yield the roughly 20% return on their investment. They tend to be highly selective on who to meet and the type of project they fund. Look for them by referral or by searching online to gleam the type of projects they have funded in the past. There are also books written by ex-VCs and ex-entrepreneurs specifically addressing the funding issues. Such publications tend to give you the best concentrated referral sources. Angel investors tend to be friends and families who would like to see you and their investment succeed. Ask for referrals on entrepreneurial and angel investor networks. Both of these networks exist on a local and national level.

Why: It really takes money to make money. Unless you can afford to lose every dollar you spend on your own venture, otherwise sharing the control and rewards is a necessity, not a luxury. Additionally, professional investors have more experiences and networks of talents than a typical starting-out entrepreneur. The right type of funding and talent pool will make the difference of a profitable or money losing project.

Who: Factory Representative

 What: This is a middleman who makes his living by facilitating the business relationship between factories and people looking to outsource their manufacturing needs.

When: The best time to search for one is when you are looking to make a professional prototype. Some factories will make the prototypes for you for very little cost. In that case it would save you time and money from paying an additional party.

Where: There are web portals such as www.alibaba.com where factories and manufacturers meet each other. In this case a manufacturer outsources the physical production to a factory. The best strategy tends to be getting a referral from someone using the same material and outsources the production. Some manufacturers will be reluctant to reveal their sources but if you befriend someone or tap into their network of inventors and manufacturers you might be able to find one who is willing to share the resource.

Why: If you outsource your production overseas, you will definitely want to leverage the contact, network, and local knowledge of a factory representative. Factory reps are compensated on a commission basis by the factory. It's true that their commissions are passed onto your cost. Yet because you do not commit to their fees, by having one finding you the lowest cost factory essentially discounts your cost of hiring their service. When compared with the time and money it costs to find a factory by yourself, a factory rep is an invaluable addition to your team. Make sure to work with only an honest and hardworking one.

Who: Product Inspector

What: This is a service company that typically has employees near the factories. The inspectors will inspect your produced goods based on a set program of checklists. Their work will ensure quality check and quantity, in addition to the prevention of unauthorized production of your products to be sold elsewhere. They are essentially your eyes when you cannot be there to inspect the factory.

When: Depending on the production rate of the factory, as soon as a reasonable quantity has been produced (e.g. 100 retail units), you should arrange for an inspector to visit. If done too early, there may not be sufficient goods to allow for random selection and testing. If done too late, any mistakes discovered by then would be costly to correct. You would let the factory know that an inspector would be dispatched by you but not exactly when so as not to allow the factory to manipulate the goods or the setting.

Where: Online searches are very easy to do. If you outsource production in China, then Hong Kong based inspection companies are typically easy to find. Be sure to ask if they have locally based employees so you don't end up paying extra for traveling and lodging expenses.

Why: Despite best intentions and communication, mistakes often happen. Hopefully production samples will take care of last changes. Yet when the products are being mass produced, there is no guarantee that the changes will be incorporated into the final product. Factories in China have also been known to steal the idea and sell extra production of products in South East Asia. The cost of the inspector is equivalent to buying insurance to avoid major mistakes.

Who: Product Testing Company

What: Testing has become a necessity by law for many products. It is important that you comply with testing requirements and be able to produce certified certificates as required by most major resellers.

When: Testing should be done before the production is complete and ready for freight. It is preferable to have at least three weeks ahead of the freight date to allow for any last minute changes.

Where: There are several large international testing companies. An online search will yield many of them. Be sure to ask about their procedure, costs, and a sample report. Test criteria required for a particular type of product tend to be uniform so the considerations should be primarily cost based.

Why: For compliance and sales reasons. Sometimes insurance companies could refuse your coverage if your product has not been shown to comply with federal product safety standards. Resellers will often require proof of compliance before they do business with you.

Who: Material Supplier

What: They procure and sell raw components such as vinyl, plastic, metal, fabric, chips, etc. to the factories.

When: As you research your production cost, isolating the components and understanding whether the product can be produced by a single factory will determine whether you might need to source a raw material supplier to work with the factory.

Where: If you will be outsourcing overseas, try www.alibaba.com. If you are interested in producing in the USA, do a search on the National Association of Manufacturers which has a buyer's guide. Another popular search site is Thomas Net which has a register of manufacturers and suppliers. There are other entities that online search will yield such as MadeinUSA.org.

Why: Typically you would not interface with raw material suppliers. However if your product requires multiple components and the factory you have selected does not normally procure some of them, then you might be required to find the raw supplier. The alternative is to trust the factory to find them and charge you a premium for the material.

Who: Freight Forwarder

What: This is an agent that arranges the logistics between the shipper (you) and a receiver of your goods. The types of vehicles include ocean shipping, airfreight, trucking, and rail, etc. that transport shipping containers within a particular route. Sometimes a freight forwarder also owns the freight vehicles as well as provides warehousing and fulfillment services.

When: It is a good idea to research their costs early on as part of your cost calculation. Depending on your production volume, you might be able to find one and schedule a shipment within a month if necessary. It is advisable to reserve freight at least three months ahead to avoid paying extra for expedited shipping. During peak seasons (usually summer) you can expect to pay more.

Where: Depending on the region of your production, there are ocean freight companies that are based in the US as well as Hong Kong. It would make more sense to select a US based freight company from online directories or referrals.

Why: Freight forwarders also deal with customs and sometimes provide warehousing and order fulfillment services. Finding one at a reasonable price would make managing these separate parts of the business easier. However, freight companies do what they do best which is to transport your product from overseas to the US.

Who: Customs Agent

What: These government agents perform random inspections of goods coming through the ports of the country.

When: In most cases you will not deal with them directly. Freight forwarders have customs brokers who are familiar with the process and will take care of the paperwork.

Where: Work with the freight forwarders to find licensed customs brokers who can clear your cargo from the customs office.

Why: All goods imported into the country must go through customs. There are associated fees to pay for the inspection. Sometimes your goods may be detained for days or weeks pending inspection. Be sure to allow extra time in your overall delivery schedule.

Who: Trucking Company

What: These companies provide land based transportation of your goods.

When: Before you make arrangements to ship from port to warehouse, or from warehouse to distributors, or even for shipping tradeshow setups from your home or office, it is best to reserve their schedule at least two months ahead.

Where: There are several national trucking companies for this purpose. Yellow Trucking is a larger one. Fleetdirectory.com is a site where smaller operators are listed. Freightquote.com is a company where you can do online reservations quickly and easily. They are essentially a freight broker who gets paid by the trucking companies.

Why: Trucking is used for transporting your products from port of entry to warehouses, from warehouse to distributors, and your booth display to and from tradeshow floors. When the items are in bulk and can be placed on skids, you will save money going with trucking companies instead of UPS or FedEx.

Who: Order Fulfillment

What: These companies handle the packaging of your product into shipping boxes and prepare them for pick up by shipping companies. They may or may not provide the frontend ordering interface for customers.

When: Most small startups tend to fulfill orders by themselves. However if you find that you are spending too much time fulfilling the orders, then it would be time to upgrade your operation to include outsourced warehouse and fulfillment services.

Where: The best sources are from referrals. This is because fulfillment is such an integral part of your customer's experience in doing business with you; you do not want to take a chance. Fulfillment and warehousing tend to be provided as a joint service.

Why: Once order quantities pick up or your temporary storage space is no longer big enough for your products, then renting warehousing space and having someone else fulfill the orders make much more sense. This way you can focus on the more important aspects of the business such as finance, sales and marketing.

Who: Shipping Service

What: These companies handle the last leg of the journey your product makes to the customer. Most will provide pickup service at your office location for a fixed fee.

When: If you are sending out packages everyday, then it is a good idea to sign up with one of these companies for a pickup service. If not, you could always drop off your packages at their drop off locations.

Where: The best known ones are FedEx and UPS. The U.S. Postal Service has also improved its service competitively by making it easier to ship with fixed rates and boxes.

Why: These established companies beat out small competitors by having global reach and well-established processes. They also provide free supplies of packaging boxes, shipping labels, and online tools to help you prepare the shipping process.

Who: Manufacturer's Representative

What: Similar to factory reps, these middlemen bridge the gap between you the manufacturer and the large retailers or distributors.

When: When your operation has matured to the point where you can handle large distributors or resellers but don't have a way to reach their buyers.

Where: Manufacturer's reps make their living by getting commission from the manufacturer. They tend to focus on mass market opportunities where the payoff is larger and more sustainable than a one-time sale. There are territories and product types to consider when choosing a manufacturer's rep. If you are lucky enough to find one through referrals then you should have an easier time in understanding how the rep works and how the distribution channels he approaches work. If not, by advertising and sending out PR statements with your product announcements, you might catch the eyes of these folks.

Why: Getting a new product from an unproven vendor to the large distributor's buyer is akin to breaking into a heavily fortified castle. Without connections or proven sales results, promotional efforts, etc. you stand very little chance of getting a buyer's attention, unless you get lucky. The manufacturer's rep has the insider's scoop on how the target distributor works, what they are looking for, what they require in terms of product specs and prices, and any other operational requirements. This is an absolutely invaluable player and is worth the commission if your product does in fact become a mass market product. Typical commission is about 5% of wholesale revenue although it varies from industry to industry. The rep will be able to help you with such questions.

Who: Industry Awards

What: For the toy industry, there are several entities that evaluate new products on a fixed interval throughout the year. Some charge a small submission fee while others play more of an informer role for their particular online followers. Most other industries similarly have awards that are given on a periodic basis.

When: When you have a functional product that closely resembles the final product or has reached the retail packaging stage, you should consider submitting it for awards. Depending on the time of year you might find several choices amongst such entities. The best time to apply is when you already have some positive customer testimonials that substantiate your claims and make your product/service appear more attractive.

Where: A quick online search for your product and "award" should yield whether there are awards given, by whom, and when. The next step would be to research these entities and identify their submission criteria, cost, and schedule. Looking at the nearest competitive products' packaging will also reveal whether industry awards play a significant role in product promotion.

Why: Awards bring validity to your product. Some award entities such as Dr. Toy also help you to list your product's descriptions on their website. This type of promotion helps your product get the feel of an "official" endorsement and can lead to the awareness of retailers, buyers, and manufacturer's reps. For the cost of submission, assuming your product wins, it is a worthwhile promotional expenditure if only to catch the attention of resellers.

Who: Direct Response TV Companies

What: There are many companies promising to produce short segments of your product in TV infomercial form. These companies also have affiliations with media buyers who would be happy to sell you a 60-second spot on a cable channel.

When: As a promotional channel, Direct Response TV (DRTV) can be an expensive option relative to your other marketing expenses. However if you have a product that generates mass appeal, then displaying it on TV might be a good choice, provided you calculate the potential payback and choose the right time and channels to display your commercial.

Where: Online search for DRTV will yield many companies that provide this service. Be sure to do comparison shopping on cost, see sample videos on quality, and get customer testimonials on their effectiveness. Another search keyword is "media buyer." Both of these terms will generate lots of options to choose from.

Why: Marketing costs vary depending on the medium. Sending out brochures, doing online advertising, and attending tradeshows all generate considerable costs. DRTV can be had for as little as $8,000 or up to $100,000 for a turnkey project. It offers some validity to your new product by helping to build brand and product awareness with the "As seen on TV" slogan. If displayed frequently enough, it might even catch the eyes of buyers. Chances are, however, that DRTV should be viewed as a highly targeted promotion for a very specific segment of the infomercial viewers population. Choosing the right programming and timeslot can make all the difference in its effectiveness. Media buyers buy up inventories of 30-second to 30-minute timeslots at drastically reduced rates from cable companies. This in turn provides you with a discounted cost to advertise on TV.

Who: Temp Agencies

What: There are talent agencies that operate like conventional temp agencies. They are brokers of service providers and usually target smaller companies that need extra help temporarily.

When: If you have a particular need for a project or situation on a short term basis, it would make more sense to hire a temporary worker. For example, for tradeshows I hired temporary workers to staff the booth while I walked around to do business development activities. At one time the industry slang "booth babes" for these temp employees actually attracted a fellow exhibitor who in turn introduced me to a manufacturer's rep for Toys "R" Us.

Where: Asking for referrals is probably the best approach. If not, online searches will yield almost too many options. When deciding who to choose, compare the agency's ability to find your specific criteria for the short assignment and ask for backup guarantees on top of comparing costs.

Why: For a specific occasion like manning a tradeshow booth, it often makes more economic sense to hire someone local. The cost of the talent runs anywhere from $15-$30 per hour. Compare this to flying an employee and paying for travel, food, lodging, and salary, the savings become obvious. At the same time, since the task is temporary in nature and relatively simple, hiring someone local who has been screened by the agency to ensure competence makes all the sense. The agency takes care of all the human resources related issues and your financial transaction is straight forward and with the agency only.

Who: Tradeshow Organizers

 What: Tradeshows are run like any other businesses. The tradeshow organizers rent physical spaces and arrange for logistics to gather the exhibitors and their target audience under one roof. Most tradeshow organizers have been around for years and have set schedules published almost a year ahead of time.

When: If you have a functional product and resale pricing established, exhibiting in a tradeshow is the best way to get industry attention on your product.

Where: Do online search for your type of product with the word "tradeshows" included. For example, if you search "toy tradeshows" you will find multiple listings of the shows available as well as toy industry associations and directories that will lead you to them. Alternatively you can also check out http://conventions.net for your particular industry.

Why: To get your product in front of specific buyers and resellers you will need to physically exhibit it at least several times. A physical product speaks louder than brochures and samples because you would be able to demonstrate its functionality in the most powerful way while interacting live with your target audience. A tradeshow intended for business to business transactions is where you will pick up most interests from resellers. One that caters to consumers is where you can sell directly to consumers locally. In this case you would need to consider the cost of transporting the inventory for on the spot sales and pickup.

Who: Direct Mailer

 What: An alternative to mass marketing efforts is highly targeted promotion. Direct mail offers the opportunity to send your product information to just the audience of your choice.

When: When you want to test out a different, more targeted promotional campaign instead of mass market approaches to see which yields higher sales.

Where: There are many direct mail companies more than happy to sell you their services. The service might include the sale of qualified leads at 10¢ -20¢ a piece on top of processing fee and postage.

Why: If your product serves a very specific niche, such as childcare centers, then you might want to consider doing a direct mail campaign just for this group. Direct mail should be used with caution. Conventional response rate has been quoted at 2% however in reality many campaigns return less than 1% or a fraction of 1%. This means for every 100 of your brochure you paid for the design, printing, handling, postage, and the cost of the leads, 99 of them will end up in the trash bin. The concept of specifically targeted marketing must be weighted against your breakeven calculation. Will the campaign breakeven, make money, or lose money if your response rates are below 1%? These are the financial considerations for this somewhat outdated mode of promotion.

Who: Advertiser

What: For a fixed cost you get to place your product on someone else's display medium and hopefully get others to notice and become interested in it.

When: Most products require advertising. Word of mouth has yet to take over traditional advertising. When you have decided that your product is ready for public display and you have sufficient marketing material to support it, then advertising would make sense.

Where: There are many media to advertise in. Online advertising on search engines or industry web portals are popular. Conventional paper-based advertising on printed publications or tradeshow journals is still an option. Less used advertising media such as buses, taxis, subways, and billboard are yet another option for new products.

Why: Even if you have a product that literally speaks for itself, it still needs to be seen by lots of people in order to get the ones most interested to recognize it.

Advertising costs vary according to the medium you choose. Online pay-per-click tends to be effective only if highly targeted. Print advertising on industry publications tends to get your product out to the business customers. Mass market advertising is not focused unless your intended population segment sees the advertising naturally. The cost of advertising is typically a few thousand dollars. The key is to create repeat exposures for your target audience otherwise you would be wasting money.

Who: Public Relations Company

What: If you are not a marketing guru with lots of industry contacts then you will need a PR company to handle your promotional activities most effectively.

When: When your product is ready for primetime, with the 4Ps of marketing (Product, Pricing, Placement, Promotion) clearly spelled out in your marketing strategy, and your operational processes and infrastructure are in place for action, then you should engage a PR company to get the ball rolling.

Where: The number of PR companies can be overwhelming. Many of these are started by new entrepreneurs who previously worked in the marketing area. Finding the right one begins with asking questions from your own network. If you end up having to screen different companies, ask about their knowledge on your particular industry, including windows of opportunity for tradeshows, public events, their contact lists, and their customer lists. The better ones will be able to tell you what to expect from each event and have somewhat of a campaign strategy for your product.

Why: PR companies serve to get your product's name, brand, and image out there where people will notice, recognize, and hopefully eventually recall what your product is. Without this type of promotional effort, your product's public awareness may be shallow and slow in coming. If growth and acquiring market share is high on your list, then you cannot afford not to hire a PR company. PR companies succeed largely not in how the promotional materials are made but in their existing relationships with other promotional outlets and medium, and their knowledge of what's happening in the market place in real time. Both of these aspects are crucial in launching your product successfully.

Who: Hosting Company

What: Hosting companies rent out their servers to you for an online presence. Beyond providing a web server, they may bundle or sell independently other services such as email, security software, eCommerce modules, website design, etc.

When: Once you are ready to present your product and company to the world, you will need to create a website. This is especially important for small startups that need to look and feel like an established company online.

Where: The number of hosting companies are also numerous. A simple online search would yield dizzying choices. There are online guides on which web hosting service have the best user reviews. Use these if you don't have a referral from someone who has a similar business to yours in size and type of product.

Why: To be without an online presence with a reliable uptime and email service, not to mention FTP (File Transfer Protocol) service and other online capabilities is a sign of immaturity for any business starting out. A professionally designed web presence (despite how many actual people are working behind the scene) can create a strong favorable first impression. Most people ask for the product's URL instead of the company's information nowadays. This is your product and company's outer appearance where people make judgments about them. Choosing the right hosting company for this critical aspect of your business is a very serious matter. You will most likely maintain a long term relationship with a hosting company because it can be a major hassle to change a hosting company without disruption to your business.

Who: Web Master

What: Web masters are people who design the look and feel of your website. They also involve themselves in additional functionalities of your website such as frontend and backend operational transactions and processes.

When: At the same time when you look for a hosting company. These functions go hand-in-hand.

Where: Hosting companies will often offer do-it-yourself design templates. Unless you are proficient with web design and the affiliated technology, it is probably best that you find a professional designer. Referral again is your best option. Otherwise if there is a particular website that you like when doing comparative shopping you can contact the webmaster listed on their pages. If your competitor can afford the quality that attracted your eyes, can you afford not to be at par?

Why: Similar to having a dependable hosting company you will want a competent web master. Having a low cost but incompetent web master will end up costing you more time, which is another manifestation of money. As your business grows and the market place changes around you, so will the web-based technology. Finding the right web master who is a professional will help you upgrade or migrate to better online business infrastructures faster and with less downtime. Non-functional websites or amateurish websites send just as strong a message to the customers as a professional one but has the opposite effect.

Who: Packaging Designer

 What: Package designers are artists who have experiences working with different types of package material, size, shape, and designs.

When: Finished packages are required to be displayed on store shelves. Often the same if not similar images are required on your website to attract attention, or on your promotional literature to be sent out or shown in public. When you are ready to promote your product in public you should consider getting the packaging design done. However, be forewarned that large distributors or resellers will often ask for changes in your packaging to optimize sales so don't commit to making too many units initially.

Where: The most efficient way to find package designers is through referrals from manufacturer's reps. This is because the reps tend to know what the buyers like in terms of packaging design and other companies whose products have been placed. The rep would have contacts that could link you to the designer behind the products that already secured a shelf space with the reseller.

Why: People judge a book by its cover all the time. In the same way, people will judge your product by the appeal from its packaging. A novel and eye-catching design will dramatically improve the chances of your product being distributed by resellers or purchased by customers. Hiring a top quality designer who is familiar with your type of product is one of the best investments you can make.

Who: Universal Product Code

What: If you ever intend on selling your product through retail stores then you will need to license UPC codes. These barcodes allow the stores to scan the boxes and perform inventory control functions at the same time.

When: While working with your packaging designer you should supply the UPC codes to him or her for inclusion on the boxes.

Where: UPC codes are licensed from a company called GS1 US. You "join" GS1 US and get assigned an identification number that appears as the first part of your UPC codes. There are resellers of UPC codes that you can also purchase from for a small quantity of codes if you have very few products.

Why: UPC codes are a requirement for most resellers.

Who: Internet Service Provider

What: ISPs provide the pipe between your business and the rest of the online world.

When: Once you decide to launch an online business the first thing you need to do is get internet service.

Where: Depending on where you live, you may have several choices or just one service provider. The service packages will differ. Choosing a business package over residential service will ensure better service but at a higher cost.

Why: You will need a website, email accounts, hosting service, and research capabilities, just to name a few. Getting an ISP that is reliable especially when your business internet service needs restoration after a storm, etc. should be your highest concern when shopping for one.

Who: Payment Gateway and Processor

What: A payment gateway is a software that is part of the eCommerce module of your website where financial information is transmitted electronically. The payment processor is an entity that approves the financial transaction and settles it between your merchant account and the customer's credit card company. Your merchant account has your banking information to deposit and withdraw money. When a customer submits his credit card information on your website, the gateway transfers that information to the processor who then settles the transaction with the customer's credit card company and your bank using your merchant account assigned by the processor.

When: This arrangement needs to be finalized and the information given to your web master to incorporate into your eCommerce module on your website.

Where: There are many payment gateway (software) providers. You have the option of buying it independently or go to some payment processors who offer free gateway software. A quick search online will reveal many credit card processing companies. The key point is to identify and add up all the fees, whether they are fixed or per occurrence, and determine which package suits your product's transaction pattern the closest.

Why: This is an essential part of the technology if you want to conduct sales online directly. The gateway is synonymous to the credit card swiping machine just as your online store is synonymous to a brick and mortar store.

Who: Patent Attorney

What: Patent attorney serves several functions. First he will give you an assessment on whether your invention is patentable. Second, he can help with patent search and filing. Third, he needs to be able to defend your patent if there is any dispute.

When: After you determine that your product in fact does have a market to sell to, you should interview patent attorneys on the likelihood of getting it patented.

Where: The best sources are inventor associations where others have preceded on the same path. Be sure to ask for referrals and compare different costs and work styles, on top of expertise that is relevant to your invention.

Why: A patent attorney gives you the reassurance that your intellectual property is at least in review by the US Patent and Trademark Office. His critical value is in defining the claims of your invention, which are the only defensible part. Without a patent attorney, you could use a patent agent and do patent search or even submit a patent application but you will not have the legal expertise to back you if your patent claims are not strong enough. This is not an area to skimp on.

Who: Accountant

What: An accountant provides tax guidance and reporting service. He can also recommend a financial management and reporting system that you will use to track and analyze your company's finances, generate purchase orders and invoices.

When: Seek an accountant as early as you can, once you have determined that it is a business you want to launch. If you engage an accountant before that, you could also pay him for his professional evaluation of your pro forma financial analysis to see if the assumptions are realistic.

Where: Ask for referral from business associates or inventor clubs. Be sure the referral is for someone who is familiar or has experience dealing with your type of product.

Why: It's possible to set up your own financial reporting system such as QuickBooks or Peachtree. However, unless you have a good accounting background or finance training, you will find that setting up all the accounts, the assets and counter assets, etc. can be confusing. You do not want to set it up incorrectly because any incorrect categorization of accounts may cause problems in your reconciliation and tax reporting. Get a professional.

Who: Banker

What: Banks are essential to set up your banking account and possibly credit cards. They also provide loans, money transfer service, letter of credit sales, etc.

When: As soon as you know that you will receive funding and establish a company name you need to set up a bank account to manage your financial transactions. You would do this after you incorporate and have your corporate tax ID.

Where: Local banks have their relative advantages when you need to perform frequent cash transactions. National banks and international banks are easier to work with if you deal with international vendors and need to wire money or use letter of credit to transact. If you use the same banks for letter of credit transactions you would save some transaction fees.

Why: This is an essential part of your business operation.

Who: Business Attorney

 What: Business attorneys address the parts of your business the patent attorney does not. This includes contracts and agreements, non-disclosure agreements, business structure, business name and other intellectual property, licensing agreements, partnership agreements, supplier agreements, etc.

When: When you decide to incorporate.

Where: By referral remains the top choice. Ask your network or inventor's club. Interview attorneys who have experience working with products or companies similar to yours in nature and size. Compare costs.

Why: Virtually all business transactions rely on written agreements. Do not make the mistake of doing deals based on verbal agreements only. Memories fade and perceptions differ even if intensions are the same when you first make an agreement. The agreements need to be professionally written to ensure your best interest is represented. Obviously if any legal issues arise you will want a competent attorney to represent you. This includes product liability issues and any regulatory matters that impact your business.

Who: Promotional Material

 What: Promotional material formats include written, sight, and sound, and now video. It is no longer limited to brochures, cards, fliers, and product images. Unless you are fully capable of producing professional looking material otherwise you need to hire a marketing person or firm to produce your promotional material.

When: After you have set up your operational infrastructure and are ready to reach out to the world to begin marketing.

Where: Marketing brochures and similar material can be produced by a marketing professional familiar with the jargon of your new trade. The physical reproduction can be outsourced to companies that specialize in printing marketing material for small business such as Vistaprint online printer. To find marketing professional you should ask for referrals from entrepreneur clubs or work with your PR firm to find a contractor.

Why: Just as people will judge your product by its box design, they will judge your company by the promotional material you send. This is a crucial area as it is intended to show your best side to the public. Make sure the marketing message speaks clearly and concisely to the target consumers, including the benefit statements for them.

Who: Insurance Agent

What: If you begin by working out of your house, you need to know that your home insurance will not cover your business activities. They include any inventory you temporarily store at home, the general liability insurance, business property insurance, and health insurance for you and your employees, unemployment insurance, workman's compensation insurance, and even business interruption insurance if you opt for it.

When: As soon as you have assets to protect.

Where: Local insurance agents are easier to work with for small businesses. Larger insurance companies have products for small businesses but you will find that using an agent is easier to compare premiums and coverage. From time to time you will have to change your coverage as dictated by large resellers. Many will ask for insurance riders with their names on it. A local insurance agent who knows you in person will be easier to work with on these changes.

Why: Insurance is a necessity. Do not make the mistake of not having liability insurance especially if you have a physical product that could cause harm somehow. It only takes one frivolous lawsuit to bankrupt a small business.

Who: Equipment and Supplier

What: Whether you work out of your house or have an office, you will need physical infrastructure to operate. Office equipment and supply vendors are as varied as the people you will meet.

When: The moment you start operating as a business you will need to separate your own equipment, space, and supplies from the business. These operating expenses are tax deductable.

Where: Establish an account with a major office supply vendor such as Staples so you can reap discounts or rewards.

Why: Office equipment can be expensive. They include computer equipment, printers, fax machines, and even water coolers, supply cabinets, desks, tables and chairs. Office supply also tends to deplete quickly once you begin business development and promotional activities. Paper, ink, writing equipment, envelopes, folders and trays, etc. are only a few to start. Consider leasing furniture until your cash flow is more established. Always weigh the options of lease verses buy before making your decisions.

Who: Business Consultant

What: Unless you are already familiar with the industry you are venturing into, otherwise it is a good idea to find someone who knows the ins-and-outs of the industry. Consultants are typically ex-employees of companies in that industry who still have contacts and are up to date with the industry dynamics.

When: In the early stages of strategy formation is when you need such expert advice.

Where: Look online for industry associations. Ask for consultant lists and interview them for their understanding. Ideally you know someone already in an inventor's club who is willing to advise you for free. However once the subject becomes involved, you should hire a consultant on a per hour or project basis.

Why: The difference of having knowledge and experience is sometimes the difference of saving a few hundred thousand dollars. A consultant who knows her stuff can help you navigate hidden dangers and find shortcuts by way of knowing the players and how the culture and processes work within a particular industry. It is money well spent if you are not familiar with the new industry.

Now that you have a bird's eye view of the business relationships and a cast of characters you're most likely to bump into, let's begin deconstructing the nuts and bolts of the commercialization process so that you can assemble and/or reconstruct your own venture. Next we will examine the process of evolving a concept to a profitable product or service in the form of a construction blueprint.

> A loner in an interconnected world is not avoiding problems but asking for them.

CHAPTER 2 ACTION ITEMS

1. Identify the ecosystem for your concept as if it were to be commercialized.

2. Do preliminary research on each player, identify the 5Ws + H (who, what, when, where, why, and how) and prepare questions by category to interview them.

3. Identify the motivation factor of each player who you will likely come in contact with, regardless of who ultimately brings your concept to market.

Chapter 3

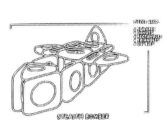

The C2C Blueprint... a Step-by-Step Approach

An architect relies on the blueprint to communicate his overall design to the construction crew. The crew relies on it to determine the proper sequence of building. There is great parallel in the way a physical structure is erected and the way a concept evolves into a commercialized product.

Most people think of product commercialization as materializing an idea into a product on a store shelf. That really is only three-quarters of the story. To reach profitability there needs to be a fourth component which is product lifecycle management.

In a corporate setting, this is what product managers do for a living. Corporations may have the resources to set up an internal incubation bed or a new product planning department, etc. These business functions tend to have established processes and procedures to evaluate and rigorously determine whether an idea is a go or no go. A product manager's role in bringing the new product to market tends to be limited in scope unless the company is small or the project involves few people.

In contrast, for someone with just a great idea and no backing of corporate resources, you would own the whole piece of pie. You would need to incubate and nurture your idea to the point of commercial market entry and then ongoing management in the full extent and definition of commercialization. If you find yourself in that position and needing moral support, you could begin by looking in the mirror for company; there will be many times when a team composed of "me, myself, and I" will be burning the midnight oil together. Many people have achieved the extraordinary by staying highly disciplined and efficient before they were able to hire help. You can achieve the improbable as well if you thoroughly apply the sequence within and the rationale behind this blueprint.

This commercialization blueprint has four phases that show the **macro-view** of a venture building process. Each phase has its particular objective. It is not surprising that the overall blueprint resembles that of a monumental physical building process.

Phase	**Objective**
1. **Building the Foundation**	Make Go or No-Go decision
2. **Planning and Strategy**	Get funding
3. **Implementation**	Build the company
4. **Ongoing Management**	Obtain profitability

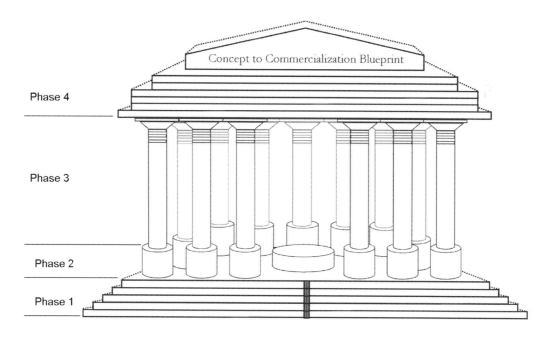

The information in this chapter identifies the "**what**" and "**how**" of the concept to commercialization process at a high level. The intent here is not to describe everything in detail (yet) so try not to get bogged down with the descriptions but simply understand the blueprint and its organization first. Much more details on exactly what should be considered will be discussed in the subsequent product evaluation chapters (4 through 7). Likewise as you read those chapters later you should keep in mind the structure and sequence of this blueprint and the progression framework so as to leverage each tool into a coherent system.

THE FIRST PHASE

In the first phase, the focus revolves around the discovery and evaluation of a new concept. The end goal is to help you determine whether you have enough justification to pursue your idea as a business venture or if you should move on to the next big idea.

At this point the emphasis is about 50/50 between product design and business issues. What you will do likewise is equally split between creative and critical thinking. You can probably simulate different product and business scenarios without risking too much financially. You also have the most control over your time and expenditure during this time. It is analogous to the dating period; you can walk away without obligations.

There are <u>10</u> <u>steps</u> involved in the foundational building and discovery phase.

Step 1 of the Foundation is Concept Development

Your objective is to be able to fine-tune your idea into something that you can

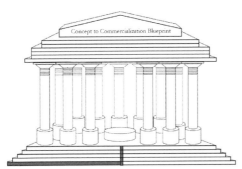

clearly describe. The more well defined and fleshed out your idea is, the easier it will be for you to move on to the next steps. However your cost should be kept to a minimum. See what you can get away with without spending money. Do just enough to enable a physical or theoretical representation for illustration purposes.

The types of activities you will do include product function and feature description, usage and user identification, and why you think it's a good idea.

Step 2 of the Foundation is Comparative Research

Your objective is to find out if someone else already developed this idea into a commercialized product or service. If someone has beaten you to it, you still might be able to commercialize it if your idea is better. This is a step within the overall market research effort. It's not the first step per se, but as long as it is done within the scope of the discovery and foundation building phase, the exact order is not critical. It helps aspiring entrepreneurs gain confidence.

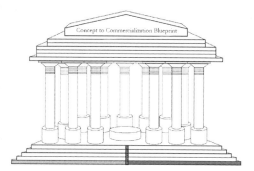

The types of activities you will do include looking around online by doing keyword searches and patent searches or by asking someone familiar with the particular industry. Keep in mind that sometimes a patented design by someone else may not surface in the marketplace for years.

Step 3 of the Foundation is Rough Prototyping/Business Modeling

Your objective is to transform your idea into something tangible. At this point the goal is to make something that is good enough to represent and perhaps

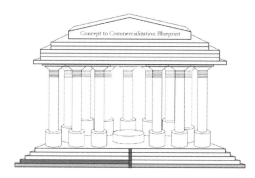

simulate how your idea works as a precursor to getting accurate market feedback. There is no need to spend thousands of dollars.

The types of activities you will do may include going to craft or hardware stores for some raw material. This is the time to experiment with different types of material that will perform the functions your product promises. Sometimes a non-functional mock-up will do as well at this point as long as you are able to effectively describe how it would have worked if actual materials were used.

Step 4 of the Foundation is Feedback and Validation

Your objective is to be objective. No mother thinks her baby is ugly. But if you want to showcase yours, then getting someone else's honest opinion is essential. You want to get opinions from the targeted user and buyer groups. Get as many diverse feedbacks as possible to validate your own assumptions.

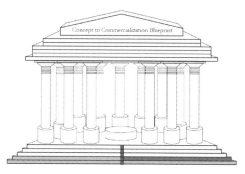

The types of activities you will do may include going to friends and families first, but definitely ask people further removed from you for honest feedback. You might also attend small groups and use them as focus groups to tell you how people perceive your idea and whether they would buy it and at what price.

Step 5 of the Foundation is Concept Refinement

Your objective is to take the feedback you got from the previous step and work it

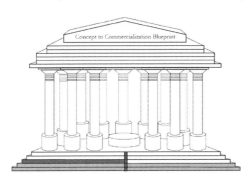

into your prototype. The closer you can achieve the desired functionality as described by the target user group the better.

The types of activities you will do may include swapping out material, eliminating parts, or research. Research how to refine your design so that it meets the functionality that will sell your product. This is the time to completely restart from a blank slate if your idea is hot but your design is not.

Step 6 of the Foundation is Market Assessment

Your objective is to understand who will buy your product and why with a market segmentation study. The result also allows you to identify competition within each segment and build custom profiles for market strategy.

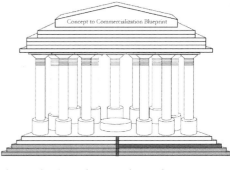

The types of activities you will do are to identify the market size, user profile, how similar products are priced, sold, and used. You will need to understand the 4Ps of marketing mix (Product, Price, Placement, and Promotion) to do a good job here.

Step 7 of the Foundation is Distribution Assessment

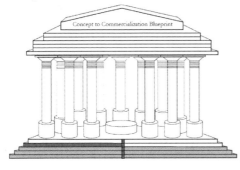

Your objective is to understand who will potentially distribute your product.

The type of activities you will do is to identify where similar products are sold, and by whom. Don't make the mistake of assuming that you will not need wholesale distributors. Even the best products use channels to get into homes.

Step 8 of the Foundation is Resources Identification

Your objective is to figure out what resources would be required to bring your product into production and commercialization.

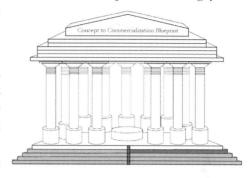

The type of activities you will do is primarily research. At this point you need to break down the collective to-do list and determine what resources are required to make each step happen. Resources are typically money, talent, and time. Money can buy talent, other people's time, and knowledge.

Step 9 of the Foundation is Financial Modeling & Projection

Your objective is to take the first critical thinking step and determine whether this idea will ever be profitable. If profitable, is it sufficient to meet your own financial goals?

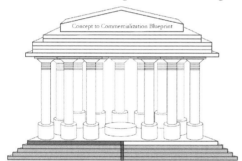

The types of activities you will do at this point are at a rudimentary level from a financial analysis perspective. You want to do a quick and dirty assessment of the cost of goods, potential price ranges, and your profit margin based on preliminary data only. You can do this by using reasonable assumptions to create different scenarios by manipulating cost, units, price, and required margin.

Step 10 of the Foundation is Determination of Go or No Go

Your objective is to decide whether your idea has the potential to become a commercial success and whether you are willing to do what it takes to make it.

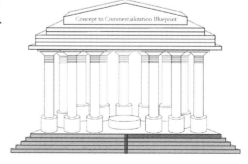

The type of activities you will do is primarily soul-searching. The financial analysis and the market research should have told you whether this is a pipe dream or if the market is real and profitable margin is achievable. Discuss with someone with similar experience if possible.

The foundational work is necessary for two main reasons. First, it uncovers real life issues for you to consider and evaluate. Moving ahead is basically a decision to be committed to a major undertaking and should not be taken lightly. Second, all the work and knowledge you gain up to this point will support the planning module in the next phase.

Whether figuratively or literally speaking, if the foundation is strong, the structure has a better chance of surviving future storms. If the foundational work is shoddy or incomplete, the infrastructure standing on it may crumble or collapse. This is the least risky phase yet holds the most implications.

THE SECOND PHASE

The second phase deals with the detailed **planning and strategy** aspects of your venture.

The goal is to optimize your chances of success by exploring every aspect of your potential business in minute details. Once the research and analyses have been done, the information you acquired would allow you to do careful planning and craft strategies from where to sell to what to say, how much to charge and how much you'll make, etc.

From this point forward you will be wearing the entrepreneurial hat instead of the inventor's hat most of the time. Incidentally, in case you have not seen one, the entrepreneurial hat has many labels. Rotating them allows you to play different roles throughout the day.

Your financial investment will increase and therefore your risk will also increase. However, assuming that you are not completely financially independent and therefore would not fund the entire venture with your own money (most of us cannot), your end goal for this phase is to produce a realistic summary of all the plans and strategies in a document called the business plan. The activities in this phase are equivalent to those of a long term relationship before tying the knot. You can still walk away but you would have invested major time and efforts already.

By the way, this is where only serious entrepreneurs should continue and casual tinkerers/inventors stop. Every step you take will cost more time and money. From now on it's real money being spent at a rapid pace. If you do not have strong confidence about your product or the prospect of financial success by the time you're through with this phase you should really consider stopping.

There are 14 steps involved in the planning and strategy phase. Each step is highlighted below. Business insights that pertain to the steps will be presented in much more details in subsequent chapters.

Step 1 of the Planning and Strategy Phase is Obtain IP Protection

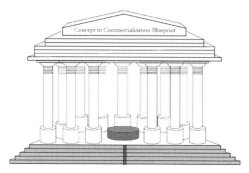

Your objective is to be able to shop your intellectual creation beyond the trusted groups without fear of someone stealing your hard work.

The types of activities you will do include patent and copyright research. You will need to trademark your product name and company name as well. Whether to protect your creation from potential theft is a decision based more on marketing considerations than on legal grounds, as most experienced entrepreneurs will tell you.

Step 2 of the Planning and Strategy Phase is Functional Prototyping

Your objective is two folds here. First, you need to prove that the design you have in mind can indeed be produced cost effectively. Second, you need your

product to work in front of other people. People will pass instant judgment on your product based on its appearance and stated functions. A real functional prototype as close to the final product as possible is highly recommended. You will be using it for promotional activities later.

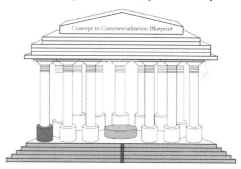

The types of activities you will do include trying out real raw components and putting together your product to test out the assembly process. If you are unable make the actual components, then you need to hire people who can. Machinists and professional prototype makers can help. Swap out parts if they are too difficult to assemble or cost too much to procure.

Step 3 of the Planning and Strategy Phase is Detailed Marketing Plan

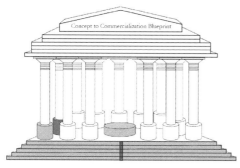

Your objective is to clearly define your product's value propositions to the target user group. The marketing work should generate a comprehensive strategy on how to tackle the market complete with the product's proposition, positioning, placement, pricing, promotion, and packaging statements. The goal here is not to implement but to understand and be able to justify your value and pricing.

The types of activities you will do include competitive research, user profile research, pricing research, and packaging research. Expect to do lots of online research, reading industry magazines and articles, join associations, go window shopping for the actual feel of competitive products and how they are presented, etc.

Step 4 of the Planning and Strategy Phase is Distribution Channel Planning

Your objective is to be able to identify the distribution network structure for your product. You need to know who's who in the industry and how the industry operates, such as any specific windows of opportunity, cycles that insiders adhere to which if you miss could cost you an entire season or year.

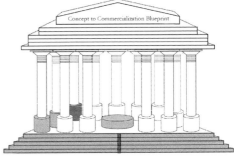

The types of activities you will do include researching competitive products to see where they are being sold. You will need to contact potential distributors and resellers and see if they have any stated requirements for new vendors. You will also need to know the margin requirements of resellers and typical quantities that they wholesale.

Step 5 of the Planning and Strategy Phase is Manufacturing & Vendor Planning

Your objective is to find factories and other service vendors who can cater to you at the minimum production quantity with the lowest cost and highest quality possible.

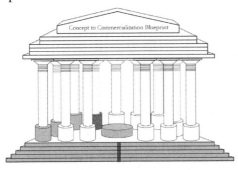

The types of activities you will do include online keyword search for manufacturers and service providers. It may include talking to professional trade associations or go to tradeshows where such service providers solicit their business. You will need to assess samples they send for quality and price. You will also need to ensure cost control, delivery arrangement, and compliance testing. If doing business overseas, you will have the extra duties of understanding export control laws, custom inspection process, warehousing, and freight schedules, etc.

Step 6 of the Planning and Strategy Phase is IT Infrastructure Planning

Your objective is to be able to handle and manage every process of your business operation from internal communications, order processing, customer interfacing, financial management, warehousing and inventory control, and any other frontend and backend operational procedures your business needs.

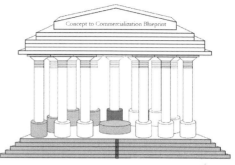

The types of activities you will do include finding and assessing vendors who provide the Information Technology (IT) systems you need. This includes telecommunications and data warehousing infrastructures such as EDI (Electronic Data Interface) that might be required by large wholesalers. You will definitely need web developers, graphics designers, and eCommerce modules if you choose to sell direct. If you sell via large retailers you will also need to research their requirements for vendors. Anything to do with voice or data communications will need to be identified and researched during this stage.

Step 7 of the Planning and Strategy Phase is Customer Interface Planning

Your objective is to establish the necessary methods and procedures that allow all customer interactions. The goal is to make it as customer friendly and enticing as possible. This area feeds into the business operations section, but because of its importance it should be addressed with utmost attention separately.

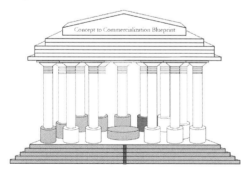

The types of activities you will do include designing and running simulations of a product sale from A to Z. You will probably use a flowchart or similar to depict the steps involved in the transfer of goods from warehouse to consumer via several layers of middlemen. You need to understand the interfaces from each party's perspective. The middlemen are resellers who are also your customers since they buy from you at wholesale prices. The interface design needs to include both frontend (purchase process) and backend (order management and fulfillment) including inventory control considerations.

Step 8 of the Planning and Strategy Phase is Company Infrastructure Planning

Your objective is to be able to conduct business activities professionally. Whether this is in your basement or a rented office space is irrelevant. The goal is to be able to conduct business activities including meetings and presentations.

The types of activities you will do include determining the type of office environment and space required. This can be done in phases as well although the moment you have employees and customer meetings you will need a professional setting. You will need to determine the location, space requirements, office furniture, rental or lease supplies, office equipment such as PC, fax, even a water cooler, etc. You do this by researching and calling for prices. You should do financial analysis on whether to buy, rent, or lease capital equipment which can be depreciated in years, if your business can indeed be sustained for that long.

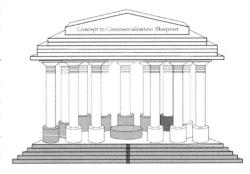

Step 9 of the Planning and Strategy Phase is Legal and Insurance Planning

Your objective is protection. Protect your company, your product, and especially yourself against frivolous lawsuits or legitimate damages.

The types of activities you will do include finding a business attorney who can

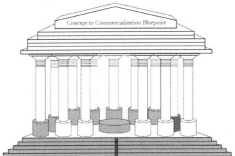

draft business agreements for you. The type of business agreement may extend from confidential agreement to sales, licensing, incorporation, shareholder, and employment agreement. You will also need to research insurance agents and companies willing to issue insurance for your type of product. The amount of insurance will depend largely on your distribution channel's liability coverage requirement.

Step 10 of the Planning and Strategy Phase is Human Resources Planning

Your objective is to be able to handle every requirement and interaction without being unprofessional. You also need talents and skills to manage marketing and sales, accounting, order management, and customer service.

The types of activities you will do include identifying the types of talent you will need and what each person's responsibilities are. You will need to determine whether to hire permanent or temporary employees and how to compensate them. You will also need to find the expertise associated with employment law and benefits, and tax reporting. You should research extensively on service providers and have a hiring strategy as business grows.

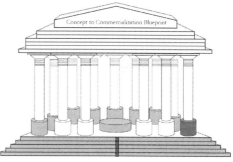

Step 11 of the Planning and Strategy Phase is Business Operations Planning

Your objective is to be able to walk away and yet the business continues to operate. You need to understand and design how the business operates at every level and what infrastructure and procedures are required. The goal is to set up a system that provides you with instructions and monitoring capability.

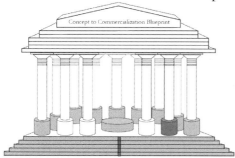

The types of activities you will do include tracing through each aspect of the business by functional areas. You need to visualize or simulate data and physical product movements and transactions. You become the brain of the different parts of the business. Your central nervous system is the continuous feedback you get from the methods and procedures you developed to ensure consistent performance.

Step 12 of the Planning and Strategy Phase is Detailed Financial Analysis

Your objective is to identify the industry standard profit margin for your type of product. You want to be sure that your cost factors are correctly identified, your asking price is realistic, and your profit margin is acceptable based on different growth scenarios. You will also want to look carefully at cash flow projections to ensure you can stay in business even when the business is slow for years, not just months.

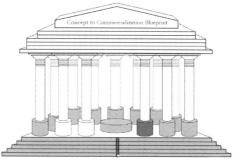

The types of activities you will do include cost factor identification and research. You will need to build a financial spreadsheet to run different scenarios based on quantity ordered and sold. You will need to know which accounting and financial reporting systems to use by talking with your accountant. You will finally determine how much funding you will need based on growth and cash flow scenarios which feed into your capital budgeting exercise.

Step 13 of the Planning and Strategy Phase is Business Ownership Planning

Your objective is to identify the right type of business entity for the venture. Based on the analyses you've done so far, is it smartest to sell the idea, license it out, partner with someone, or take it all the way by launching a business around your idea? Depending on funding choices and business operation responsibilities, company ownership and shares need to be clearly spelled out.

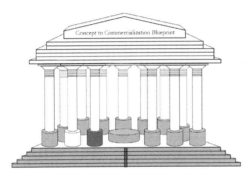

The types of activities you will do include assessing whether the business should be a sole proprietorship, partnership, or corporation. You need to research the pros and cons of each and consult with an accountant based on the projection of your earnings and the level of protection you need. If you decide to seek venture funding, you will also need to determine business ownership based on the level of funding. If you decide that you prefer to outsource the entire business operations to product launch companies then you will need to understand the pros and cons of profit sharing, which would be royalty in that case.

Step 14 of the Planning and Strategy Phase is Funding & Business Plan Writing

Your objective is to be able to promote and sell your business idea to potential investors.

The types of activities you will do is mostly collecting all the research and analyses you have completed and compiling them into a convincing promotional document called the Business Plan. You will need to research the most suitable formats for your particular type of business. You will need to research and identify potential venture capitalists or angel investors who are most likely to fund your type of product. You will need to spend time writing the business plan and rehearse pitching the value propositions before you have secured funding meetings.

The planning and strategic efforts take a formal approach to assessing the commercial success probability for your idea. There are a few groups of people you need to convince to cross that bridge. First is yourself. By doing all the factual research and objective analyses, you should have developed a clear-eyed sense of whether this is something you would want to invest your life in.

Investors will ask the same questions and need justifications on why they would hand their money to you. People you recruit will want to know that the company is sustainable, market is real, and product is good. Lastly, the people you sell to need to be convinced of the product's value and justified price points.

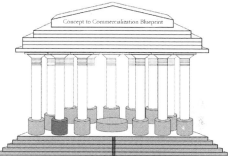

Concept to Commercialization Blueprint

All your research and earned understanding will go into writing those promotional literature and salient sales points that get your product into the right distribution channels and on the shelves.

As you will now see, the planning modules provide the underlying support for their corresponding counterparts in the implementation phase, albeit in reversed order. Graphically this is how the foundational work supports the planning modules.

THE THIRD PHASE

The third phase deals with the **implementation** aspects of your venture.

All the planning and analyses in the world won't do an ounce of good if not put into action. Starting in this phase you will spend lots of real money on building up the product and the business.

If you had done your planning well, most if not all of your to-do lists would have been identified. The nitty-gritty decisions of business operations such as methods and procedures, employee relations, specific aspects of any operational strategy (marketing, sales, infrastructure, financial, etc.) need to be identified, properly designed, and determined during this phase.

The implementation activities are in effect carried out in reversed order from their planning counterparts. This makes sense once you see that planning takes a top-down approach while building takes a bottoms-up approach.

Implementation is more about spending money based on the strategy you have set. The order of activities also centers on money by beginning with who owns what, down to monitoring the expenditures, and spending it to set up the rest of the infrastructures.

It is imperative to identify any prerequisites of each stage and make sure that the proverbial cart isn't put before the horse. Do not make the false assumption that more people will get things done faster all the time. After all, it takes nine months to give birth to a baby, having nine women does not get it done in one.

The implementation activities are listed in this order:

Acquire funding

Incorporate business and shareholder agreements

Setup accounting/financial reporting systems

Setup business operations (frontend/backend) processes

Acquire human resources

Acquire legal and insurance protections

Setup company infrastructure

Write out customer interface processes

Setup IT infrastructure

Acquire manufacturer and service vendors

Acquire distribution channels

Execute marketing strategy

Begin limited production

Graphically this is how the foundational work supports the planning modules which in turn align the implementation activities.

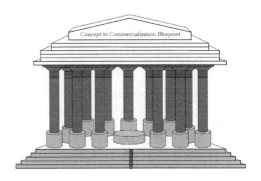

THE FOURTH PHASE

The fourth phase deals with the **Lifecycle Management** aspects of your venture.

Assuming you have successfully placed your product on some national retailer's store shelves, profit is still not guaranteed. In business unexpected events happen frequently and only those who are on their toes can manage changes as soon as they happen. This is where ongoing product lifecycle management comes in.

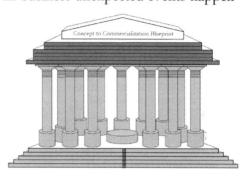

In this ongoing phase of business management, it is important to point out a few things which might as well be set in concrete:

Cash flow needs to be monitored constantly. It could cripple your business even if you have major accounts, pending orders, but unable to make payments.

Eventually you will want to consider the next phase of the business, whether to license, IPO, acquire, or sell. This can be driven by investors and shareholders.

People management issues need to be addressed everyday. People are hired, trained, transferred, promoted, or fired as situations change.

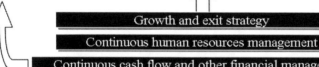

Growth and exit strategy

Continuous human resources management

Continuous cash flow and other financial management

Market expansion management

Continuous cost, process, quality improvement

Continuous market change analysis

You will either grow or shrink. It is almost impossible to stay the same size. If you choose to grow, every aspects of your business will be impacted.

Market conditions constantly change. What works today may not work a few months from now. It is necessary to continuously monitor and analyze changes.

Costs tend to rise, which makes it necessary to improve processes and quality to compete.

The four phases of product commercialization together form a system. It is a process which tackles issues in a logical and sequential manner. You need the foundation discoveries to support the planning modules. The planning modules in turn ensure the proper alignment and sequence of the implementation activities. Together they uphold the product lifecycle management and form the blueprint.

The Concept to Commercialization Blueprint

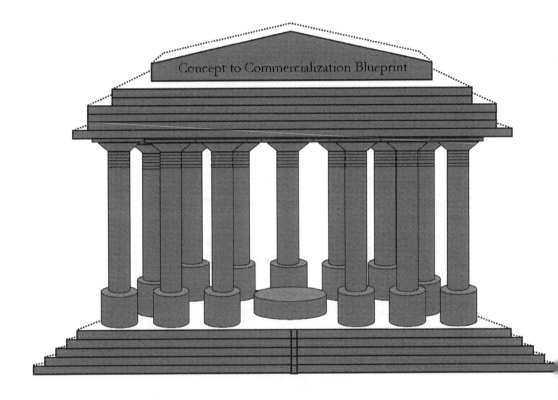

Appendix 2 shows a consolidated master blueprint.

Appendix 3 lists the commercialization stages in a quadrant format.

Concept Evaluation within the C2C Blueprint

Just as inventions are a part of the innovation process, concept evaluation is the first part of a venture creation process. It uses simulation and analysis without involving actual risks associated with launching a business.

As mentioned in Chapter 1, there are significant differences between pure concept evaluation and commercial viability assessment. Pure concept evaluation can be done without involving much of the planning, strategy, implementation, and product lifecycle management phases of the blueprint. Therefore its function is necessarily limited. The best time to use a pure concept evaluation is when you have an idea that you need to investigate but don't know if it is good enough to merit the rigorous approach recommended in the commercial viability assessment process. If you are quite sure that your idea will be successful, then you should immediately use the commercial viability assessment questionnaire in Appendix 4.

Graphically a pure concept evaluation looks like this:

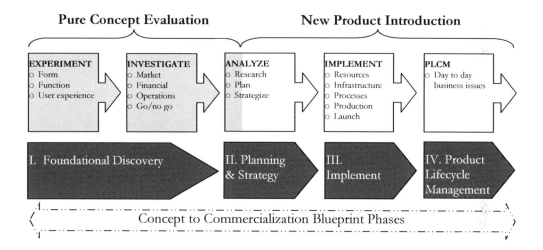

Notice how evaluating a concept involves activities that map primarily to Phase I. of the C2C blueprint. It includes preliminary research, planning, and analysis of the data to arrive at the Go or No Go decision. A concept is not advanced to in-depth analysis and beyond until it has been declared a Go. The entire blueprint describes from ideation all the way to market and ongoing management, which is far beyond the evaluation process.

How Business Emphasis Shifts Over Time

In the earliest stage of an idea most people tend to focus on the product or service attributes; as time goes on their emphasis shifts towards more business-related issues.

The following table shows an approximate percentage of emphasis across time and business areas. What it means is that two dynamics are at play here. First, the amount of time you should spend on each business area (e.g. R&D) changes over time as you move from stage to stage. Second, while within a stage (e.g. Lifecycle

Management), you should allocate different emphasis or your attention on the various aspects of the business.

This table is also more geared towards consumer products than service based businesses. Nevertheless there is much that can be applied for the service business. Simply substituting R&D for service definition and everything else continues to be applicable.

Recommended Approximate % of Emphasis (Resource Allocation) at Each Stage of the Concept Commercialization Process

% Emphasis / Stages / Business Area	Foundational Discovery		Planning & Strategy	Lifecycle Management
	Idea Formulation	Commercial Viability Evaluation	Infrastructure Planning & Implementation	Business Growth Management
R&D	70%	10%	5%	5%
Marketing	20%	50%	30%	40%
Finance	10%	30%	50%	25%
Product Lifecycle	0%	10%	15%	30%
	100%	100%	100%	100%

How to Read this Chart

For example, **R&D** should take up most (70%) of your attention and resources in the idea formulation stage. By the time you get to your venture's lifecycle management phase you use about 5% of your resources on it instead.

Likewise, during the **commercial viability evaluation** stage, most of the emphasis should be on marketing considerations (50%) followed by financial considerations (30%).

Keep in mind, of course, that this is a generic model used to describe a dynamic. Its purpose is to stress that business is not static. Different products and services will obviously have different allocation percentages but the overall process should be the same.

By the way, if you apply the logic behind this system, the optimal sequence of the 20 spastic questions first identified in Chapter 1 would become:

1. What does the entrepreneurial path look like at a high level? (*understanding*)

2. Is there an example of a product idea that got commercialized? (*case study*)

3. I have an idea. (*concept development*)

4. Does it already exist? (*comparative research*)

5. How do I make a prototype? (*rough prototyping*)

6. What do others think? (*feedback & validation*)

7. What is my marketing strategy? (*market assessment*)

8. What do I need to make it happen? (*initial resources identification*)

9. Will it make money? (*preliminary financial modeling*)

10. Should I take the plunge? (*determine Go/No go before detailed analyses*)

11. How do I protect my creation? (*IP protection*)

12. Who can make a functional prototype? (*functional prototyping*)

13. Who can I pitch the plan to? (*distribution planning*)

14. I got the funding, what's the next step?(*incorporating*)

15. What do I start building first? (*setup business infrastructure*)

16. How do I build the right team? (*acquire human resources*)

17. How do I find a manufacturer? (*acquire manufacturing capability*)

18. What marketing activities do I do? (*execute marketing strategy*)

19. Where do I start selling my product? (*acquire distribution channel*)

20. How do I become profitable? (*product lifecycle management*)

A systematic approach ensures better chances of completion without reworks.

CHAPTER 3 ACTION ITEMS

1. Perform high level investigative works to generate the information needed during the foundational and discovery phase. The information will help you decide whether your idea has merit and should be pursued further or dropped altogether.

2. Follow the 14 steps of the planning and strategy phase and gather the data you need to do preliminary planning. The knowledge you gain here will help you formulate any workable strategy.

3. Generate a draft business plan based on your preliminary research data from phases I and II.

4. Simulate the implementations steps with your concept to see what resource requirements you will need. At the same time determine how you would potentially obtain those resources.

5. Determine what ongoing product management skills it would take to nurture a new venture based on your idea to profitability. Do this even if you intend on licensing; it will give you an advantage in negotiations.

6. Develop a realistic expectation of how your idea would move through the phases and what different business skills it would require over time.

7. Reorganize or reprioritize your own set of questions from Chapter 1 so you can develop a preliminary roadmap.

Part III

THE NUTS AND BOLTS OF COMMERCIAL VIABILITY ASSESSMENT

"Details create the big picture."

Sanford I. Weill

Chapter 4

Marketing Preparations... Doing Your Homework

Contrary to popular belief, marketing isn't all glitzy and glamorous. In fact, a successful marketing campaign often requires similar efforts presumably as those of a military campaign. Business at times is war.

Both types of campaign require a great deal of efforts founded on tirelessly strategizing and tweaking before their actual implementations.

The amount of information to be covered in a marketing campaign is rather extensive. To make it easier to digest I have split the information between this and the next chapter. In this chapter we will explore the foundational work of marketing and sales which is getting to know the territory and the people involved. The next chapter will dive deeply into the outward facing aspects of marketing and sales.

The target landscape is divided into three categories. They are:

    (1) The industry that your concept will be launched into

    (2) The competition that will greatly influence your actions

    (3) The target customer base your concept will cater to

Each of these critical areas needs to be analyzed based on solid information. Such information will then feed into individualized sub-strategies which are then rolled up into a coherent marketing and sales strategy.

CHAPTER ORIENTATION

The primary purpose of this and the next three chapters is to provide you with sufficient information to rate the evaluation questions in Appendix 4. The secondary purpose is to expose business knowledge and insights that an aspiring entrepreneur must become familiar with.

We will focus on what you need to know or insights that only experience can dispense. Therefore if you need more explanations on any business topic I would encourage you to do more research. There are excellent business text books as well as plenty of online resources on business terminology just clicks away.

If possible you should have a copy of Appendix 4 on hand as you read Chapters 4 to 7. If that's not practical, the evaluation questions have also been replicated at the end of each subsection for your convenience.

You might notice that the order of the evaluation questions does not match the order of the business knowledge contents exactly. This may seem puzzling at first but it makes total sense if you simply compare the table of contents between them.

As real life does not follow text books so the evaluation thought process does not mirror the business knowledge structure exactly; the order of the evaluation questions reflect the typical thought process of an inventor and aspiring entrepreneur, from idea creation to financial assessment. The chapter contents, on the other hand, follow a logical sequence that builds up the knowledge pertaining to each business subjects.

Be forewarned… the knowledge contained here is collected from over 20 years of professional experiences, three startups, and a MBA education. The information is necessarily extensive. I would recommend that you scan through Appendix 4 to get a sense of the questions before reading these business knowledge chapters.

Likewise it is most useful if you already have a concept to evaluate with. If not, another option is to use an existing product and "trace through" its developmental steps with the questions. Otherwise you might find it difficult to read through. The easiest way to navigate through them is by looking at a map on the following page.

We will cover from **The Elevator Pitch** to **Customer Profiling** in this chapter. The work done in this chapter will naturally support the second half of the marketing and sales evaluation efforts, namely the marketing mixes in Chapter 5.

> The preparation efforts behind marketing outreaches are every bit as critical as the foundation of a physical structure.

Marketing & Sales Activities Map

4.1 THE ELEVATOR PITCH

4.2 INDUSTRY ANALYSIS
- **Revenue size**
- **Market characteristics**
- **Market dynamics**
- **Market segmentation**

4.3 COMPETITIVE ANALYSIS
- **Competitor profiling**
- **Barrier to entry**
- **Differentiation**
- **Substitution**

4.4 CUSTOMER PROFILING
- **Research**
- **Demographics**
- **Usage pattern**
- **Sources of influence**
- **Identify customer's values**

MARKETING MIXES
- **Product/Service**
  - R&D
  - Design
    - Customer friendly
    - KISS principle
    - Physical design factors
      - Function
      - Form
      - Material
      - Quality
    - Ergonomic
    - Design for the future
    - Safety and liability
  - Making prototypes and models
  - Feedback, validation, refinement

MARKETING MIXES (continued)
- **Positioning**
  - The importance of relevance
  - Value proposition
    - Need vs. want
    - Value and worth
    - Core value vs. secondary
    - New vs. improved
  - Writing positioning statement
  - Branding, naming, logo
  - Getting noticed
- **Pricing**
  - A baseline understanding
  - Dispelling a myth
  - All about psychology
  - How to set prices
    - Cost plus approach
    - Benchmark approach
    - Maintaining margin approach
    - Value based approach
    - Supply & demand approach
    - Intangible based approach
  - Pricing adjustment
- **Packaging**
  - Physical considerations
  - Display considerations
  - Techniques
    - Using surprises and bonus
    - Value vs. price
    - Licensing
- **Promotion**
    - Objective
    - Audience
    - Message
    - Delivery
- **Placement**
    - Anatomy of distribution
    - Sales
- **Overall Strategy**
  - Lifecycle management
  - Go-to-market strategy

SNAPIT! AS A TOOL FOR ILLUSTRATION

We will use a hypothetical invention at its conceptual stage to help clarify some business concepts in the next three chapters.

Let's call this invention "SnapIt!" SnapIt! is a power hand tool idea that anyone who does housework or a bit of woodworking can come up with. It is similar to existing power hand drills but does a lot more so its unique value propositions are attractive to a wider audience.

As we explore each stage of the development, evaluation, and potential implementation of your concept, we will simultaneously develop this hypothetical invention and assess its potential for commercialization.

To begin, we will first identify the overall objective, or the scope of a concept introduction.

4.1   THE ELEVATOR PITCH

AN INSIDER'S INSIGHTS

This is an executive summary that succinctly describes your concept in a readily understandable manner for your target audience.

Your ability to concisely describe your concept in its functional and value terms is directly related to your ability to attract investment, talents, and ultimately customers, and revenue.

To get the message across you should focus on these topics:

Positioning	How will you position this product? More importantly, does it meet other people's expectations of your concept?
Target market	Have you clearly identified who your target market is?
Function	What is the function of this product or service? What does it do? How does it work?
Value	Can you specifically describe what values and benefits your idea brings to the target audience? Why is this product or service useful? What is its potential price range?
Time-to-market	How long before you think you will have a functional model or a finished product?
Distribution	Do you know how you will get your innovation to the market place?

An Example

SnapIt! is a versatile around the house power hand tool designed to make everyday chores much easier to handle. It is meant for anyone who cleans the house by scrubbing, polishing, or brushing and works just as well as a light duty power drill in the workshop.

Its main value is in saving time and doing a more effective job than using manual labor. By adapting the power of a hand tool to do everyday chores you can do them quicker and better without using anymore strength. The projected price range is about $40 to $55 dollars based on current research. I expect this product to be ready with all its accessories for sale within 18 months. The ideal distribution channel will be hardware stores as well as kitchen and home goods stores.

Evaluation Questions: Appendix 4 Section 1-1

- How well can you describe the essence of your innovation in one minute or less? Measure your delivery against the ABC rule (Accuracy, Brevity, and Clarity) of communications.

HOW DID YOUR CONCEPT DO?

Ideally you will have covered all the major points effortlessly and be able to expand on any of the points you mentioned.

Potential Challenges and issues may arise when you have not prepared to give the speech when the opportunity presents itself, or worse yet, your information is inaccurate and obviously so.

4.2   INDUSTRY ANALYSIS

- **Revenue size (4.2.1)**
- **Market characteristics (4.2.2)**
- **Market dynamics (4.2.3)**
- **Market segmentation (4.2.4)**

SECTION OBJECTIVE

The first question that comes to mind to someone who has come up with a great idea is whether someone else has already brought it to market. Even though this is instinctive and seems to make sense, it isn't necessary right.

What if the answer is "yes," will you then automatically give up pursuing your idea further? It's a fact that the majority of new product rollouts are improvements on existing concepts; true innovations are relatively rare. What if yours is better in many ways, do you then assume that you should commercialize it? Again not necessarily.

Competitive analysis is only a small piece of the marketing detective work you will do. The objective of this section is to raise issues for you to consider and resolve for your own concept. You would probably not march into an industry that you have no idea is growing or shrinking. How would you know what needs to be researched? The answer is embedded in the summarized steps below:

1. Once a concept has been defined, it's time to look into the industry it belongs to. In other words, do **industry analysis**.

2. The most important thing is to figure out if the **market size** is large enough to invest your efforts in. If payback isn't enough, you will not get your money or the investor's money back.

3. The next question is whether the industry has any special **characteristics** that place constraints or requires unusual attention. For example, seasonal buying timeframes of the school supply industry will dictate the marketing campaign timeframe.

4. Look at the **dynamics** of the industry. Has it been expanding or contracting? Is it under unusual constraint due to raw material, uneven forces of supply and demand? For example, the plastics industry was facing unprecedented price increases due to the global demand of oil. Given that plastic is a byproduct of petroleum, its availability also fluctuated with the oil market.

5. Next do a market **segmentation** to differentiate behaviors within an industry. For example, a life-size construction toy like AeroBloks can be marketed to several distinct sub-segments. It can be marketed to schools as an educational toy, the pediatric occupational therapy segment as a therapy tool, the toy segment (which further divides into specialty and mass market), and the childcare segment as indoor play equipment. Each segment needs its own marketing strategy. Segmentation allows you to customize your marketing strategy. In doing so you will create higher relevance to your target segment and ensure better reception of your product.

6. Pick out the segments of interest then perform a **comparative analysis** to see if your concept already exists in that segment. Sometimes your product already exists as a product but in a different segment, in that case if you can find competitive advantages you can still bring it to market. For example, the SnapIt! drill with different attachments would compete

directly with entrenched competitors in the hardware segment, but will meet little competition if marketed to the household chores segment. The initial finding that a concept already exists is not an automatic sentencing of non-introduction. Digging another layer deeper is a more intelligent approach.

7. Once you determine that there is opportunity for you to enter, despite competition, then you can begin building **customer profiles**. In the customer profile you don't want to rely on just statistics but engage in primary research if possible. If not possible, define each profile in as specific terms as possible, covering from:

   a. where they get their information (your promotional channel),

   b. how they use the product (your product features and functions),

   c. what they want out of the product (your value propositions), to

   d. who they are in terms of age, gender, income, location, and occupation, etc. (your general assumption about the typical habits of the segment).

All this information will be used in your marketing strategy starting in Chapter 5. Let us now dive deeper into each subsection.

4.2.1   MARKET AND REVENUE SIZE

AN INSIDER'S INSIGHTS

Market size represents potential revenue for businesses. It is a data point that needs to be identified and analyzed to provide the answer to whether the industry is one you should consider getting into.

As a rule of thumb you DO NOT want to be investing your valuable resources in dying industries. You could have the very best product or services in that industry but if the revenue is drying up, yours will also despite your best efforts. It would be like paddling a canoe up stream towards a dried up dam.

An entire industry dying out is less likely the case but an entire product line moving towards obsolescence is likely. Take the example of the computer keyboard. In all likelihood it will be replaced by the touchpad technology in combination with voice recognition. Investing hundreds of thousands of dollars or millions making "better" keyboards may not be a good idea now. Would you want to be the last person who bought out the entire payphone franchise just when everyone else is getting cell phones? Or be the person who created a better payphone at around the same timeframe?

A market or industry in decline limits your earning potential at best. At worst it destroys your business. There is a reason why people call it a "falling knife."

You can find the size of an industry and its financial performance trends by using tools like Google[5] Finance®. For example, if you developed a medical device and need industry research, you could use Google Finance® to enter the stock symbol of an existing company in that industry. On the same page you can find the industry's information (in this case Healthcare). Clicking the link on the industry displays a stock performance chart that can be set to specific time intervals. The overall trend should tell you whether it is growing, stagnant, or dying.

You should also be aware of substitution technology at work. The payphone example is a perfect illustration when wireless technology takes over landlines.

Industry size is also displayed on the same page or thereabouts. This obviously is not the only tool but is suggested here as an example.

The next step is to figure out your potential revenue.

Resist the temptation of a common error that uses a percentage of market method as the basis of your revenue source. For example, the US toy market is $21 billion dollars and your toy invention just needs to capture 0.001 or 0.1% of it which is $21 million. Sounds within reach, but wait until this number is translated to the units sold, then it will become apparent that your projection is way off. If your toy is retailed at $20, it would take 1,050,000 units to meet this revenue target. This type of estimate may make sense for a large corporation with entrenched distribution channels and resources but makes no sense at all for a startup business.

Market research can be done by purchasing data from market research firms for the specific industry you are looking into. It can be from government sources which are free. It can be done by researching competitive products on their prices and their company's financial performance if they are a publicly traded company. Annual reports, 10K and other financial reports are readily available for viewing on Yahoo[6] Finance® or Google Finance, along with stock performance and news about the product or industry.

Another potential research venue is through trade journals and magazines. The trick here is to monitor advertising rates. Rates will increase over a few issues if the demand is high, meaning the industry is doing well. The reverse is also true.

---

[5] Google Finance is a registered trademark of Google Inc.

[6] Yahoo Finance is a registered trademark of Yahoo Inc.

Interviewing potential customers about their likes and dislikes on existing products will shed lots of insights for your own concept. Likewise interviewing potential distributors on the number of units they might be willing to buy from you is also a more down to earth approach.

Evaluation Questions: Appendix 4 Section 1-4

- How did you determine total sales of the industry and its growth rate? Is it expected to grow in size, remain constant, or decline?

- How large is your market size/potential revenue? Can it support your operational costs, production costs, marketing costs, management costs, etc. and absorb new market entrants without causing major shifts?

HOW DID YOUR CONCEPT DO?

Ideally you will be able to find solid data on the industry that your concept is in. The information will be freely available and accurate. You would also be able to reach sufficient number of distributors and get their rough estimate on the units they are willing to distribute. Altogether you will be able to understand the industry size and accurately project your sales revenue.

Potential Challenges and issues may include the inability to find accurate data. More likely it will be difficult to get the specific data that represents your particular concept. Such information could come at a high research report cost. You could also run into problems getting potential retailers' estimates on the number of units they might carry in a year to do your projection.

4.2.2 MARKET CHARACTERISTICS

AN INSIDER'S INSIGHTS

Certain industries have unusual business characteristics and cycles that an outsider may not realize. Some of these characteristics are unique to the particular market and drive the behaviors of the people within. For example, some industries have their own timetables that everyone abides by. Some follow the natural cycles of seasons, and some are dominated by a few major players. A monopoly is a market characteristic, and so is an oligopoly. Both of these have to do with industry structures.

Unfamiliarity can become a disadvantage. For example, seasonal buying nature of the school supply industry will dictate the marketing campaign timeframe. If your product is geared towards the school market and you are not aware of this characteristic, then you may end up missing windows of opportunities.

Another example may be that your product is revolutionary but implementing it would mean destabilizing the existing market structure where a few dominant players control the market. If you don't have the huge amount of resources to break the tight reign, then you could be wasting your time regardless of how much better your product is.

If you can identify these particular characteristics which some will undoubtedly be key drivers of business transactions, you stand a much better chance at penetrating the market.

Key drivers of success come in many forms. They can be relationships, the way business is conducted (e.g. via manufacturer reps only), size, seasonality, and any cyclical nature, etc.

The way to find out is to ask. Ask a potential retailer or distributor of your future product how they find out and order new products. Are there just a handful of suppliers or manufacturers that the industry uses? Knowing the answer can help you direct your attention on how and where you do your promotions.

If the industry is seasonal, then you need to find out what the windows are during which the sellers and buyers meet. Furthermore, find out when goods exchange hands. Knowing this information allows you to schedule your own timeframe in terms of when it is best to contact buyers. Seasonality also impacts your labor requirement. Missing one window often means missing an entire year in industries that have seasonality built in.

If the industry is cyclical, meaning that it is in synch with the health of the economy, then you would also plan ahead on when to launch your product. You don't ever want to launch at the low point of a cycle when people are not buying your particular type of product or service. Examples of this type are automotive parts, travel goods and supplies, and large expensive items.

A less obvious but more disheartening situation involves markets that you have no means of penetrating. An industry of limited powerful players may have the incentive to keep the status quo and prevent any innovation from entering. In this case a superior product is irrelevant if established competition has a firm control of the market place. For example, a cloth that never needs cleaning may not succeed in the market place because people's established lifestyle and industry infrastructure would be completely disrupted, dislocated, or destroyed.

It is rare, but if your innovation falls into this category, your risk is extremely high even as you think your financial return is also high. This reality has been imitated by art in the 1951 movie "The Man in the White Suit" where a scientific discovery was made into a fabric that never needs cleaning or wears out. While the invention was hailed as a huge success initially, the established garment industry made sure it never saw the light of day.

So what if your innovation is potentially disruptive to the status quo? Do you automatically give up or give in? Not necessarily. If your concept is a game changer that has the potential to upset an entire industry, then the strategy would be to find someone with lots of resources, especially distribution networks that can penetrate the market efficiently and eventually replace the incumbent products.

In all likelihood you would need to work with an industry insider. Of this potential pool of manufacturers or distributors of existing products, identify and work with the ones that would benefit most from the innovation. The value and benefits must be specific and clearly stated. The insiders can simulate any cost savings or increased unit sales attributable to the innovation with their known production numbers or sales figures respectively.

Often the number one player is not the best choice because their interest may lie in keeping things the way they are. Maintaining their current position is less work than introducing a disruptive innovation. This is especially true of well-established industries that have been around for a long time. The better candidates are those eyeing to topple the top player and have the resources to do so. The disruptive power may be just what they need to succeed.

Evaluation Questions: Appendix 4 Section 1-4

- Do you know the key drivers of success in your market?
- Are there market factors that can dramatically impact your profits?
- Are there seasonal effects or cyclical natures that exist in your industry?
- How does your company and product fit into the industry?

HOW DID YOUR CONCEPT DO?

Ideally you develop a good grasp of the ins and outs of the market, its special characteristics, any unusual requirements for new entrants, etc. At the same time you are also able to control your resources to match the special requirements of the markets your product is in.

Potential Challenges and issues may include the lack of information on the market. You could research all you want but not get the right answer because you didn't ask the right sources. Seasonality is a challenge and requires great planning skills. Cyclical nature is harder to deal with because you wouldn't know exactly when the cycle is low. If you happen to miss either the buying season or jump in at the low cycle then you could be wasting a lot of time.

4.2.3   MARKET DYNAMICS

AN INSIDER'S INSIGHTS

Market dynamics describe a general class of conditions that may create unique opportunities or produce potential threats to your product or service concept beyond the usual known business environment.

Forces that can drastically alter the course of your projected business path exist in various forms. They can be obvious or nebulous. If you don't perform due diligence thoroughly to identify them you could end up getting sideswiped at the most critical moment and lose everything you have worked for. This was the nightmare we faced with the AeroBloks venture.

In business there are many factors that are within one's control then there are those too powerful or too vague to deal with. Timing and luck come to mind for the latter type of dynamic.

Dynamics are relatively easy to spot market changes that if you pay close attention to what is happening and ask enough consumers you would be able to pick them up. They may impact your product's appearance, function, promotional media choices, and even where you sell your product. Paying attention has major payoffs; ignoring them will be at your own risk.

Something that does not change too often but has a more serious impact on your proposed concept is regulation. The person that invests heavily in plastic shopping bags when the regulatory trend is moving towards the "green" way will invariably suffer financial losses. Regulation is especially hideous in this respect because a product at least has some sub-segments of the market who might buck the trend and allow it to survive or exit gracefully.

If and when government regulations begin to mandate and enforce new laws that work against your concept, its components, or even the market you serve, then the situation could turn quite ugly. Imagine if gambling were suddenly outlawed while you were designing a slot machine that leverages the social network frenzy and promises huge payoffs for you. You could lose everything. Fortunately under normal circumstances it takes a while for a regulation to pass through. You would likely see some warning signs before it is enacted into a law.

Environmental concerns in recent years have become a hot topic. Social trends such as using text messages and tweets instead of picking up the phone and calling people have produced both opportunities and threats. If you are able to spot trends (by reading a lot) then you can create a new concept to take advantage of them. If you have already developed a concept, then figuring out whether the trends are friends or foes is something you must consider carefully.

Market dynamics may be "out there" from a product design and market study perspective, but if you ignore them then you subject yourself to potential surprises and not in a good way.

The most difficult type of dynamics may be timing and luck. I have met a few genuinely experienced (and humbled) inventors-turned-entrepreneurs who attribute their success to good timing and great luck. In one case a struggling entrepreneur friend was ready to call it quits when someone introduced an opportunity to sell her products into the military. It turned out that her products had tremendous appeal to families that are separated because of the recent wars in the Middle East. That one contact completely changed her business into a very respectable entity. Was it all luck? According to her it was. I on the other hand believe that timing was good and by luck she was in touch with the right contact.

Does this mean that timing and luck can only happen to you and not necessarily be effected by you?

I believe that with sufficient study of the market trends and global forces such as rising costs of oil and "bubbles" you can at least anticipate somewhat the potential threats and avoid poor timing.

Luck is a harder thing to obtain but I have learned that if you are prepared, you can increase your odds of finding the right combination of people, places, and circumstances by expanding your circle of contact and influence. After all to get lucky meeting the right people with the right resources they would need to be able to find you. To improve such chance meetings you may want to think about how to increase your circle of contacts.

Evaluation Questions: Appendix 4 Section 1-4

- What are the current market trends? Are there windows of opportunity or special circumstances that make your product or service concept especially favorable now or in the projected timeframe of your product launch?
- Are there foreseeable potential threats for your type of product or service?

HOW DID YOUR CONCEPT DO?

Ideally you will have a well-founded understanding of your target market's current happenings before you spend too much resources developing your product, market, or launching it. The information you gathered would be validated by the news media, industry reports and analyses. You would be able to determine whether the market dynamics create opportunities or threats for your concept.

Potential Challenges and issues may include the fact that you are not familiar with the industry and have not done your due diligence on researching its dynamics thoroughly. Another problem may be hidden dangers in the future that you or others simply cannot see because it is just forming as you are forming your concept or company. Some problems arise suddenly and if you don't have enough resources to wait it out then you could lose everything.

4.2.4 MARKET SEGMENTATION

AN INSIDER'S INSIGHTS

Market segmentation is a technique used to subdivide an industry or market into segments that share similar attributes.

Segmentation study allows you to essentially divide and conquer an otherwise diverse market place. Since the so called market place is nothing more or less than a collection of people, and people have varying interests and needs, it makes total sense to put them into subcategories. The risk of not doing this or doing it incorrectly is that you could be literally barking up the wrong tree when trying to position or promote your concept turned product/service. Your efforts and money could be completely ignored.

The basic premise of segmentation has to do with optimizing communication. If you customize your message and deliver it to a particular group of people whose likes and dislikes you have become familiar with, then you would be better able to get their attention and induce them to buy your product or service.

Marketers are nicknamed "spin doctors" for good reasons. Your product's intrinsic value stays the same, it looks the same, works the same, but it may hold different appeals to different groups of people. This is especially key in your packaging design(s). For example, with the AeroBloks construction play set we were able to identify several distinct segments amongst our target market of children 4-10 years old.

To do segmentation you begin by asking the question about your concept, its design, and its intended functionality. Is it meant for the masses as in commodities (e.g. toilet paper) or does it have more specialized functions that not everyone needs (e.g. spy pens). If your concept serves a niche market within personal electronics, the next question would be whether there are sub-segments within this niche. For example, is the spy pen more attractive to men or women, kids or adults, people who enjoy classic spy gears or people who just want the newest gadgets, etc? By answering these probing questions you begin to identify different groups of people.

Each segment shares same characteristics such as price tolerance level, usage, durability requirement, and storage issues, etc. Sometimes by doing segmentation study you will find that you can serve several different segments with slight modifications of a single product, thereby creating multiple product lines and market them as such.

Here is an example of a segmentation study on the AeroBloks product lines. This is what we discovered through interviewing people within each segment:

◆ General toy segment – Price needs to be low for a toy, which is a "want" and not a "need." Most parents tend not spend a lot of money on toys. Disposable toys are hot, others are not.

◆ Specialty toy segment – Prices can be above $100 but the packaging must demonstrate its higher value. Dramatic play is worth more than educational play.

◆ Pediatric occupational therapy segment – Price sensitivity is not as high. The product must be positioned as a therapy tool and not a toy. The packaging must be designed to show how the product can be used by children as a therapy tool.

◆ Special needs segment – It is similar to the pediatric occupational therapy (OT) market but the emphasis also needs to focus on the educational benefits.

◆ Museum stores segment – We must stress its uniqueness as a life-size construction play system. The appeal is in the creativity and education, not on recreation. Dramatic play is not as enticing as creative play in this segment.

◆ School segment – It has considerable budget constraints. Teachers tend to pay for the product themselves and use it as an educational tool. They would need to have curriculum built-in to the play system. Price must be low.

◆ Childcare and preschool segment – Their biggest concern is storage. Children generally do not build but rely on onsite caretakers to build. This poses a major problem as most employees follow pre-established routines and tend not to build structures on demand. Complicated construction is an automatic no-go. This is not because the children didn't want it but because the workers wouldn't build it.

My lessons learned:

Each segment has a distinct characteristic. They include usage pattern, children's physical, mental capabilities and corresponding complexity preference.

Evaluation Questions: Appendix 4 Section 1-4

● Does this product have mass market appeal or is it better suited for specialty, niche markets?

● Are you able to identify market segments and their characteristics?

HOW DID YOUR CONCEPT DO?

Ideally you have a keen understanding of your target market and are able to clearly segregate different groups and identify their particular needs and preferences. Furthermore you are able to leverage this understanding in your product design, positioning, promotional message, and even packaging to maximize your product's appeal to each target segment.

Potential Challenges and issues may include missing the entire point of segmentation or doing it incorrectly. There are few possibilities:

1. Designing the product based on your own likes and dislikes

2. Pricing the item based on your own assumptions or just copying the nearest competitor's price

3. Taking a shot-gun approach, promoting to different segments all at the same time

4. Not providing enough "relevance" in your message to the segments; what you offer and what they want are different

5. Too much generalization or customization without considering the subtle differences between groups

6. Failure to understand that a market is made up of people who have different needs and preferences

4.3   COMPARATIVE ANALYSIS

● **Competitor profiling (4.3.1)**
● **Barrier to entry (4.3.2)**
● **Differentiation (4.3.3)**
● **Substitution (4.3.4)**

SECTION OBJECTIVE

Before jumping in head first to bring your concept to the market place, you need to find out if someone else has already developed the same idea into a commercialized product or service.

Even if the answer is yes, you might still be able to commercialize it if your target market perceives yours as superior. The tendency to say no is a carryover mentality from inventors where the question should have been rephrased "does it already exist in a patent?" But even so, it doesn't mean that the existing patent is the best design. If you can come up with an improvement that proves superior in function, feature, cost, usage, etc. you can bring it to market.

Entrepreneurs will ask if it exists, and if so how they can compete against the incumbent. These are two different mentalities and the latter is what's needed to succeed in business.

If you don't do the due diligence, you could be setting yourself up for failure by:

◆ Wasting time, money, and other resources building prototypes or an actual product before realizing the market is already satisfied with existing products.

◆ Working on an inferior product and not even know it.

◆ Walking into a battle you can't win from the very start.

◆ Infringing on someone else's design and end up being sued.

◆ Contributing to someone else's success by carving a market segment for them.

4.3.1   COMPETITOR PROFILING

AN INSIDER'S INSIGHTS

A competitive analysis that builds a profile of the competition allows you to formulate strategies to compete successfully. Knowing your own strengths and weaknesses as well as those of your competitors gives you an edge on whether to compete, how to compete, and even the when and where to compete or not.

Competition is a natural part of life especially when someone else decides to make money on a product or a market segment you have created. Not knowing the profiles of your competitors is a vulnerability you can't afford.

The information you gain from research will tell you how your product is perceived against theirs, thereby allowing you to modify your marketing approach and improve your product's chances of success.

Competitive profiling also exposes potential threats that you might never even realize, especially if the potential threat comes from a substitution product that isn't even considered to be a competitor.

You begin compiling a competitive landscape by asking the question of whether your concept already exists in the market place.

How to Search, Where to Look?

There are at least two sources to begin. First is to use keywords that represent your concept or potential product and do an online search on Google or Yahoo. Browse through online or print catalogs or magazines that might carry products similar to what you are thinking. Second is to do a quick patent search on the U.S. Patent and Trademark Office website (www.uspto.gov) or Google Patents (www.google.com/patents) using the same keywords. You always have the option of asking others if they have seen or heard anything like what you are considering.

Who Are They, Where Are They?

Competition comes from multiple sources. Existing competition is easier to identify than potential competition or worse yet, hidden competition.

Existing competitors are those who already have a product in the market that delivers the exact function your concept proposes. They pose an immediate threat because they compete for the same consumer dollars. However, other products in the same category that work slightly differently can also become your competition.

Potential competitors are those who can enter into your particular market segment if they choose to. There are those who have the means to enter the market when you've done all the work pioneering the field. They can rise from any source and sometimes may not even appear on your radar screen. They don't even have to be in the same industry. This type of competitor is nebulous and needs more anticipation on your part.

How Do They Compete?

Products tend to compete on: function, appeal, features, benefits, price, quality, and usability.

Companies compete on their weaknesses and strengths, which may include their distribution channel capability, brand awareness, resources level, pricing flexibility, bureaucracy, minimum production and sales quantity, response rate, and margin requirements. These are all competitive advantages or strengths they have. On the other hand, depending on their size and product design, and maybe even relationships with their distribution channel, there may be weaknesses that you can exploit.

There are some advantages of being a small or late comer:

1. Pricing, for instance, is largely dependent on production cost. Production cost in turn is based on manufacturing process. Manufacturing process is driven by the product design. So if you have a simpler design that improves existing product designs, then you stand to reap a pricing advantage.

2. Product performance is similarly tied to the simplicity and functional design of the product. A product with fewer parts to assemble has less reliability issues.

3. Service is often another area that a large competitor may suffer from. Usually the larger the competition, the less able they are to offer personalized attention and services. Here is where being small and nimble can help win over existing customers if your product has a service component to it. If the manufacturing process does a good job in producing a simple design that works, then your corresponding product warranty can also in theory be better than your competition's.

The Competitive Circle of Death

If you imagine a radar scope of companies producing the same category of goods or services, you could probably position them along similarities in their offerings such as price, function, features, and locale.

An Example

Toys historically compete on different price levels. There is the $4.99 or less disposable income level such as plastic figurines. There is the $19.99 or less discretionary spending level for birthday toys and other events. Then there is the $49.99 or less level for "really good" boys and girls. When the price hits $99 and above, the toys are considered premium.

What happened to the premium toy market in time was largely unseen by most toy makers. There was the oil price crisis that impacted most toy production costs for sure. Yet the real category killer was the handheld video game consoles and games. Classic toys were slaughtered by these games while a molasses-moving debate within the industry continued on whether to classify videogames as toys. By the time the debate subsided, most premium toys were bypassed for videogames in the same price range. Even kids as young as 4 years old were asking for videogames instead of classic toys.

This trend became worse for classic toys as videogames evolved to include social and online aspects. In AeroBloks' case we were benchmarking against other construction toy makers. The focus then was on educational and pretend play value propositions.

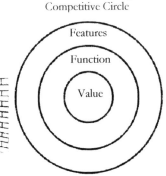

Premium Classic Toys
Competitive Circle

Features

Function

Value

Who could have known that we should have been comparing apples and oranges when traditional wisdom told us to measure against other apples? The only similarity was price which hovered around $100-$300.

In time the handheld video games spelled the demise of premium classic toys.

This lesson is clear but not easy to apply. While looking for competitive products, it pays to look beyond the immediate circle of competition and see if any emerging technology could spell death for your own idea.

Evaluation Questions: Appendix 4 Section 1-3

- Do you know your competitive landscape and can you identify their strengths and weaknesses?

- How do you compete in terms of price, performance, service, and warranties?

- Do you have significant resource constraints, such as lacking in branding, established customer base, cash reserves, favorable location, and experiences?

- If you plan to take market share, will you become a me-too, best in class, or just picking off the table crumbs?

HOW DID YOUR CONCEPT DO?

Ideally a competitive landscape analysis will include both enemies seen and unseen. This is relatively hard to do but not impossible. Products compete for consumers' attention and dollars. The analysis will be complete if all the criteria have been identified and ranked amongst existing and potential competitors, including those that might do a cross-industry jump and compete on price and function. With this profile complete you will be better able to judge whether to enter the market or not.

Potential Challenges and issues could include the fact that after the analysis you decide that it simply doesn't make sense to commercialize your concept. This can be caused by many reasons, amongst which could be that existing product is meeting market needs at great prices, or that you simply cannot produce the quantity to reap the economies of scale. It's just as likely that you don't have the distribution muscles to compete.

4.3.2   BARRIER TO ENTRY

AN INSIDER'S INSIGHTS

The concept of barrier to entry is fairly straight forward to understand but difficult to implement. It is about what an entrant to the market has to overcome in order to compete. Depending on your position in the market place, if you are entering into an existing market then the terminology begs the question of how you plan on breaking down the barriers. If you are the sole occupant or have carved a place in the market, the question becomes how you will erect barriers to prevent others from coming in.

Barriers are an effective way to ward off competition. If you do nothing to erect them you are basically opening the door wide open to invite others to compete in your niche. If you do not identify them when you are trying to break into a market then you might end up wasting all your efforts if some of them become impossible to penetrate.

There are different types of barriers that can be set up to prevent a business from entering the market segment. Some are easy to achieve while others can take years.

Think of barrier to entry as the walls of a castle. If the walls are low, not only you but anyone else can get in. Once you get in, it is in your best interest to try to raise it higher.

Being the first to market with a low barrier of entry is generally not a good position to be in. Nevertheless you could still succeed, provided that you focus on a few critical steps:

> First, if your concept is somewhat innovative but not overtly unfamiliar to the market segment, then you would need to establish a strong brand with emphasis on product positioning and promotional activities.

> Next, you will want to secure a network of distributors as quickly as possible in order to lock out others.

> Then, you need to focus on your service delivery system to make sure the customer experience is in alignment with the expectations you set and the brand you establish.

> Most importantly, your strategy needs to enable the business to quickly reach a critical mass where you can influence the market. This critical mass often requires a certain number of customers, users, or subscribers that has aligned with your brand.

These are just examples of the barriers that you can erect. Superior product design, water-tight IP protection, exclusive relationships with prominent distributors, locked-in cost advantages with manufacturers, etc. are just a few possibilities.

It's not uncommon for others to be lurking around and observing your performance, then at the right moment replicate your business model or with a knock off product offered at better terms to steal your hard work away. There is no law against unethical behaviors, and all that you have done to build up market awareness and acceptance of your type of innovation would have been done for the benefit of those who steal them from you. This is a very real threat if your idea indeed has a very low barrier to keep others out.

An Example

Let's suppose that you created a new cookie cutter with the ability to imprint custom shapes by clicking together different geometric shapes or animal parts. Suddenly instead of making 50 different shape cutters you have a kit that can do the same and create strange creatures to boot. Would that be an exciting product for mothers and young kids to play with? For sure it would be.

Before you decide to invest your money and time into making this unique product (I haven't seen it anywhere as of yet), what if someone else also decides that it's a great idea but can reproduce the same effect much cheaper? There really isn't much you could patent on the shapes other than perhaps how they are clipped together. This means that the design barrier is very low; it can be surpassed or modified easily. Suppose that someone else came up with a system that uses bendable plastic strips with pre-made molds that the strips can conform to, thereby forming the same shapes that your cookie cuter can. Yet because of his design's simplicity his cost and therefore retail price is much lower than yours. In this case the low barrier to entry presents an enormous risk for the money you invest in it.

The situation would be different if an existing kitchen products company with well established distribution channels came up with the idea. In that case the sheer volume of the number of units that can be sold, coupled with any brand awareness, could in fact deter someone else who might even have a superior design.

> A barrier to entry is a double-edged sword; it can be used against you or your competitors.

Evaluation Questions: Appendix 4 Section 1-3

- Do you have a strategy to overcome any existing barriers to entry into the market your concept is geared for?

- How easy is it to create a knockoff replicating your innovation's function with lower cost material and design?

- What barriers of entry can you erect to prevent future competition from eroding your market place?

HOW DID YOUR CONCEPT DO?

Ideally your concept or the business supporting it has a natural barrier to entry, such as a function that is difficult to replicate. Additionally you may have existing relationships with distributors who can blanket the market overnight with your product. Likewise your design could already be perfected with the simplest configuration such that others find it impossible to knock off at a lower production cost. If your concept possess all these qualities it would also be easy to break down existing barriers set by others.

Potential Challenges and issues may include existing barriers that are simply too difficult to break down. A tight network of distributors and existing manufacturers leaves new entrants almost no room to stand. Your production cost may also not be low enough because you don't enjoy the economies of scale from having large quantities produced. Another possibility is that your concept is so simple that it cannot be patented and simply has no way to erect a barrier to entry so someone else cannot copy it.

4.3.3   DIFFERENTIATION

AN INSIDER'S INSIGHTS

Differentiation describes the difference between your proposed concept or its materialized product/service and that of existing competition. It is used to help identify your value proposition.

Consumers love options and choices. This is a fact of life. Side by side comparisons are natural when there is competition. Winners are chosen by their attributes that are important to the person making the selection. If you fail to identify what attributes are important to your target market and fail to point them out in explicit ways, you may lose a sale. If you do this across your entire product line, you may lose your business.

When a customer looks at your product verses one that is next to it on a store shelf, what will she be thinking about?

What is the difference? Which one is better, assuming the prices are comparable?

There may in fact be differences but do the customers care? In other words, do the differences contribute to your value proposition? For example, suppose your concept involves creating a hand sized massager. If all things being equal, your version has 4 prongs while the other has 3 prongs. Does it really matter to the consumer and can that difference translate into more dollars in your pocket? If not, then it is not a differentiator.

On the other hand, if you can justify that a four-prong design can apply more even pressure to the sore muscles and you explicitly state that on your packaging then you will have a noteworthy differentiator.

The point is that you don't want to be another "me-too" product but a "me better" product or even a "me only" product to get the attention of distributors. Value propositions need to be obvious; it should be something that can be digested within seconds.

Your concept may be new or newer but that doesn't make it necessarily better, and depending on the degree of newness may even have significant drawbacks.

Knock-Offs and Differentiation

Although knock-offs are a fact of life, when one shows up, it is still a very upsetting event. Watching someone else stealing the concept and developments you poured your life into and getting away with it is like being robbed in day light and no one can do anything about it.

I experienced this first hand when a competitive product was introduced into the life-size inflatable building system segment a year and a half after our launch. Competition in itself is not a crime and may even be healthy, but it became infuriating when some of our structures posted online were copied onto theirs. Worse yet, they blatantly stole our brand on Google and Yahoo advertising. When someone entered AeroBloks, their advertisement would show up right on top. This pure form of theft is not punishable because bad ethics are not punished in the business world.

The only way to fight back was to emphasize our differentiation of AeroBloks such as the transparency, structural stability, movement, and realism that parents really wanted. In fact we received many customer comments that they immediately saw that ours was a superior product. This went on even as the competitor's distribution channel was wide-reaching due to their existing relationships. Within two years time that company went bankrupt.

> Regardless of how you feel about it, knock-offs are a fact of life. Business is not about ethics or the lack thereof.

Evaluation Questions: Appendix 4 Section 1-3

● In what ways is your concept better than the competition? Is it function, design, style, user experience, convenience, safety, cost, or overall value?

● Is there sufficient differentiation between your proposed concept and an existing product to justify developing yours, or are people already happy with the existing?

HOW DID YOUR CONCEPT DO?

Ideally your concept has clear differentiators from the competition in meaningful ways to your target market. You are also able to identify them and explicitly display them in your promotional and positional statements.

Potential Challenges and issues may include the fact that there is very little differentiation between your concept and someone else's. Or, the difference is so minute (even if obvious to you) that it is not noticeable to the target market. Another problem may be that your differentiation may be obvious in design and function but is no competition to their distribution muscle. Ultimately it's not about the product but its marketing efforts that lead to sales.

4.3.4   SUBSTITUTION

AN INSIDER'S INSIGHTS

Substitution products are those that can compete against yours in function, price range, or general characteristics but do not exist in your product's same category.

Substitutions are different from knockoffs but pose just as much of a threat or even more. An unforeseen enemy is more dangerous because you would not have made any preparations.

Most times when we think of competition we tend to draw a line or a circle and keep those whose products are in the same category as ours within the region. Competition is therefore mostly from similar products and compete on price, features, or appeal.

When something outside of that region becomes a replacement of your product, that's when a substitute becomes a competitor. For example, if you are trying to sell a Honda sedan to a customer who's weighing his decision against a Toyota sedan, and suddenly he decides to buy a motorcycle instead, then a substitution product has entered the competition. In this case the competition was between car manufacturers but a motorcycle which is a substitute transportation mode entered into the race and took away the customer's money.

Substitutions are not the same product (e.g. two soft drink brands) and may not even be in the same product category (all soft drinks). This is particularly true when the purpose of the product is wide in scope such as for entertainment purposes.

Their physical forms are most likely nowhere near your patent drawings and claims. You may not even realize the potential threat. Therefore they may easily render any patent protection you think you have useless.

Substitute products are harder to identify but not impossible. The trick to identifying them is to widen your definition of function and purpose. If your concept is of a mechanical design then its function may be more straightforward. A hammer's function is to drive something with blunt force. There are not that many substitution products for a hammer. But for entertainment products or services, substitutions abound. Someone may opt for a book instead of a movie on a Saturday night. In this case it is much harder to anticipate and prepare for it.

Evaluation Questions: Appendix 4 Section 1-3

- Are there any obvious substitutes for your product/service?

- What are other substitute products or advances in technology that can affect your product?

- Do you have a strategy to prevent substitute products from taking away your market share?

HOW DID YOUR CONCEPT DO?

Ideally you can map out who the potential competition is early on, including (1) products in the same category as yours, (2) obvious substitution products, and (3) some not obvious but similarly functioned products. At the same time you have a positioning strategy that defends why your product is better at delivering the function that a substitution might be able to do.

Potential Challenges and issues may include the fact that you simply have no clue what substitution products can take away your market share. Similarly you may have some idea or can make reasonable assumptions but have no means of countering the potential loss of market share.

> Substitute products can come from any direction. Use your creativity and imagination to see how you would substitute for your own product or service.

4.4   CUSTOMER PROFILING

- Research (4.4.1)
- Demographics (4.4.2)
- Usage pattern (4.4.3)
- Sources of influence (4.4.4)
- Identify customer's values (4.4.5)

SECTION OBJECTIVE

Whereas market segmentation is about dividing and conquering the industry, customer profiling is about taking the next step to study your mark and subsequently hitting the bull's eye.

To build a profile you will need to clearly identify distinct traits of your target customers. The work involves doing detailed research and analysis to generate data that describe your subject's demographics, their sources of influence, what they value, and how they use products or services like yours.

The type of information you gather can be grouped into three major categories:

- ◈ **Physical** profile includes anthropometric data and usage patterns.

- ◈ **Social** profile includes information flow and sources of influence.

- ◈ **Psychological** profile includes what is appealing and considered valuable.

A Sample Profile of the ***Childcare*** Segment from AeroBloks

Physical Profile	
Age	3-5 (children), 18-40 (caretakers)
Anthropometric Data	Measurements on average height, hand size, finger strength, and weight lifting limit.
Usage Data	Children use product mostly for sitting and carrying around. They do not have the physical height to build large structures. Caretakers occasionally build simple structures but never complex structures.
Social Profile	
Information	Children gravitate towards cartoon characters from movie, TV, and video games.

| **Influence** | Influenced by what can be seen, as in guidebooks. Typically do not come up with new building configurations. |

Psychological Profile

| **Appeals** | Color, transparency, cushiness, bounciness, lightweight. |
| **Value** | Easy to deflate and store, safe. |

This profile suggests that to successfully sell into the childcare segment, we needed to focus on the value that they care most about, namely storage function. Large structures are typically not used indoors because of space constraints. By emphasizing on the ability to deflate and store in sheets, the value proposition got their attention because they now have something to do indoors on rainy days.

At the same time the product had to serve two user groups: the children and the adults. Children care about color while adults cared about transparency so they can keep an eye on the children when they're inside a large AeroBloks structure. The product was designed with the children's finger strength in mind while the adults could also use without physical limitations.

The research also indicated that creating new structures was not a strong preference for this group. Therefore compiling and including an activities guidebook that included mostly simple structures with a few complex ones was essential in selling the concept to them.

After the data has been collected and compiled, a clear picture will emerge that describes your customer's likes and dislikes which will give you a clue on how best to "communicate" to them. This marketing step precedes the actual selling and is covered in detail in Chapter 5.

4.4.1 RESEARCH

AN INSIDER'S INSIGHTS

Good market research provides you with data to create intelligent strategies. It helps you identify your target market, build profiles, see trends, identify opportunities and threats, and reduce unnecessary risks.

The quality of research will directly dictate the effectiveness of your executions. Good data ensures better results. Without market research you would be proceeding blindly.

First thing first, never assume that your personal taste, preferences, likes and dislikes are representative of the general market. Even if you decide to describe yourself as average and typical, they are still uniquely yours. They most likely do not necessarily reflect the broader target market of your product or service.

There are three stages of managing useful information: acquisition, evaluation, and putting into action. The key to getting just the information you need without getting overwhelmed is to define what you need then deciding where the best sources are.

In general market research can be broken down into primary vs. secondary research. Both types can be fee-based or free.

Primary Research

The best kind of feedback you can get is directly from would-be users of your concept. This type of primary input is extremely valuable and provides raw material for you to apply in anything from how to market, where to distribute, and even how to set up the operations system for best customer experience. It is especially useful in financial projections if you can get estimates of orders from the distribution channels.

For SnapIt! the sources of research (survey) would be home goods stores and hardware stores. Obviously this type of research is time consuming and limited in reach. But if you consider the accuracy of the information, it may be just what you need to make preliminary assessments.

Aside from doing standard internet search, buying industry reports, paying consultants, etc. you can also donate your products directly to some users in exchange for their feedback.

For example, we provided free samples to OT professors and well-known practitioners who in turn gave us very valuable feedback.

Another source of primary research is online forums of people with the same interests or issues. This is often a goldmine for information leading to what people like and dislike, as well as opportunities to improve existing products.

Secondary Research

Short of having the first person contact opportunities, most of us end up doing online keyword searches. This may mean hours of narrowly defined keyword searches on the web, or flipping through trade magazines. The trick to selecting the right keywords is to put yourself in the consumer's mind frame. The keywords need to reflect both benefits as well as features. If you simply enter the functions or features then you would be missing half the story.

For example, if you were to put in the words "convertible hand drills" for SnapIt! market research, then you would not find information related to scrubbing sinks and tiles which are presumably major usages of this innovation.

Moreover, keyword searches can reveal how much interest there is by looking at the number of search result returns.

For example, as of this writing the keywords "power car scrubber" returned 410,000 results from Google.com, but "power sink scrubber" returned only 71,300 results. "Power tile scrubber" generated a return of 2,460,000 results at the same time. This very quick research reveals that more people are interested in scrubbing tiles than they are in the other two applications. This has an impact on how to position SnapIt!

Secondary Research Sources

Besides keyword searches, there are specific locations where reports are compiled. Government sites provide an array of amazing and rich contents for free. The problem is often with digging them out from layers of structure.

General information is easy to find but specific information takes more work. If you need information catered to your own situation, the best source may be highly focused reports compiled by market research companies. Cost of such reports range in the low thousands of dollars.

Here are a few useful and free government research sites:

- ❖ US Department of Labor – Bureau of Labor Statistics www.bls.gov compiles information on employment and wage, consumer price index, and consumer spending data with which you can derive trends and overall economic health. This is critical if your concept is a cyclical item.

- ❖ US Department of Commerce – Economics & Statistics Administration www.esa.doc.gov provides free information on economic indicators that you can extrapolate to project macroeconomic trends relevant to your industry sector.

- ❖ US Department of Commerce – International Trade Administration www.trade.gov has reports on industry analysis pertaining to manufacturing and services sectors and much more.

- ❖ US Department of Commerce – US Commercial Service www.buyusa.gov provides assistance on exporting and market research data for international trading.

- ❖ Here is an example of a private market research firm and its available reports on demographics research and the range of prices www.marketresearch.com.

Evaluation Questions: Appendix 4 Section 1-4

● What is the degree of difficulty in getting accurate and up-to-date data that is specific to your research needs at a cost you can afford?

● What is the quality of your market research? Does it cover industry size, trend, competitive analysis, cyclical behaviors, windows of opportunity, cost of marketing, and approaches to promotion?

HOW DID YOUR CONCEPT DO?

Ideally you are able to conduct the market research you need to gather the information within your budget. Your data should come from both primary and secondary research. The quality of the data should be accurate and allows you to formulate your marketing strategies.

Potential Challenges and issues may arise because you have no resources to obtain the exact type of research you need. You may also not be willing to conduct primary research by contacting direct potential customers and retail buyers. Your data could be mostly secondary and present only generic information which are not fine-tuned enough to produce a meaningful marketing strategy.

4.4.2 DEMOGRAPHICS

AN INSIDER'S INSIGHTS

Using demographics to market a product/service is a common practice. It allows you to better define your target customers' profile and reach them. The common traits used in demographics study include but are not limited to: age, income, dwelling, home value, period of residence, gender, marital status, number of adults in household, children in household, net worth, credit, and ownership of different types of products.

When used correctly, demographics data can be a powerful marketing tool. It allows you to focus your promotional dollars on specific channels with specialized messages. It makes your offering relevant and appealing than if you were to take a shot-gun approach and blast your message through common media, otherwise known as a hit or miss approach.

Making sense of the demographics data is much more important than collecting the data.

The baseline assumption behind using demographics data is finding similarities amongst a population of people and making sense of the finding. How you use a criterion also matters.

For example, the "Age" criterion is more useful when used to identify health related issues than for car buying tendencies.

The same can be said for the "Gender" criterion. In general, do all men buy dark colored clothing? Probably not. Do all women shop more than men? Statistically yes. These answers will then be used to target women on coupons and other shopping promotions.

Individually the data points are of limited uses, but when combined they form a more meaningful profile. In fact the data points become most useful when they are used to validate a predefined customer profile instead of creating a customer profile.

If you have a profile in mind, you can use the demographics data to fine-tune your promotional strategy. You will be able to know what zip codes to send your promotional literature, what cable channels to advertise on and during what timeframe, and where to find the young, hip crowd that loves everything made by Apple Inc., for instance. Each of these promotional channels can identify a specific target demographic profile that they know is their hard core audience.

Having this information allows you to design your positioning statement which will cater to their profile. You can then launch a promotional campaign which will grab their attention from their favorite sources of information.

What to Do With Demographics Data

First, identify who your target market is. Create a profile of this segment, including physical elements. Describe every demographics such as age, gender, marital status, income level, physical size, education level, usage preferences, shopping habits, where they get their information, likes and dislikes, and behaviors as much as you can. Each of these characteristics gives you a clue on how to reach them and what to say.

While your goal is to identify statistics that offer clues to what your target consumers are like, you should keep in mind that beyond demographic data there are living, breathing people who have wants and needs just like you. Statistics measure averages and norms which are good for generalization about a population but not necessarily good for what you need to dissect and do segmentation exercises on the buying behaviors.

The word "market" is a figurative term. It is as representative as the word "company" or "community." All these are just descriptive terms of groups of people sharing some homogenous traits. The physical buildings and infrastructures do not make up the essence of these concepts. It is the people within them that you need to understand.

For example, if your product is geared towards the elderly because it helps them manage their daily medicine intake, then you should build a profile of them including their physical conditions, age range, habits, lifestyles, and other demographics that will allow you to better understand their needs and thereby creating an accurate value proposition for them.

At the same time you need to understand the difference between primary and secondary users, and between customers and users.

Primary users will use your product's function predominately whereas secondary users will use it as a matter of course. Customers are the people who pay for your innovation while users are those who benefit from it.

For example, the medicine management device mentioned here could be used for the benefit of an elderly woman. Yet her husband is the one who manages the organization and dispensing of her pills. Meanwhile, the trend is for the adult children to buy such gadgets as presents for their aging parents. In this case the primary user is actually the elderly man, the secondary user the elderly woman, and the customer their adult child.

Your target customer profile needs to clearly spell out who the primary user and the customer are.

Evaluation Questions: Appendix 4 Section 1-4

- Have you defined who would be most interested in your innovation?

- Have you identified who will actually pay for this product or service? Who are the primary user and the primary buyer? Who has greater influence?

- What are the demographics of your targeted customer base? Are the demographics of your target customer reachable?

HOW DID YOUR CONCEPT DO?

Ideally you can identify who the primary and secondary users and customers are, their demographics, and how best to reach them.

Potential Challenges and issues may include the fact that you have no idea where to begin searching for demographic data. Additionally you don't have a profile to leverage the demographics data to help you reach your target audience. It is also likely that even if you have the profile, the data, and a strategy, that it is too expensive for you to reach them.

> We all march to different drums. Even if you might think of yourself as normal, typical, or average, your preferences are not representative of the population at large.

4.4.3 USAGE PATTERN

AN INSIDER'S INSIGHTS

A usage pattern study describes in what ways the target population of your product or service will most likely use it, with or without your written instructions. It is a methodology leveraged to shape or improve your concept development.

How the intended end users use your potential product or service has huge implications on how you go about designing, positioning, and promoting your concept. Without properly identifying and understanding the rationales behind usage patterns you risk going down the wrong path and wasting your valuable resources.

Ergonomics is a field of study that examines the usage pattern of products or services in detail, and for very good reasons.

Products that are more intuitive to use will naturally be accepted more readily by the end user. Anything awkward and difficult to handle or apply will quickly be rejected unless you hold a monopoly. But then substitutions will invariably arrive to correct the situation.

The way to ensure that your proposed concept will have a future audience is to share it with them in prototype stage or have them use it and give you feedback at the functional stage. As you observe how people use your product, you should pay attention to how they go about handling the product, using it, and how much time they spend learning how to use it the way you have intended. For a service product, the same principle applies but instead you should measure how much time and missteps happen when a potential customer goes through your business delivery process.

To do this correctly you will need to design your product according to the physical specifications of the intended user group. It is in your best interest to research ergonomic design principles applicable to your concept whenever possible. This will help you design your product or business flow in intuitive ways.

Intuitiveness may be natural (such as flipping open a bottle cap) or may be learned. In the latter case a good example is learning to text on a tiny cell phone keyboard which is as unnatural as it can be. But once a standard has been set, anything that deviates too much from what people have grown accustomed to will not get endorsed.

Usage patterns will also point out areas of your concept that are deficient or needs improvement. If men say that the SnapIt! product feels ok but most women reply with "too heavy" as a hypothetical market survey feedback, then it would be time to revisit your design if your primary application is tile scrubbing instead of drilling wood.

There may also be a difference between an end user and a purchaser. For example, a mother buying a toy for her son is quite different from the child who buys the toy for himself.

In that case you need to create two separate profiles. The profile for the end user should be used to generate the benefit and value statements. The profile of the purchaser should be used to generate how to promote and reach them.

An Example

When AeroBloks was launched into the childcare market, we designed the positioning statement to emphasize benefits for the children. This turned out to be a wrong strategy.

It appeared that such positioning statements were more relevant to parents and teachers but not to childcare. Childcare is a for-profit baby-sitting commercial entity whose workers are hired to watch over children for a specified period of time. For sure some of the caretakers love children and would go the extra mile in caring for them. However the vast majority of the workers did not fit this profile.

When the product failed to sell as expected, we sent sample blocks to both a Japanese distributor and a childcare within the US to get usage feedback. The results were quite revealing.

Apparently the children could not build large structures so instead they carried each individual block around with them all the time. Rather than using them as large building blocks they treated the pieces as air cushions to sit, jump, and lie on. The childcare workers, on the other hand, were fully capable of building large structures but lacked incentives to build beyond the first or second structures that satisfied their initial curiosity. It was too much work for them to crawl around the pieces and build castles, boats, airplanes, even as the children craved for them. Since the workers were in charge, the product was never used in the way it was intended. This was the same feedback from Japan as well as the first US test center, and from other subsequent facilities we donated the product to.

My lessons learned:

What we should have done in hindsight was to target the positioning statement towards the workers and supplied them with easy to follow building instructions that can be done in minutes. We could have emphasized the ability for children to play for hours indoors by themselves with an AeroBloks castle, which would have alleviated the caretakers from going outside in inclement weather or having to keep a constant watch over the children.

Evaluation Questions: Appendix 4 Section 1-4

● How well can you clearly identify how someone would use your proposed product or service, including when and where they are most likely to use it?

● Is the proposed product usage intuitive for the intended end-user and not just for the designer? If learning is required, how easy is it for the user to learn to use your product?

HOW DID YOUR CONCEPT DO?

Ideally your concept will be developed into a product or service that is highly intuitive to use by your intended end users. The concept would be familiar even as it is innovative, requiring minimum learning efforts and contains no awkward operating positions. You should also have plenty of opportunities to observe your concept turned product or service in a real world situation before you launch it commercially.

Potential Challenges and issues may occur if you lack the opportunity to observe a working prototype of your concept in the real world. Likewise you never get the opportunity to improve your product before launching it commercially. Both situations may subject your concept to stagnate in sales.

4.4.4   SOURCES OF INFLUENCE

AN INSIDER'S INSIGHTS

More often than not people make purchase decisions based on peer recommendations and social influences. Peer pressure, peer review, consumer test results, product review sites, celebrity endorsement, and advertising are just a few well-known sources of product information and influence.

By understanding what can influence the purchase decision of your concept and where your target market gets its information you will be able to optimize your promotional strategy.

Identifying the sources of information and the degree of influence they have on your target end user group is a precursor to your promotional efforts. It dictates where you should focus your promotional dollars and who you will need to get endorsements from.

For example, if yours is a beauty product, then getting endorsements from the celebrity circle where beauty is of utmost importance can make the difference between a sale or not.

Children's products are often imprinted with licensed characters to entice more sales so children can relive their fantasies and dramatic plays with movies and show characters and stories.

If yours is a household product most suitable for home-shopping network presentations, then you would not want to spend money advertising on the radio or local newspapers.

Sources of influence include pop culture, icons, celebrity, peer influence, and social trends. These affect your branding and packaging strategies as part of your promotional efforts.

Conventional sources include TV, radio, print articles (magazines and papers), tradeshows, and good-old word-of-mouth propagations such as in-home product parties. In today's commerce environment, the sources have largely gone online. Most people are able to find product reviews quickly and efficiently via online shopping sites. There are also product reviews available on online video sites, private blogs, or public forums. Today's consumers often rely on word-of-mouth peer comments to make their purchase decisions. The social media channel has become a dominant force to reckon with and to leverage for commercial gains. The key is to realize that we are currently living in a transitional era where conventional and the new channels of information and influence coexist.

The key to leveraging the knowledge of social influence is to identify how purchase decisions are made and influenced for a particular type of product. Not all products are subject to social influences or the same channels of influence. Commodities tend to compete on price where quality is similar. Niche market product sales tend to be heavily influenced by a particular group of people through social media channels such as Facebook, Twitter, MySpace, Linked-In, etc. If your concept is a product or service that is geared towards a specific niche of the population, it would make most sense if you define the characteristics of that niche. This includes the channels it uses to communicate so you can apply your promotional strategy using the social media accordingly.

Evaluation Questions: Appendix 4 Section 1-4

- Is your concept one that is heavily influenced by peer reviews or is it one that can be sold independently of market influences?

- How well can you identify the sources of influence and channels of information that your target segment relies on to make product or service purchase decisions?

HOW DID YOUR CONCEPT DO?

Ideally you can determine the degree of social influence behind the potential sale of your concept and act accordingly. If yours is one that is subject to heavy social influence, then you should be able to identify the sources of influences and the channels by which they communicate. You can then allocate your promotional resources and dollars to get the biggest bang for your buck.

Potential Challenges and issues may occur if you are unable to determine whether your concept is subject to social influence. Even if the answer is yes, you might not be able to pinpoint the type of influences behind the potential purchase of your product or service. Additionally you might not be able to afford what it takes to get endorsements from the influencers.

4.4.5   IDENTIFYING CUSTOMER VALUES

AN INSIDER'S INSIGHTS

Identifying what is important to a customer is not the same as assuming what it is. The goal here is to obtain benefits that customers explicitly state are of the highest priority to them.

With a verified list you can align your version of the product's or service's value propositions and prioritize them. This achieves the highest relevance of your message so your target customers would likewise pay attention.

What you might assume is the most important feature of your concept may not be as critical as you think. Most inventors or first time entrepreneurs assume that price of a product/service is the most important factor. This isn't necessarily true at all. In reality, besides commodities, price is sometimes that last thing to be weighed. Making a purchase decision is often justified by the paying price but not necessarily driven by the paying price.

A product has many attributes to consider. The benefits that consumer products tend to emphasize are: function, time saving, space saving, money saving, size, durability, safety, appeal (color, shape, craftsmanship, uniqueness), and convenience, etc. Consumers may also consider the fact that their friends already have one, what it would mean in terms of social status, and bragging rights, etc. as their real reason to buy something.

Therefore the conventional wisdom that lower price wins is not true all the time. Price only comes in the end (maybe a fraction of a second to several days later) that justifies the purchase. The buying experience is not always rational.

Nevertheless the prudent thing to do is to at least identify what attributes are important to your target segment, and prioritize them in terms of importance.

Doing this helps you to write your value proposition statements, design your websites and fliers, and especially when designing your package.

The key point is that each segment has similar needs but the needs are not considered in equal importance. Some will consider safety more important than function, and others will consider social status as a "must have" at any price. Your detective work needs to identify common benefits that are important to all the segments but prioritize them differently to customize for each one.

An Example

We identified in AeroBloks that storage is the number one concern for almost all the segments we were targeting. Other than the mass market segment, price is actually a secondary concern. This was completely not expected.

In fact when we pitched the product against fixed life-size structures that often cost several times more the strategy backfired. The lowered price caused a perception that AeroBloks was flimsy when in fact it wasn't true. Each block could withstand up to 180lbs of standing weight. In the end we realized that different segments placed different values on what they want. There was not a silver-bullet solution but many solutions. Here is a quick breakdown of what each segment thought was more important than price:

- Specialty toy segment – packaging must project high value
- Occupational therapy segment – durability is most important
- Special needs segment – ease of use by children
- Museum stores segment – creativity and educational potential
- Schools segment – educational tool first
- Childcare and preschool segment – storage, storage, storage

Evaluation Questions: Appendix 4 Section 1-4

- Are you able to identify and prioritize a list of features and benefits your intended customers care most about?

HOW DID YOUR CONCEPT DO?

Ideally you can determine the factors that are important to each target segment then prioritize them for use in your marketing approach.

Potential Challenges and issues may occur if you fail to realize that your value proposition is not the same or not in the same order of priority as that of your target customers. You could also be singing the wrong tune to a segment with a bona fide value proposition that they don't find relevant enough to pay attention to.

CHAPTER 4 ACTION ITEMS

Use the detailed questions and insights in Appendix 4 to help you tackle these action items.

1. Perform industry analysis including the target market revenue, size, dynamics, and segmentation.

2. Research competitive landscape including barrier to entry, differentiation, and substitutions.

3. Identify primary target customers including their demographics and create profiles.

4. Determine your concept's function(s).

5. Identify your concept's value to the target market.

Chapter 5

Marketing & Sales... Meeting the Great Expectation

Having done the legwork on the industry, competition, and customers, you will now be able to tackle the outward facing marketing aspects. We will dissect each of the conventional marketing mixes as pertained to evaluating a concept's commercial viability. I will also point out impacts of the new paradigm shift from yesterday's marketing and sales approaches to today's online and social media channels as appropriate.

THE ESSENCE OF MARKETING IS COMMUNICATIONS

The goal of marketing is to make your intended message known, to entice audiences, to grab and retain that message, and to use it to influence their thoughts and/or actions. As such the first step of good communications is to set proper expectations. Essentially marketing activities build customer expectations while sales activities fulfill them.

Effective marketing creates desired perceptions. This is a field where <u>perception is reality</u>. Interestingly the perception may have little to do with the intrinsic value of the goods or services. For instance, if I perceive a product as valuable then it is valuable to me and I would probably pay more for it. In all likelihood I would have been impressed by an expressed value of that product somewhere along the way via some clever advertising.

If this sounds unrealistic, just imagine someone walking around in a grubby T-shirt, ripped shorts, and sandals. What impression would he leave? What if the same person were dressed in expensive designer clothing with dashing jewelry and accessories?

Which expression would leave a more positive impression of the exact same person? How will you then perceive his social status?

Unbeknownst to the naked eye there is much more going on than a simple exchange of offerings for money when someone buys something. Understanding the underlying dynamics and applying it to your advantage will cause a paradigm shift in your thinking, approach, and effectiveness in conducting marketing and sales activities. It may even drastically change how you think about your business operations infrastructure in light of this "expectations" paradigm. Take a look at the following questions to see why. It may help if you look at them from the customer's perspective.

EVERYTHING COMES DOWN TO MANAGING EXPECTATIONS

- ❖ The question of the day is… "What did you expect?"
- ❖ If you didn't expect anything, would getting nothing upset you?
- ❖ If you weren't expecting but received a gift, would that be a good surprise?
- ❖ If you expected to pay fair price for something you purchased but come to find out that it wasn't the case, would you be upset?
- ❖ If you expected consistency in quality and taste but didn't get it, would you go back to the same restaurant and order the same dish?

All these scenarios share one thing in common, that to "trust" is to believe that your expectations will be met. Broken trust is the leading cause of ditched relationships. This applies in everyday life and in business because as long as you are dealing with people, business is just another everyday transaction.

If marketing is about communications, then a great marketer has to be a great communicator. Someone who has mastered the art of communications will therefore understand that to be effective she needs to:

(1) *Have enticing content*

(2) *Understand her audiences' expectations*

(3) *Be able to maintain their interest level*

(4) *Execute the delivery flawlessly,* and

(5) *Not promise anything she can't or won't deliver*

Above all things she realizes that she sets future expectations with her messages. The audience will come to expect what she says is true and trust in her future delivery. Focusing on setting the right expectations is winning half the battle.

THE ESSENCE OF SALE IS TRUST

Successful salespeople will tell you that sale is about building relationships. But it's not just about any type of relationship; it has to be one built on trust.

Let's look at the underlying mental process behind a simple transaction. For me to pay for your offering is for me to expect a certain value from you that I will exchange with some form of currency. I will expect that the value is as represented by you, meaning that I trust your description. I may choose to do this repeatedly if you continue to uphold my trust in you. In that case we have a business relationship built on trust. If I didn't have any transactional experience with you, then I could rely on someone else's experience, which is why most people seek referrals.

eBay has the genius to pioneer and harvest such a system to become a superpower in retail. It has provided consumers with a database of merchant rankings that represents the level of trustworthiness in the product's quality or the service's quality. This ability to view merchant ranking gives a consumer the power to decide whether she can trust the merchant in fulfilling the merchant's representation, and therefore her expectation of the product. In a nutshell, the rankings imply the level of trust and therefore the quality of a potential business relationship with a particular merchant.

The overall selling process boils down to a trust building exercise. It begins with setting expectations followed by building a relationship. Just like any other type, such a relationship needs to be nurtured. Once the trust is built, the exchange happens. Why else do you think an unproven vendor's best chance to reach a corporate buyer is often through referrals?

APPLYING THE EXPECTATION PARADIGM

How does this relate to building a company or running a business? Recognizing that building a relationship of trust based on setting and meeting proper expectations is just the beginning. How you nurture the relationship with your methods, processes, and systems in the customer interface design is the next step.

The expectation of the level and quality of your product or service is set by your marketing communications. How you fulfill it is part sales and part business operations design. This is why if you understand this dynamic well you will shape your product, marketing, sales, and business operation approaches to be a coherent whole and meet customer expectations consistently.

MARKETING MIXES / CHAPTER ORIENTATION

5.1 Product/Service
- R&D
- Design
  - Customer friendly
  - KISS principle
  - Physical design factors
  - Ergonomic
  - Design for the future
  - Safety and liability
- Making prototypes and models
- Feedback, validation, refinement

5.2 Positioning
- The importance of relevance
- Value proposition
  - Need vs. want
  - Value and worth
  - Core value vs. secondary
  - New vs. improved
- Writing positioning statement
- Branding, naming, logo
- Getting noticed

5.3 Pricing
- A baseline understanding
- Dispelling a myth
- All about psychology
- How to set prices

- Cost plus approach
- Benchmark approach
- Maintaining margin approach
- Value based approach
- Supply & demand approach
- Intangible based approach
- Pricing adjustment

5.4 Packaging
- Physical considerations
- Display considerations
- Techniques
  - Using surprises and bonus
  - Value vs. price
  - Licensing

5.5 Promotion
- Objective
- Audience
- Message
- Delivery

5.6 Placement
- Anatomy of distribution
- Sales

5.7 Overall Strategy
- Lifecycle management
- Go-to-market strategy

SECTION OBJECTIVE

Conventional teaching tells us there are 4Ps (Product, Price, Place, Promotion) of marketing management. In practice, I found that separating out packaging and positioning from the conventional mix was much more practical, so there are actually 6Ps to work with.

What worked for me was to draw six parallel lines, each representing a particular sequence of activities. These activities are interrelated like task groups in a project plan.

To begin, you would define the <u>product</u>, decide on the <u>positioning</u> strategy, figure out the right <u>price</u>, create the appropriate <u>packaging</u>, identify the most effective <u>promotional</u> channels, and then finalize your <u>placement</u> (distribution) strategy. Once the distribution strategy is clear, you can begin pursuing your sales activities.

It may help to think about these separate but interrelated activities as 6 trains leaving the terminal. They will all converge at the final destination, but each one carries different contents.

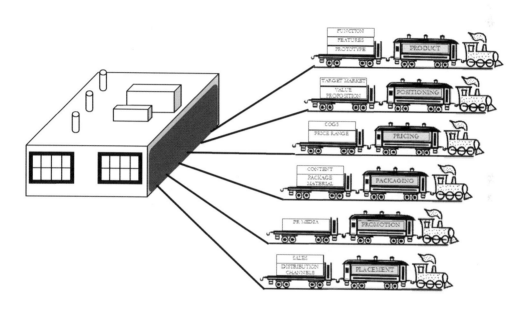

The trains may leave sequentially from the station, but sooner or later one will pass the other and back and forth; this is the real tempo of a business. When all have eventually arrived at the same stop it is then that the business is ready to launch.

Chapters 4 and 5 cover individual components of the marketing and sales considerations for evaluating a new product or service. Together they can be combined to form a high level checklist, which may be something like this:

> Marketing activities are not necessarily serial; they are interlinked within the whole marketing strategy.

<u>Checklist</u>

☑ I have done the **industry analysis** (section 4.2), which includes **market segmentation** (section 4.2.4)

☑ I have done **comparative analysis** to isolate opportunities (section 4.3)

☑ I have assembled **customer profiles** for the target segments (section 4.4)

☑ I am ready to create a **marketing strategy**

◆ I have defined **product**/service functions and features (section 5.1)

◆ I want my customers to think of my concept as best, cheapest, most luxurious, most fun, smartest… (**positioning** - section 5.2)

◆ I want them to believe that it has great value (value proposition, as part of **positioning** - section 5.2)

◆ I want people to remember my product (naming, branding, as part of **positioning** - section 5.2)

◆ I want them to be willing to pay for my product (**pricing** - section 5.3)

◆ I want the product to attract people's attention (**packaging** - section 5.4)

◆ I want them to know about my product (**promotion** - section 5.5)

◆ I want them to buy my product easily (**placement** - section 5.6)

◆ I am ready to make money (**sales** - section 5.6)

5.1   PRODUCT/SERVICE

AN INSIDER'S INSIGHTS

The first "P" of the marketing 6P is PRODUCT. By product I refer to the physical characteristics as well as the functions, features, raw material, and design considerations.

A product's characteristics are the foundation upon which the entire business venture is based on. If the product is designed carefully and correctly, the entire business building process will be coherent and efficient. If not, mismatches between what the product actually is (or can do) and its marketing promises will drive away business opportunities.

In a corporate environment where making money is always the driving force, the product strategy often drives the other activities. The product strategy itself is influenced by the company's line of business, resources availability, market conditions and demands. The strategy will include deliberately chosen marketing specifications that spell out which benefits are necessary in the design and should be pursued. The marketing specifications in turn drive the functional specifications that list the functionality and features required to meet the market conditions. The functional specifications then direct the design specifications where technical details are generated and eventually built.

The corporate process may look like this:

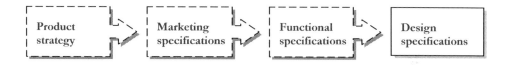

An inventor, on the other hand, tends to come up with an idea and proceeds to work on the design of the idea as a first step. If the design works, he then identifies potential applications and then tries to justify them with benefit statements. Rarely does one have a product strategy to begin with.

This situation is entirely understandable even as it is not optimal for money making. A product strategy would consider whether a concept should even be developed, or maybe when it should be developed (when the market or related technology/infrastructure is ready). It is a well known fact that some inventions sit on corporate R&D shelves for decades before they are commercialized.

The lack of a product strategy does not have to be a deficiency if an inventor follows the C2C blueprint steps to evaluate his concept before moving step-wise towards finalizing his design. In the process he will define the product's physical characteristics by answering the evaluation questions. This has the same effect as having a product strategy.

The contents of this section propose to do exactly that…to help draw out considerations and answers during the physical product creation process. The content is divided into three sections:

    5.1.1 Design considerations

    5.1.2 Making prototypes and models

    5.1.3 Feedback, validation, and refinement

5.1.1 DESIGN CONSIDERATIONS

Coming up with an exciting idea is not the same as coming up with the best design for the idea. Designing involves much more than the creative process and the mechanical process. A successful design at the very least ensures low product maintenance costs from a business operation's perspective.

There are many considerations involved in creating the winning design. Some of them are listed here for further discussions.

(1)   **A customer-friendly design process**

(2)   **Adhering to the KISS principles**

(3)   **Physical design factors**

(4)   **Ergonomics considerations**

(5)   **Designing with the future in mind**

(6)   **Safety and liability reminders**

1 A Customer - Friendly Design Process

Always design with the end customer in mind.

The ultimate goal is to sell the product which means to produce what the target market wants and needs. To do this you should begin with a marketing requirements listing or document. In such a document, you should list benefits to the end users.

Benefits, of course, are not to be confused with features. Features tend to be what the product's characteristics are but stop short of saying why a customer would care about it. For instance, a prominent feature on a steering wheel may be that all the stereo controls are situated in a single area. The benefit to the customer is that she can now control them without using both hands or taking her eyes off the road. Both convenience and added safety are benefits.

Let's use the imaginary SnapIt! concept to illustrate the translation between benefits, functions, and features.

SnapIt! has a motorized base unit which has the capability to drive a host of attachments much like an existing electric hand drill. The attachments serve everyday purposes from light drilling, vacuuming, to scrubbing with various sizes and shapes of brushes. It even has a waterproof pouch for use in wet conditions, including wrappers for extension cable contact points similar to the underwater photography cases used by point and shoot cameras.

All attachments snap on and off with a user friendly patentable design. The base looks and works just like a typical hand drill, but can also pivot or rotate from the typical pistol grip to a horizontal position. The two positions are used depending on the type of work required.

Using SnapIt! As an Example

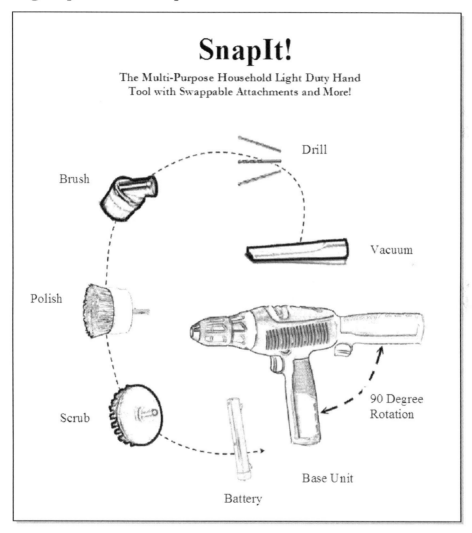

Sales revenue would come from the base unit with a few standard attachments. Additional attachments and extra battery packs, as well as other accessories such as the water proof pouches are also additional revenue sources.

It would be the ultimate hand tool, the only one anyone will need for household cleaning chores and light duty workshop activities.

A Sample Design (Thought) Process for SnapIt!

Marketing Benefits	Functional Requirements	Design Specification
Multi-purpose	Adaptors	Foldable handle in 90/180 degrees with snap-on capability.
Wet/dry conditions	Wet pouch	Water resistant on electrical contact points.
Portable	Battery powered	18V lithium-ion rechargeable.
Powerful	Comparable to hand drill powers	120V corded.
Convenient	Designed for easy assembly and storage	Hand sized base and finger sized attachments in storage bag.
Works on cars, sinks, tiles, light workshop duties	Modular with adapters suitable for polishing, scrubbing, drilling	Accessories must fit motor power while providing sufficient contact points without destroying surfaces.
Ergonomic	Anthropometric data	Dimensions and weights need to be at 95 percentile.
Optional accessories	Extra battery and water proof pouch	Battery is swappable at handle base. Water proof function.

Ultimately whether the unit sells or not depends on the end user's decision. If the guesswork on the product's appeal is taken out, and the value propositions are clear, then the likelihood of a customer buying this product is much higher. On the other hand, if the packaging and marketing messages focus on the features list or even the design specifications, then the product may not even get a chance to be considered.

It's not the product but how you market it that determines its success. This is because of a simple but profound truth that we all live with. As a friend of mine likes to say, we don't live in a meritocracy, which I agree wholeheartedly. If there were absolute justice in our society, then the best products would consistently be the most financially successful. Instead, ours is one where the most heard, loud, or popular wins. Here folks in marketing and sales have a better understanding on how to make the product "shout" or standout.

2 Adhering to the K.I.S.S. Principle

The Keep It Simple Stupid (**KISS**) principle has far reaching implications when it comes to designing a product.

The most obvious is that, for the same function and performance, a simpler design has fewer parts. This translates into several cost saving measures.

For one thing, material cost is lower. Conceivably the manufacturing cost and assembly costs are correspondingly lower as well. For another, fewer parts typically mean less likelihood for breakage or need for maintenance. This too translates into less maintenance costs for both the company (in the form of warranty repairs), and happier customers (less hassle, perhaps even avoiding return shipping costs).

Another issue often overlooked by first time inventors is that a simpler design could bypass a patented design that performs the same function (granted the designs are dissimilar) with lower market introduction prices. In other words, your product may be patented but if someone else comes up with a simpler design that does the same thing then you risk being driven out of the competition.

Here is an actual example...

> With one of the AeroBloks lines I was forced to cut production cost or face its extinction. I reengineered the connectors and was able to shave $0.25 per building block. This may not seem significant at first, but if you multiply that savings by 12 pieces in a set, that was a $3 savings in production cost. With a 40% gross margin, the cost to a retailer was lowered by $8.33. Using the keystone method translated to the retail price being lowered by $16.67. This price reduction allowed me to keep that product line's retail price below the critical psychological price barrier of $100.

By the way, your concept may be a business service, or a service based on a physical product. The same KISS principle applies in designing your service delivery model. The more simple and transparent your service delivery model is, the easier it is to troubleshoot issues. Customers will also appreciate the ease of doing business with a company whose service model is easy to understand.

3 Physical Design Factors

When designing your concept you need to experiment with various types of pattern, form, function, and material. Choosing the right one often comes with tradeoffs and balances. For each of these design aspects you will need to ask yourself several questions.

FUNCTION

- ◈ What is the intended function of this product or service?

- ◈ How will it improve the lives of the end users?

- ◈ Will it work as intended, and consistently?

- ◈ What features should be included?

- ◈ Are there compliance issues because of what the product does?

- ◈ Is the product designed to comply with regulatory specifications?

- ◈ Will it deliver better functions than competitive products?

- ◈ Am I possibly infringing on someone else's design or patent?

- ◈ If it's a combination product, am I diminishing the function or safety of the original products or introducing new hazards? Sometimes in combining functions you might diminish the functions of each and double the liability of both. A dual-functional product can be a double-edge sword.

FORM

- ◈ What would be the right appearance of the product?

- ◈ Where will it be stored? How will it be stored? Space constraint in America has become a major issue for large items.

- ◈ Is the form appealing to the target market? What color, shape, touch, and feel sensation will the customer experience?

- ◈ Will the form fit into the packaging size required for the store shelf?

- ◈ Can the product be assembled or disassembled easily?

- ◈ Is your product a single item or can it be enhanced with add-ons and accessories for use in different or additional applications?

- ◈ Will you develop additional product lines based on the same design? Single product companies have a huge disadvantage since buyers tend to shy away from the time commitment for a single product when they can kill multiple birds with one stone by dealing with companies that showcase multiple items.

MATERIAL

- ◈ Are there any shortages in the raw materials you will use now or in the foreseeable future?

- ◈ Does any of your raw material or component have legal compliance issues, now or in the near future?

- Are there substitution materials that you can leverage to make a better quality, cheaper cost, modular, or multi-function version?

- Can your product be produced with today's technology and manufacturing capabilities?

- Does the material you choose impact your ability to position your product? For example does the material make your product seem cheap even as you decide to produce a high quality item? Or, are there misperceptions about your material that can impact its ability to be sold, such as using plastic in environmentally friendly cultures.

QUALITY

- Should your product be a high quality or low quality product? Does it match with consumer expectations and price limits?

- Is your product subject to production quality control issues?

- Is your product's durability designed to last forever or break soon?

- Is it in alignment with consumer expectations? Some products are designed to break over time, some need to have high durability. The decision depends on the cost/price and function. Takeout boxes are disposable; fine china is not. Both are not durable but one is a valued property. Items that provide repeated usage needs to be durable to meet "expectations" especially if positioned this way.

4 Ergonomic Considerations

- Will you design your product according to the target user's physical dimensions (anthropometric data), usage pattern, and preferences?

- How easy is it for the user to learn to use your product?

- Has the design incorporated ergonomic principles on safety and repetitive usage?

- What is the preferred user-interface for your product or service?

5 Designing with the Future in Mind

- Be sure to have incremental improvement ideas now. Once you commercialize the product, most of your time and money will be spent on chasing sales. Product improvement becomes a necessity only to ensure continuous sales.

6 Safety and Liability Reminders

❖ Is your product safe in the way it is intended as well as unintended to be used?

❖ What safety features and concerns would you have?

❖ Are there hidden dangers or liability with your design? Put it another way, what are ways that people can get hurt with your product?

❖ It's important to evaluate any product's safety features on the outset. Failure to do so correctly exposes you to potential product recall and lawsuit situations which could be costly at best and wipe out your business at its worst.

❖ Anything that involves potential physical injury should be looked at by a safety expert early on, even while at the prototype stage.

5.1.2 MAKING PROTOTYPES AND MODELS

Before you spend a dime on professional prototype makers and modelers, you need to ask yourself if you have already determined that your concept has the means to compete with any existing competitors.

Naturally you would strongly believe that there is a market for your concept. The harder part is to bravely accept the possibility that someone else already beat you to the punch and/or is difficult to topple over, which renders any fees you pay now potentially a waste of money. You really don't want to spend thousands of dollars just to come to that conclusion.

Prototypes are used for various purposes. At the base level they are used to illustrate or demonstrate what your concept could do if it worked. Given that the goal is to minimize unnecessary expenditure during your concept evaluation process, it would make most sense if you can produce the basic forms of representations of your concept using verbal descriptions, drawings, PowerPoint presentations, or even a short video clip on home-made models. For service ideas, usually a flowchart depicting how different parties will interact and transact will get the message across. There is no need to spend a lot of money at this point; the amount of money you spend should match your objective.

If you have successfully obtained meaningful feedback using a rough prototype, the next step would be to refine it with modifications and working parts if possible. Even at this stage you might be able to get away with not paying a professional prototype shop or the manufacturer if your concept allows you to "borrow" working parts from some other objects and put them together.

Ultimately if you are sure your concept should go to market, then a final prototype, or a working sample, should be professionally produced to do demonstrations for potential buyers. It is only at this last stage of prototyping that you should be spending thousands of dollars. Any money you spent earlier than that you risk having zero returns.

This ideal path may not work for everyone every time. Once in a while you will

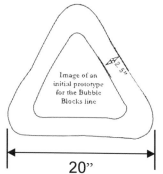

have to produce the prototype in a more final state than anticipated because of sales opportunities. Very few buyers will consider the buying decision until they see the shelf version of the product, usually including packaging.

Your final prototype will also be used for promotional purposes. You will use its images on marketing literature and possibly produce a video clip showing its functionality.

For a service business model, simulation of transactions can be very powerful. There are tools available online to help with simulation of interactions. Transactions can be traced via flowcharts or other forms of presentation. Again, depending on where you are along the evaluation path, such models can typically be done without spending money using professionals.

It should be mentioned that a secondary purpose of making prototypes and models is to learn about the product's design and function. In the process of making prototypes, it's not uncommon that you will try different designs in order to optimize its function. For AeroBloks we went through 7 iterations of building block size, connector location, and different materials while going through the prototyping/modeling stage. The total cost of overnight shipping from the Chinese factories in order to correct manufactured mistakes was several thousand dollars. In the process we learned about the cost of different designs and were able to use that information to refine our financial projections.

I believe we have had our fair share of prototyping nightmares working with overseas manufacturers. It is important that if you choose to produce overseas that you keep a running version control of your modifications and use them to illustrate new changes as a way to minimize miscommunications and unnecessary wastes.

To find a manufacturer who can produce a prototype you can try the Thomas Register of American manufacturers www.thomasnet.com. Alternatively you can find overseas factories via the Alibaba portal www.alibaba.com. Making prototypes overseas can be a lengthy and risky process. Miscommunications alone can cost you several thousand dollars. Another option is to look at products using the material you think you will use and ask their retailers who the manufacturers are. There is also a tradeshow listing published by Job Shop Technology that hosts contract manufacturers capable of producing all kinds of prototypes www.jobshoptechnology.com.

What to Consider Before Building a Professional Prototype

There are different types of representation you can use to convey your idea:

| Verbal description | Pictorial or video | Simulation | Rough model | Non-functional prototype | Functional prototype | Manufactured goods |

To use the appropriate one you should ask these questions:

- ◈ Why do you need it?
- ◈ When do you need it?
- ◈ Who are you showing to and what do they need to see?
- ◈ Is a home-made prototype good enough to illustrate your concept?
- ◈ How much will it cost?
- ◈ Is the cost worth the objective?

Questions you need to consider when making the prototype include:

- ◈ What is the right size?
- ◈ What materials can you use to make the initial and subsequent models?
- ◈ Can you find materials from hardware or fabric stores to build a model?
- ◈ Is a non-functional but illustrative model good enough?
- ◈ Can you substitute working parts from another product for now?
- ◈ Where will you make the prototype?
- ◈ How much will it cost to develop a functional prototype?
- ◈ Can you find machinists and professional prototype makers to make your prototype?
- ◈ Does the prototype maker have the right credentials?
- ◈ How long before you think you will have a functional model or finished product?

5.1.3 FEEDBACK, VALIDATION, AND REFINEMENT

Just because you think an idea is great doesn't mean it is. Let others help you honestly evaluate its intended purpose and the likelihood of achieving the functions.

Your need for something doesn't mean it's a universal need. Even if you just wanted to serve a niche market, it is always better to seek out candid opinions from that market before investing precious time and money into making a working prototype. A functional prototype of a bad concept doesn't make the concept any better.

Here the intent is similar to dipping your toe into the water before deciding whether to jump in. Many people have skipped the steps recommended in this section only to realize later that they could have found out earlier whether they should have gone as far down the path as they did. Here too you are trying to limit your own exposure before involving outsiders whose interest may not coincide with yours down the road. In other words, you have just about total control and decision making up to this point.

1 Who Are They, Where to Find Them?

Just as a concept can be represented by a range of display media and models, feedback can also be received from a variety of sources based on where you are in the process.

Conventional marketing uses the focus group as a formal market testing and feedback mechanism on new products. This approach has its drawbacks, not the least because it is expensive to run but also because the selection process may be skewed.

With technology the focus group has migrated online. There are market surveys that designated focus group members can respond online, thereby at least cutting down the travel costs and refreshment costs. But this is only one of a handful of choices.

Once again the type of people you plan on getting feedback on should map to the purpose of your inquiry and the stage of your product evaluation process.

The most informal feedback can be received from friends, families, or neighbors. This feedback provides some initial value but may be tainted with subjectivity. The next group is your local invention association or business club. These folks will hopefully have the expertise to judge your concept at a professional level.

Beyond these two physical groups you can also tap online resources. Social media forums that discuss products similar to your concept will be filled with people who are interested in your concept. You can post hypothetical questions and get responses that way. Amazon.com offers feedbacks on different products. By browsing the good and the bad you can glean much market intelligence.

Blogs that discuss your type of concept often have reader responses that reveal what people are looking for. There might also be useful links to other sites that talk about your type of product or service; there's much you can gleam from such sites. You could always hire a business to organize an online focus group, but this should not be done until you have a pretty good idea what your concept is and are just looking for validation.

The best answers will come from potential customers and distributors. If you are able to ask at least a good sampling of these people you will have better than average data points to work with. In essence when you involve others you have migrated to a different paradigm, one that is driven by social media and online strategy. The focus groups of yesterday become substituted by the online forums and the comments from anyone and everyone. Effectively you have changed your mode of operation from a closed loop to a wide open environment where people who provide feedback become part of your product development team, for free.

Regardless of which group you seek feedback or concept validation from; there are a few common questions you need to ask them:

2 Group Makeup

- ◈ Does the group have the proper expertise to offer practical feedback and validation?

- ◈ Is a test group's size large enough, independent, and representative of the target market?

3 Feedback and Responses

- ◈ Does the group agree that:

  - Your positioning is accurate?

  - The production cost is realistic?

  - The projected retail price is acceptable?

  - The perceived value is reasonable against the price?

  - Your concept receives an overall favorable response?

- ◈ Did the feedback:

  - Indicate that there are no technical feasibility issues?

  - Reach a consensus on the time-to-market feasibility?

- Raise any red flags in terms of product safety and liability concerns?

- Signify that the functions and features meet the expectations of the test group?

- Give realistic suggestions on practical safety features?

A final question is for yourself, namely will you be able to verify the validity of the feedbacks and implement them in your revised design?

4 Refinement

Assuming that you were able to ascertain the quality of feedbacks you obtained, the next step is to implement them into the prototype, marketing message, or even financial projections.

More often than not, because you did not pay verified professionals or actual customers to get your feedback, you will need to do a little more "data scrubbing" on your feedback.

It's important to realize that just because someone gave you feedback in a forum or group setting it doesn't mean you are to accept his feedback completely. If the marketing feedback is coming from an engineer who has no experience in marketing, you would be no better off than to ask anyone randomly. The astute thing to do is to take the feedback and do more research.

Once you are ready to modify your concept, model, or prototype, you can start the process of swapping out parts and assumptions and use validated information instead. At this point you need to run your financials to see if it still makes sense to go forward.

There is always the possibility that people hate your idea. This isn't necessarily a bad thing. It's probably a lifesaver, although sometimes what people reject is not your idea but your presentation. Make sure you clarify that this is not the case if you are thinking of junking your entire concept because of the feedback.

It is always a good approach to come up with a good idea and let it sit and simmer for a while. This works for marketing ideas, business models, or product designs. The first iteration is never the best or the final version. Don't cheat yourself out of the opportunity to optimize your chances of success by presenting a less than perfect product to the final group.

Stay realistic in terms of scope and functionality. This is just the beginning of the product commercialization path. Set your objective in terms of what exactly you are trying to prove, accomplish, and then stop for a breather.

Test your functionality again and again to ensure consistent outcome.

Refinement is both a philosophy and a way of life if you intend on keeping up with the competition. Continuous improvements throughout the product's lifecycle are necessary to increase value and decrease costs.

Evaluation Questions: Appendix 4 Section 1-2

Research and Development Questions:

- Do you see challenges or difficulties in developing your concept into a physical product or a business process?
- What is the total cost on expected research and developmental expenditures?
- Does your concept require continuous R&D expenditure to keep up with competition or updates in technology? If so, what percentage of budget will it be?
- Are you possibly infringing on someone else's patent?

Product Design Questions:

- How well did you apply the KISS design principle?
- Is your design based on a user-centric approach that incorporates what the market's needs and wants are?
- Do you have a clear formulation of the design's function, form, material, quality, safety, and liability requirements?

Prototyping Questions:

- Do you have a prototype making strategy that maps to your presentation objective, including where and how to source the materials and skills?
- Do you know the type of material and costs associated with the various forms of prototypes you will need?

Appendix 4 Section 1-5

Feedback, Validation, and Refinement Questions:

- Is your source of feedback qualified to give you substantiated comments and concept validation?
- Did your concept receive positive feedback on its form, function, material, safety, marketing positioning, production cost, retail price, and financial projection, etc.?
- Are you able to validate the feedback and implement them onto your prototype or business modeling?

HOW DID YOUR CONCEPT DO?

Ideally you are able to answer each question with substantiated data points. Your costs and prices are within expectations, your assumptions are reasonable, and the feedback is generally positive to go forth.

Potential Challenges and issues may occur if you fail to produce information necessary for feedback. Your assumptions could be immature or faulty. Your cost projections could be unrealistic. Your price points may leave you without any profits or with no customers. Your product could be too dangerous to produce. You could be wasting other people's time because you were not ready.

5.2 POSITIONING

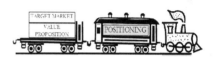

AN INSIDER'S INSIGHTS

Positioning is the first step in marketing communications. It is essentially how you have chosen to describe your product. Good positioning statements reflect a product's most attractive attributes in a relevant, easy to remember manner that resonates with customer expectations.

This section contains the following topics within the positioning strategy:

5.2.1 The importance of relevance

5.2.2 Your value propositions

5.2.3 Writing your positioning statement

5.2.4 Branding tools

5.2.5 Getting your product/service noticed

Positioning is the precursor to promotional activities. If done correctly, it has the power to capture market share, topple competition, and maintain leadership. If done poorly, the product may never take off.

Marketing leverages a lot of what we understand from the field of applied psychology. Much of what drives marketing strategy has to do with understanding the target market's psychological makeup. For example, the concept of using the "foot in the door" technique is borrowed from social psychology and widely used to introduce new products.

Marketing positioning leverages perceptions; it specifically relies on induced perceptions of the customers. Consumers make a great number of purchase decisions (especially on newer products) based on perceived values.

A positioning statement is what a marketer generates to identify with a product. In the statement it will describe what is of interest and relevance to the customer. Beyond the benefits, it may not be based on reality at all.

This is a field where perception is more real than reality.

The best examples are found in luxury items where nuances in marketing message prevail. BMW famously came up with a slogan that positions it as "The Ultimate Driving Machine." This message is seared into the minds of not only automobile enthusiasts but also consumers who want the highest performance. Whether it is in fact superior is debatable.

Likewise, when L'Oréal came up with the advertising slogan "Because you're worth it" in 2009, it captured a lot of attention. The basic premise was that luxury beauty products should not be limited by money; every woman regardless of wealth deserves to be pampered by luxury beauty products. This sentiment echoed across economic sectors and resulted in sales that otherwise would not have occurred.

Therefore, what you suggest with your positioning statement is exactly how you want the customer to perceive your product or service; it is all in the mind and much more than just describing the product.

Avis car rental adopted a repositioning strategy and famously issued the slogan "We try harder!" as a way to relate to the No.1 car rental company Hertz. Their strategy was to inject the perception that they work harder at servicing customers. Whether this ever happened is immaterial; their market shares went up dramatically afterwards. It's a true testimonial to the power of positioning.

5.2.1 THE IMPORTANCE OF RELEVANCE

Even if your market is in an English speaking environment, you may need to re-learn English as a second language (at least in marketing terms)! Just as a writer needs to write at the reading level of his target audience, when you wear the marketer hat you need to use everyday language that your customers can readily relate to for your marketing efforts to succeed.

Putting it another way, if there is a specific lingo or jargon pertaining to that niche then you need to incorporate it into your product description and maybe in the positioning statement as well.

I made this fundamental error after switching from a high tech to a consumer retail environment. I started noticing some blank stares at our first tradeshow when I tried to explain that AeroBloks was a *modular building system of inflatable building blocks*. A few shows later I noticed the repeated usage of the words "blow-up blocks" from would-be customers. At first I resisted the words because of the connotation of explosion and leakage, which would be disastrous for the product's image. Soon I realized that "when in Rome…you must speak Italian as well." I started closing more sales once I adopted the wordings. Wish I had known this earlier! It was an expensive mistake in the way I positioned and described the product. Don't let that happen to you.

The "Relevance" Test

Before issuing a positioning statement you need to double-check its relevance to the target consumer's way of life and quality of life.

To stay relevant you will need to study the target user in detail and not simply grab some demographic data and call it a day. You may not need to use as much detail as a time-and-motion study typically conducted in ergonomics research, but the more actual observance on the way the product is to be used in your test market the better.

Something is highly relevant if the test subject can readily relate to or remember it afterwards. In other words, the message needs to "stick."

Depending on any subculture, the positioning statement needs to generate perceived (hopefully real) benefits that resonate with the customers. This might even involve laying out the promotional material with images or icons, color, fonts, etc. that are familiar to the customers' subculture.

One way to induce relevance for a physical product is to relate it to something that already exists. After I finally gave up using my own words to describe the AeroBloks building system to the specialty toy market, sales also increased. The magic phrase was "think of it as a giant LEGO building system."

Keep in mind that even though perception may be outsized from reality, there still needs to be a real dose of facts in your product description to make it relevant.

5.2.2 YOUR VALUE PROPOSITION

 Need vs. Want

Thanks in large part to American psychologist Abraham Maslow, the concept of a hierarchy of needs is commonly known. We can leverage this analysis loosely to assess the degree of demand your product may generate.

There are baseline physical needs such as food, water, and security, and then there are the social need of being connected to others and the emotional or psychological need of getting fulfillment. Does your concept provide for any of these needs or is it a fad that will come and go?

If it's a product, is it driven by a proven need from someone else? If you invent a product then try to find a market for it, then you are doing it backwards with no guarantee of demands. This is a fairly common first time mistake.

Since there are plenty of free resources on the internet that explain the difference between "Needs" vs. "Wants" and the concept is fairly straightforward we will not spend much discussion on it. Instead we will dissect the concept of "value" which is the basis of someone wanting or needing a product or service.

2   Value and Worth Examination

Most everything has a value. The value can be subjective (as in one man's trash is another man's treasure) or more objective (as in a commonly agreed upon significance). The value is defined by the recipient just as beauty is in the eyes of the beholder.

Before the arrival of the internet, office workers would sometimes gather around the water cooler and socialize (gossip). This used to be looked upon as a waste of company time. The value of the gossip was generally low for business and high for the people who needed to socialize and be "in the know."

The internet technology changed all that. Now there are blogs and forums, or the "digital water coolers." There are now millions of blogs that talk about anything under the sun. Some of them carry business intelligence while others stick to traditional gossiping. Both types and everything in-between provide value to their viewers. Blogs have even been known to be sold for money. Imagine someone trying to sell a water cooler spot for money years ago, it would have been the joke of the day. This development demonstrates that value has a price.

The value of anything is measured by its worth which translates into what others are willing to pay. This is no different than any other transactions in the marketplace. The implication for you is that if your goal is to make a profit from your idea then you need to focus on what can increase the worth of a value that your product or service can deliver.

For example, if you have created an improved version of a commodity product, then optimizing its worth means designing it to achieve the lowest retail price possible. This may impact your choice of material and packaging. Since people often choose lowest priced commodities, relative to competing products yours will have the highest value. The "worth" to a customer is more even as she pays less.

> One man's trash is another man's treasure; don't automatically assume that what you value is the same as that of your customers.

If your concept is for a new medical equipment, then its effectiveness and safety features will generally outweigh price when others determine its worth. The following table lists some examples on how to increase your idea's worth:

If Your Idea Is For:	Its Primary Value Is:	Then Optimization Means to Focus On:
Creativity	Aesthetics	Style, color, shape, design, branding
Industrial equipment	Function	Reliability, durability, predictability
Medical technology	Life saving	Effectiveness, safety
Alternative energy	Cost saving	Production, installation, operating costs
A better mousetrap	Improvement	Usage, efficiency, price, maintenance

The best products are those designed specifically for the intended users; the most persuasive presentations are those tailored to the target audiences' interests. Often the invention process or accidental discoveries work the other way around; the idea comes before the application.

To compensate for this, you should focus much of your energy on defining the concept's value propositions and increasing the worth in the eyes of the end users. Think from your customer's perspective. Why should they care?

3   Core Value vs. Secondary Value

With all the benefits that your innovation can potentially boast about, how would you know which ones are the most important?

The strategy comes down to putting the greatest need in the center of your proposition. The primary need can be physical or functional, or it can be psychological and perception driven. It all depends on the type of goods or services you provide.

> Different types and classes of goods or services have different value propositions. There is no one set that fits them all.

Let's take a look at the following diagram to illustrate:

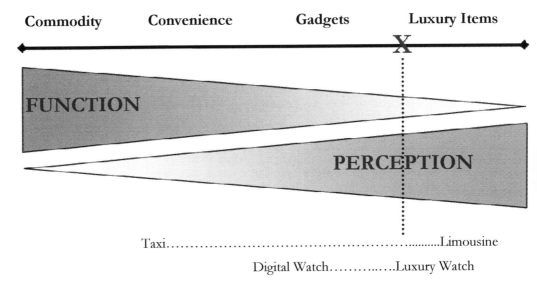

If your product or service is strictly a commodity, then your positioning statement should focus primarily on its functionality, which is the value it brings to your customer. If what the customer is willing to pay (its worth) equates with its real or perceived value, then the price is considered reasonable.

If your product is a pure luxury item then you should focus primarily on the projection of the perception that you intend to invoke. Its worth to the customer is measured by how much of the perceived benefit (e.g. social status, image, position, fantasy) the customer receives. The price they are willing to pay is equivalent to the degree of the perceived value they get.

If your product (X) lies closer on the spectrum to luxury than to commodity, its positioning statement needs to contain a proportional mix of the two values. In the illustration the X could represent a retro spy gear that doubles as a camera. Its function as a spy gear would be outdated and its function as a camera would be substandard performance. Yet its appeal as a gadget from another time and its scarcity can command a high price as a collector's item. In this scenario the positioning statement would contain much more perception based than function based descriptions.

For example, it could be something like *"With a surreptitious click of a finger you could transport back to a time when spies captured secret images to save their countries"* for a statement. This statement would invoke the perception of patriotism, time travel, secrecy, bravery, and adventure while touching on its function as a camera lightly. Its appeal would be on-target for people who fantasize about another era and the spy trade. These would be the real reason why they buy, and certainly not because the camera works.

With attention span becoming ever shorter you need to identify the real reason why someone might want to pay for your product or service and put it where it belongs.

Isolating the most desired need for each sub-segment as the core value is critical. Unless the core value proposition is met, otherwise by pitching secondary values repeatedly may actually drive your customers away. In other words, even though telling people that your product can last longer and is cheaper may not matter at all if all they really care about is the perception that the competitive product projects.

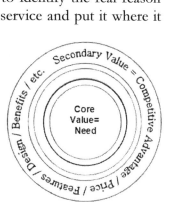

4 New vs. Improved Implications

There is a little secret that not many people will tell you; perhaps it's because they don't know it either.

It is the notion that "new" is not necessarily a good thing.

Believe it or not, when people say they want something new, they actually mean something vaguely familiar but with a new twist. If a product is totally new, they become reluctant to commit to it. Incrementally new is the real deal for getting products sold.

This is because most people tend to shy away from unproven concepts and products, preferring to let others be the guinea pigs. It is a well known fact that true innovations often go through a period when only the early adopters will make the purchase. The degree of "unproven" usually correlates with the length of time during the early adoption period. This is particularly true in technology products.

Realistically speaking the reality is that very few things are truly innovative today. Most new ideas are derivations or improvements of existing concepts. Nevertheless there are different degrees of "newness."

Notice that a lot of products have "New and Improved" claims go hand-in-hand in their promotional messages. It literally means new modification by improving an existing product or concept.

It's important to realize that if your concept targets several different segments, that you will need to develop segment-specific position statements. For example, the AeroBloks play set was different things to many people. For the education segment, it was a construction system that promoted spatial creativity. For the occupational therapy segment, it was a therapy tool that helped kids to cope with hyper-sensitivity issues. For the specialty toy segment, it was a life size pretend play type of structure. Depending on which market segment your innovation targets, your product description needs to resonate with your target audience's existing understanding and expectations.

5.2.3 WRITING YOUR POSITIONING STATEMENT

Technology gives people power, capabilities that they otherwise could not have. It's amusing to watch how some people act as if they are invincible with their newly acquired technology toys. With tech toys they can suddenly create hot or cold air, communicate across vast distances, get information they need within seconds, be well informed and connected at all times, and even mobilize armies of workers with a single call. In other words, they have become the demigods of legends. Such power can be addictive, which is the reason why so many people continue to flock to the latest and greatest gadgets.

If technology can do that for its target consumers, <u>what</u> <u>does</u> <u>your</u> <u>product or service</u> <u>really</u> <u>do</u> <u>for</u> <u>yours?</u>

If you can answer this question then you can create the most appealing positioning statement that combines its perceived value and actual functionality.

Positioning should be driven by what your target users really want instead of what you assume they want. If you don't do this, you will end up doing much work trying to hard sell instead of experiencing effortless sales.

If you were to rate a positioning statement, the most successful one (measured by customer's response) would be the most relevant one with simple to understand and easy to remember statements. The key is **relevance** and **simplicity**.

Positioning statements are often launched with advertising campaigns. It should be printed consistently on all marketing material, especially the packaging and possibly on the product itself.

- ◈ If you have a household product – Say what it is, don't make up fancy descriptions just to sound smart or different; it will backfire.

- ◈ If you have a commodity – The value is usually in saving money, time, or space.

- ◈ If you have an improved version of something – Begin your description by relating it to the existing as an improved version.

- ◈ If yours is a new technology or scientific discovery – Focus on the function and capability before finalizing on its potential applications. Sometimes what you think is the primary application may not be the optimal commercialization path for it.

Regardless of which category, ascertain how it is better in the minds of the consumer. People need help with framing unfamiliar products. Use simple, easy to understand words to do so.

Possible answers include:

- A better mouse trap (an improved X)
- Improved efficiency
- Reduced cost
- Improved quality of life
- Improved safety
- Improved convenience
- Improved learning

I was looking to buy a foot massager a couple of years ago. After several hours of reading online reviews, I noticed a product with lots of negative feedbacks. As luck would have it, it was not exactly a foot massager but an electro-physiotherapy stimulator that sends mild electrical impulses from your feet to the rest of your body's nerve endings. The product was worth at least $300 but was marked down to less than $100.

Apparently most people thought it was a foot massager and when they received the mild electric shocks they thought the product was defective. And no wonder why! Whoever did the marketing and positioning of the product for this South Korean made device absolutely botched the job. They named it a foot massager even though the insert describes the electrophysiology function. This product remains one of my favorites to this date, and is absolutely effective as a physiotherapy product.

Apparently the product launch in the US market was completely bombed because of incorrect positioning. To prove this point, at the time of my purchase there were only three units left at liquidation prices. Once we told a physical therapist about it, she immediately snatched up the rest of them. She could not believe her good luck! Imagine what could have happened to the sale of this excellent product if the marketing positioning was done correctly?

The moral of the story is that it's not the product that matters but how it's positioned that matters the most. Any unique features must be called out and get noticed. If yours is truly unique and has superior functional value, then you need to be able to demonstrate it perhaps with online video clips.

5.2.4 BRANDING TOOLS

For an inventor trying to break into the market with his invention, or an entrepreneur with a new business idea, a strong brand of an existing competitor is a formidable barrier. On the other hand, for the same competitor, a strong brand is an extremely valuable asset. This formless asset exists in the minds of the target consumers.

A brand carries with it a powerful association (perception) of the product's assumed attributes like quality, status, reputation, and the set of expectations behind that signature. It is an integral part of the positioning strategy of a company.

Brand building takes time and a lot of work. It is often accomplished by promotional efforts like advertising and product displays in prominent areas. It is an expensive proposition and undertaking, that's why branding and name are highly protected by trademarks.

Consumers will often buy products from one brand instead of the other even without knowing the specifics of the product. Someone who gravitates towards a GE brand of washer from other less known brands may have no idea about the differences in machines but makes his purchase decision solely on the strength of the brand.

People are willing to pay more for branded goods even if a new competitor produces higher quality. Again business relationship and ultimately sale is built on trust and expectations.

As usual, trust takes experience to build. Customer expectations need to be set up appropriately. As a manufacturer, you build your brand upon consistency. If you want to build a strong brand, spending millions of dollars in promotional events may get you temporary attention and a spike in sales but they will not last. Consistency in quality, delivery, and meeting expectations builds a lasting brand which in exchange earns you customer loyalty, repeat sales, referred sales, and even the right to raise prices just as your competitors cut theirs.

Of course, as a promotional activity, branding requires strategy. You cannot simply have a strong brand because you want to. Strong brands happen when customers collectively and overtime endorse your brand. To do this you must have a branding strategy that includes slogans, catchy and easy to remember value phrases that are consistent with your product's benefits, your company's operating philosophy, and anything that is publicly visible.

1 Naming

Picking the right name for your product or service is no easy task. A strong name will carry with it meanings and projections, perceptions and expectations, and a slew of other invisible attributes that will be associated with the product or service for as long as it exists.

A name is suggestive and brings up images. One good example is perfume. A fruity name conjures sweet scents of fruits while the name of a spice does the spicy thing. In reality the two perfumes may not differ too much but the imageries are there.

Naming is as much a part of the positioning strategy as branding. An appropriately named product or service saves promotional dollars. International Business Machine (IBM) for example, projects a global presence, giant machinery, and a business attitude which were all very appropriate during the climate of its establishment. Over time its brand has become a household name for computers and its initials are as easily recognized as most other retail giants like GE, GM.

Naming does not need to be done in isolation. In fact for consumer products it is actually more advantageous to ask would-be customers how they would describe the product as a first impression. Names that are easy to recall go hand-in-hand with brands that are easy to recognize.

If you were developing a product or service in the hospitality sector, your core value propositions might include convenience, easy, hassle-free, cost savings, personalized service, and friendly which all give the assurance of a pleasant experience.

If you provide a streamlined reservation system, it may consist of easy to deal with, one-stop shopping, with expertise, insider's scoop, and local advantage attributes.

When it comes to providing such services, yours is the expert, specialist, authority, professional, the go-to-guy, concierge service, and connoisseur.

Any of these words can be used to conjure up images of your product or service and their value propositions. The best selection would do both.

2 Logos

It should be mentioned that a logo is a visual cue of a company and its brand. Think of it as a written representation of the company's name. It is a part of branding which is a subset of positioning strategy. So choosing a logo must be in alignment with your overall positioning strategy.

Your logo must project the same imagery as your positioning statement. It is much more than just picking the design and color scheme that looks right. Once set, a logo is like a name and a brand, it becomes costly to change especially if your brand grows. People will come to recognize and associate all your positioning statements with the logo.

Apple products have a common signature design that is sleek, black and white in soft contrast, and looks like jewelry which denotes elegance. Overtime the theme has been copied and now has also come to represent technology in a sexy way.

When designing your logo for your concept you should select from a theme that fits your company's image.

5.2.5 GET NOTICED (AMONGST COMPETITORS)

There is clear advantage to be the first to market from a positioning perspective. Customers tend to remember the first product that carves a mental category in their minds. If your concept is truly unique, as AeroBloks was the first of its kind, then you must stress that attribute in all your positioning statements using words like unique, first, original, etc. This will ensure its first position within how people remember.

If you already have competition then you must accentuate on what makes your concept different (not unique). That difference must stand out in your positioning statement so customers will remember it. For example, SnapIt! is certainly not the first electric drill-like hand tool, it is also not the first home scrubbing tool. However, it is one that easily converts to both tools. The positioning statement for SnapIt! may then be "The First Dry/Wet Interchangeable Hand Tool for Your Home."

Consumers tend to form mental categories of products and remember one or two companies per category, which tends to be the market leader. Mercedes, BMW, Coke, Pepsi, IBM, Apple, Hertz, AVIS, are all examples of the top two contenders in their categories. Number three and below are often forgotten.

Evaluation Questions: Appendix 4 Section 2-1

● What is the degree of relevance in the consumer's mind for your product or service, in terms of what they look for?

● Can you specifically identify the primary and secondary values and benefits your idea brings to the target audience?

● What is the level of familiarity your target market has towards your invention's function and usage. In other words, what is the effort required to become familiar with your invention?

● How well does your positioning statement entice your target market to buy your product/service?

- Do you have a branding strategy that is in alignment with your positioning strategy?

- Does the concept have a name and a logo (identifiers) that are highly relevant and easy to recall by the target customers?

- Are you able to easily differentiate your creation from those of the competition?

HOW DID YOUR CONCEPT DO?

Ideally you will have developed a positioning strategy that encompasses all the critical elements discussed in this section. Each element should have been carefully considered and incorporated into its own strategy. Specifically you will be able to identify the relevance in your target customer's minds, leverage the improved aspect correctly, identify what is of primary value and focus on its worth, know how to build a strong brand with an easily recognizable name and logo, and be able to differentiate successfully from your competition.

Potential Challenges and issues may be caused by a slew of factors. A positioning strategy can be easily botched by the most innocent mistakes. Failure to identify value and relevance is the basis of going down the wrong path. Not incorporating the intended perception or projected image onto your branding strategy will cost more money in trying to promote your product. An incorrectly launched positioning statement may cost you your business. Names and logos that have no relevance to your concept or the central theme of your positioning strategy serve no real purpose.

5.3   PRICING

AN INSIDER'S INSIGHTS

Pricing is a part of the overall marketing strategy and is an integral part of the consumer buying process. It sets a cost point where consumers must decide whether it is reasonable to exchange their currency for the goods or services.

This section will include these topics:

5.3.1   **A baseline understanding**

5.3.2   **Dispelling a myth**

5.3.3   **It's all about psychology**

5.3.4   **How to set prices**

5.3.5   **Pricing adjustments**

The right price will optimize your profit. The wrong price will preclude sales or cause business loss.

Pricing your goods or services is more of an art than a science. Selling and buying transactions are about people interactions; it should come as no surprise then that pricing leverages psychology more than rational buying behavior. If the price is set incorrectly, you may never make a profit. In other words, pricing is difficult and the implications are serious.

Where does that leave a first time entrepreneur? Most likely in a state of anxiety caused by high uncertainty.

In response, most people set out to follow a couple of the tried and true (but not necessarily right) approaches. The most common one is the most straightforward, which is to add a certain amount of profit above their total cost, otherwise known as the cost-plus approach. The second most popular method is to price slightly above or below a similar product that's already in the market, a practice known as benchmarking.

Neither one of these basic approaches meets the goal of maximizing profit, which presumably is the reason why people go into business. As we examine the rest of the approaches this claim will become clear.

There are five major points that will illustrate what needs to be considered in a pricing strategy.

5.3.1 A BASELINE UNDERSTANDING

Pricing is **more of an art than a science**.

In science, predictable outcomes can be generated by manipulating the input variables. But since we are dealing with fickle human beings, there is not a guaranteed or consistent sales outcome each time you tweak the price.

With practice and experience (assuming you are afforded such opportunities), in time you will be much better at setting the right prices. It is the same as in art; a master artisan will get something right the first time but amateurs need to try it a few times.

Price is the **gatekeeper of your customer's wallet**.

Customers make purchase decisions on many levels, not just on price. Yet price is the gatekeeper that either opens or shuts the customer's wallet.

Price is NOT the enticing agent. Attractive products and packaging entice, positioning statements entice, messages entice, and price justifies. The purchase justification can happen even before a product is evaluated if there is a budget to be kept, otherwise it happens after all the other attributes have been considered and weighed. This mental process can take seconds to minutes.

People don't buy things because they are cheap or on sale. They buy them because they think they need or want the item, and a lowered price simply tips the scale. If this weren't true, then every low priced item would be bought the moment they become available.

5.3.2 DISPELLING A MYTH

Most first time entrepreneurs make **the mistake of thinking that if they can make a lower priced product they will topple the existing competition**.

This notion may be true for commodities but in most other cases the pricing strategy is not so simple and straightforward. It is important to realize that price is only one of the many factors people consider when making a purchase.

Something that most business owners also don't realize immediately… lower prices tend to attract value shoppers whose loyalty lies not in brand but in prices. The moment they find somewhere cheaper for similar products they will leave. No one can afford to consistently be the lowest price provider unless he has a huge war chest and bargaining power based on economies of scale. Being the low price provider therefore has its risks.

5.3.3 IT'S ALL ABOUT PSYCHOLOGY

Successful pricing leverages consumer psychology. It uses comparisons, perceptions, expectations, valuations, and ultimately reasonableness as yardsticks.

We witness this behavior everyday. Sometimes even the difference as small as a penny can cause a consumer to drive a mile to a different store. This makes no sense from a rational perspective since the cost to do so already exceeds the savings. But it has more to do with how a person feels with the price. The sense of "right, reasonableness, fairness, and not getting gouged" will almost always justify going the extra mile. It's as if pricing is the catalyst that initiates a quest based on principle.

What is right, fair, just, and reasonable has to do with the perceived value of the product or service. As mentioned earlier, a product or service's worth is measured by how valuable the target buyer feels. The amount of money that she is willing to spend has to be equal to or less than the worth she assigns to the product or service.

There is no universal judgment on the value of any product or service, going back to the saying that "one man's trash is another man's treasure." This is half the reason why pricing is subjective and an art. The other half has to do with perception, which is why positioning statements are so crucial in moving goods and services.

The key term in pricing is PERCEIVED VALUE. **Perception** drives **value** assessment while assessment is based on reasonableness and reasonableness is all about **fairness**.

If I perceive something to be highly valuable because I believe in the positioning messages, then I would most likely place a high worth on the item. When I was younger I salivated over BMW cars. I believed that they were worth a lot and therefore the higher prices (150% or more of other comparable sized cars) were right and in fact reasonable considering that BMW was the "ultimate" driving machine! So for me to pay that much money in return for all its advertised features and benefits was fair.

Years later after having owned the least expensive line of the BMW series, I began to realize that a lot of cars can do 0-60mph faster, take corners better, and cost cheaper to drive and maintain. Is it still the ultimate driving machine? I have my doubts especially since lower priced cars seem to perform better in some areas. Nevertheless I continue to be in awe of the power embedded in the BMW positioning statement even if it's not entirely true.

If I were not convinced by their claim, I don't believe I would have ever considered owning a car at that price range. This is a testimony to the inter-related mechanics of pricing, positioning, and sales. I didn't even need to hear the car salesperson; I went there determined to own a BMW. His job was easy.

On the other hand, I would never consider forking over the large sum of money for a Lexus despite their excellent reputation. Their price ranges are an automatic stop sign for someone like me who believes that a car is a vehicle designed to transport. It should not be a luxury item. Just to clarify, this does not violate my rationale to buy the beamer; I bought the "ultimate" driving machine, remember? It meant that I got the best value possible for its promised performance.

Lesson learned… your price should seem like a no-brainer to the customer so as to allow her to focus on your value propositions. The more someone lingers on deciding whether a price is "right" the more likely you will lose that sale. This is another way of saying that you should find the expectation and then meet it. If you were to do an online survey, the right price point will be the one that has the most people voting for it.

Price is the gatekeeper of your customer's wallet because it either immediately prevents her to even look into your offering (as in the Lexus cars for me), or as one that is weighed after the perceived value is evaluated (as in the BMW case for me).

At the end of the day it is all in your head. Don't believe it? Just look at the exorbitant prices some teens are willing for pay for a T-shirt. Sometimes the T-shirts they buy have a price that can pay for a sleeping bag. This is where pricing really becomes irrational and is totally based on perceived value. In this case the value is in social status (as in I can afford it), social acceptance (as in all my friends have it), or simply in impulse buying.

5.3.4 HOW TO SET PRICES

There are different types of pricing strategy. Some are based on the type of goods, some are based on cost, some are based on perception, some are based on value, and some are totally irrational.

For example, commodity pricing is quite different from specialty item pricing. By definition a commodity is generic in character and appearance, and has similar levels of quality and function regardless of who manufactured it (think paper plates). In this case price would be the primary determining factor of whether your product wins the sales or not. If your product is a commodity and you want to charge more for it, then your price has to reflect the additional value in concrete terms.

This is not the case for specialty items. Think about a pair of designer shoes. The price charged (the worth assigned) is based on the perception of its value. Perception here means more than function. Shoes pretty much perform the same functions although a good pair of shoes will be more comfortable, durable, and attractive. The last characteristic of attractiveness is subjective and therefore subject to perceptual differences amongst different people.

In that case, pricing needs to reflect the perceived attractiveness and so it works like a double-edged sword. Price it too high and hardly anyone buys it; price it too low and its perceived value drops and potential customers also walk away.

Whether the perceived value ends up being associated with a strong brand, a status symbol, or something more nebulous, the pricing psychology for specialty items is entirely different from that of commodities.

There are different pricing strategies to set the initial price. We will look at six of the most common ones:

    (1) Cost plus approach

    (2) Benchmark approach

    (3) Maintaining margin approach

(4) **Value based approach**

(5) **Supply and demand approach**

(6) **Intangible based approach**

1 Cost Plus Approach

Pricing must cover your cost basis if you are to make a profit. There must be wiggle room for you to raise prices without sacrificing so much of your profit margin that you drive yourself out of business.

Everyone knows that everything has a cost to produce/provide. Nobody expects to pay unreasonable prices; they expect the producer to price based on the cost. But those who actually price based on production cost risk not charging enough to cover their expenses when costs increase and at the same time a price ceiling exists.

Most people start with the cost of production, and then multiply by 4 or 5 times to get an estimated price point. This is a classic mistake. Pricing should never be based on cost alone but instead should be used to determine if cost is within your capability.

For example, if your closest competitor's price is $25, then you would divide by 5 to get the maximum production cost you can absorb, namely $5. If you are unable to keep your production cost below $5, it becomes highly questionable on whether you should even enter the market with your concept because you are already at a cost disadvantage.

You need to recognize that product cost quotes from factories are just a piece of your total cost. There are others like packaging, freight, warehousing, and standard business operations expenditures that your final retail price (revenue) must support. Let's not forget about the amount of marketing promotional cost which will dictate whether you attract any customer or not.

This approach leaves very little wiggle room. You might end up having cost controlling you and not the other way around. That is essentially leaving yourself vulnerable to unforeseen forces that potentially could cripple you.

2 Benchmark Approach

Many first time entrepreneurs find the nearest competitive product and price their own product slightly above or below, thinking that consumers will feel that the price is "in the range." Some then invent value statements to justify the price difference. Unfortunately this is a strategy filled with holes. It isn't necessarily a wrong approach but does require more strategic thinking to "plug the holes."

A better strategy would be to focus on providing a better value than your competition so any higher prices can be justifiable.

Competitive pricing begins with looking at the customer profiles and figuring out how they evaluate the value and assign a worth on the attributes of your type of product or service. When you benchmark you basically treat an existing product's price as a market tolerance reference point.

Some of these product attributes include quantity, size, quality, function, form, and ergonomic features, etc. Once you have some idea of what they consider is important, you may have the option of either embedding more value and charge the same price or price lower and provide less value. This is a strategic decision.

The next step is to generate the positioning statements that will create the desired perceptions for your product in your customer's minds. Your price then reflects that perception. For example, "SnapIt! saves you time every time!" would be used in its pricing evaluation against a competitor's product. If SnapIt! really does save more time than another sink scrubber, then you could price it higher.

With today's technology you can always test out your price assumptions and value propositions against an existing product's price by surveying potential customers on social networks or user forums. Give a simple description and price ranges and have people pick a range. The multiple choice format will allow you to sort the responses more easily. Use the price range that most people agree with, then zoom in to refine the price within the chosen range, and do it again until you get to a popular price point.

3 Maintaining Margin Approach

The need to maintain a profit margin is universal amongst businesses. Sales revenue pays for direct costs associated with making the product and getting it ready for distribution.

Revenue minus direct costs generates the gross profit. The gross profit in turn pays for sales, general and administrative costs including salaries. The ratio of gross profit divided by sales revenue is called the profit margin or gross margin. For construction toys the gross margin is around 45%. This is a key financial number that businesses pay attention to.

Taking the approach of maintaining a particular profit margin level is similar to the cost-plus method. In this case you would figure out what your profit margin needs to be and calculate what price you need to charge in order to cover your costs and meet the profit margin level.

This method allows you to measure your business operation's effectiveness relative to your competitors in the same industry. The company with the highest profit margin selling the same goods or services in the same industry obviously has a stronger financial position to weather potential storms.

If your concept is in high demand at least for the short term, you could leverage the opportunity and start pricing with a high margin. Overtime your product's margin will erode as a natural course of its lifecycle. More detailed discussions on profit margin are available in Chapter 7.

4 Value Based Approach

Setting your price based on perceived value is easy in theory but more difficult in practice. This is because it's a culmination of multiple steps.

First, your product or service must have intrinsic value that serves the target segment. Beyond that you need to come up with a powerful positioning statement that hopefully creates a memorable and convincing perception in your target customers' minds. Next, your product descriptions need to include substantiated value proposition which are benefits that hopefully you are able to identify by soliciting feedback from relevant sources. Finally, you need to experiment with different price ranges and narrow down to a price point that your target customers have agreed on by popular vote. This sequence ensures that your product will have been "scrubbed" clean of any false assumptions along the way. This is probably the most rational approach and begets predictable outcome although nothing is a guarantee.

5 Supply and Demand Approach

As a general rule of thumb, the more scarce and hard it is to get something the more people are willing to pay for it. This economic law should tie into your production strategy.

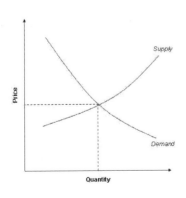

Many entrepreneurs start out assuming that they will mass produce their product. You should consider the demand for your product and determine whether mass production is the right idea. Sometimes a product can be kept artificially low in supply to drive up the price if there is a strong demand and no substitute for it. A truly unique product would fit in this category. Think about rare bottles of wine that command several hundred dollars each. They fit into this category.

The recent price of crude oil is a good example of

this. Although it is a known fact that crude supply does not fluctuate wildly each day, as its price does. This is yet another indication that price is more psychologically driven then reality driven.

Intangible Based Approach

How much should you charge for a timepiece? How about a digital alarm clock with unusual features to wake you or put you to sleep? Neither one of these can command extravagant amounts of money but a designer watch can. Would you consider paying several thousand dollars for a designer watch? Some people would.

In fact the world's most expensive watches cost in the millions of dollars per piece. Beyond function (timekeeping) and form (same size as regular watches), these prestigious luxury watches add jewelry. Even with the jewelry's intrinsic cost, the total production cost is nowhere near a fraction of the asking price. Yet someone will buy them.

Social status, peer influence, peer pressure, trendy items or fads will drive goods often at prices much higher than everyday products. If your concept is one of these, you should be aware that pricing no longer follows the traditional rules of thumb. Instead, pricing becomes even more of a black art. If the demand for your product is strong enough, you can get away with astounding amounts of profit.

High margin products like jewelry and other luxury items have this unusual "problem" to solve. Low margin products like computers and most electronics do not. In this case it all goes back to perceived value. What can your product do for your customers? Is it prestige, status, popularity, acceptance, or all of the above? The key is to find out how much they would be willing to pay.

5.3.5 PRICING ADJUSTMENTS

Pricing is not fixed forever. It used to be that if you priced your product incorrectly you could kill your business. In the days before eCommerce this was true as there was no inexpensive way to get feedback while a set price drives all your operations and marketing activities. Thanks to the internet we're looking at a lot more flexibility in testing different price ranges to find the sweet spot.

One way of looking at pricing is to see it as setting a currency exchange rate. Your currency is the goods

	Number of MP3 Players per Box		
Number of Boxes	1-25 units	26-50 units	51+ units
1-3	$39.95	$44.95	$49.95
4-6	$37.95	$42.95	$47.95
5-9	$35.95	$40.95	$45.95
10+	$33.95	$38.95	$43.95

and services you offer. The customer's currency is their payment.

In currency trading the value of a particular currency changes daily. In commerce, the value of your goods and services also fluctuates, although not on a daily basis. There are factors that force the change of your price, the most notable one being new competition.

A quick word on pricing strategy...pricing is never fixed for long. The initial pricing point is critical, but then so is the flexibility to adjust it up or down based on market conditions. Not many new ideas are for commodities, so the assumption here is that your product or service's pricing strategy is more flexible and therefore should be based more on value and perception instead of a cost-plus based approach.

There are ways to adjust or change your pricing to improve sale. One technique is to test your price range periodically by posting questions online in forums or social groups. If you are a mother inventor, there are plenty of websites and forums devoted to helping mothers launch their business and inventions. Try asking about different price points and see what the responses are. Another method is to sell on Amazon.com and vary your prices by a few cents or dollars every week and track your sales results. Doing this will help you find the sweet spot for your product.

There are several ways you could manipulate price after the initial setting:

- ◆ Set a fixed price with rebates or manufacturer's coupons

- ◆ Offer a low price on a limited time (on sale)

- ◆ Buy 2 get 1 free promotion to induce the sense of getting something free or extra

- ◆ Give your base unit away for free or at a low cost then charge on proprietary consumables (e.g. Gillette shavers and blades, Swiffer mop and refills)

- ◆ Volume discount

Price increases may or may not upset customers; it depends on how you approach it. Making small increases at a regular basis makes sense since people expect costs to rise. A big jump is always a shocker and can drive customers away. An increase bundled with added value can sometimes offset some of the shocks.

> The difference between right and wrong pricing can mean life or death for the consumer products business.

Evaluation Questions: Appendix 4 Section 2-1

- Do you have a pricing strategy that takes into consideration your product's intrinsic value, the perception your positioning statement creates, your cost, competitive price ranges, and your profit margin?

- Will you be able to execute your pricing strategy in concert with the rest of your business activities such as marketing, finance, and operations support?

HOW DID YOUR CONCEPT DO?

Ideally you will be able to produce a pricing strategy in concert with your marketing strategy, operational capability, and financial goal. Your pricing strategy will have included the identification of your product or service's intrinsic value, its competitive strength or weakness, the target customer's value, your marketing positioning statement, your product cost and margin requirements, and a plan to test and verify price ranges to narrow down to a popular decision.

Potential Challenges and issues may include bumping into difficulties in any of the tasks mentioned above.

5.4 PACKAGING

AN INSIDER'S INSIGHTS

Packaging is the strategy behind creating the best presentation of your product. It is an integral part of the larger marketing strategy. As such it is a form of communication.

Whereas positioning is to create perceptions, packaging is to display such perceptions. It is a visual communication about your goods when one-on-one interactive selling is not practical. It is essentially the spokesperson for the inner content that cannot promote itself.

A package design is the key to attracting a customer's attention and hopefully leading to a sale. It is the last piece of the sales process without any human intervention. If done poorly, all the previous steps would have been done in vain.

The purpose of packaging is to entice, impress, and invite to buy. It has many jobs to do in a very short amount of time. Assuming that it can attract the attention of a prospective customer, with one glance, that potential customer needs to understand all the benefits and value propositions.

To do this successfully the packaging strategy must involve several techniques. Since the most effective mode of communication is interactive, an optimal design would invite a potential customer to interact with it. This comes in the form of an experience that could entail touching, feeling, or pressing a button to get a demonstration of what the product can do. For example, toys and children's books often have the "try me" button to produce a sampling of lights and sounds.

The package design considerations can be quite involved. It is far beyond just putting some artwork on a box or a bag. The package must bring out the most appealing aspect of your product's value proposition, which may not be its function or purpose, but the perception that you want the customer to absorb.

A strictly descriptive package design is missing half of its potential. This is the same rationale behind why real estate agents place so much emphasis on a property's curb appeal before showing it to the buyer's market. The difference between a good "packaging" in this case can mean selling a house or not.

People often make purchase designs based on packaging. Sometimes the packaging itself is considered as part of the purchase value. It is no doubt an effective competitive weapon.

STRATEGY COMPONENTS

The packaging design considerations can be divided into three main areas:

 5.4.1 **Physical**

 5.4.2 **Display**

 5.4.3 **Technique**

5.4.1 PHYSICAL CONSIDERATIONS

Sometimes a product does not need packaging, such as a chair. But any label or sign attached to these items serve the same communication purposes. In most cases products are enclosed in protective coverings that can be used to display messages. For these products the design strategy begins with the content.

The first question is always whether the product needs to be packaged or not. If it doesn't need physical protection, then a hanging sign or a removable labeling will do. But if it does, then size, shape, and number of units that should fit inside a package all need to be decided.

When we designed the initial batch of AeroBloks retail boxes, we were also beginning to combat a vicious trend of rising costs. To minimize ocean freight cost, we designed the retail boxes to be as compact as possible, thereby fitting as many as possible into a master carton. This in turn allowed us to squeeze in the maximum number of master cartons onto the pallets. At the same time we had to play around with the dimensions of both inner boxes (retail boxes) and the master carton in order to just make it under the height limit of the freight container. Meanwhile we also had to balance the master carton's weight against the legal limits of lifting weight per OSHA guidelines (www.osha.gov).

This seemingly logical step ended up costing us thousands of dollars in return products due to leakage. What happened was that in order to compact the individual pieces of building blocks, the factory folded them several times. Not only did this create creases along the folding lines, it also caused the air valves to be bent since bending along the air valve was easier.

Over time we started getting returns from disappointed customers. The blocks were leaking, but there was no hole that they could see. After doing some testing on the returned merchandise, we found consistent microscopic leaks along the creased folding lines. This problem exasperated as time went on. In the end we had to dispose a large proportion of the new blocks in order to avoid the costly return process and generating a bad reputation for the building blocks. It is ironic since our stringent testing requirement made sure that every single building block was inflated for at least 48 hours before being carefully packaged in individual plastic bags, which prevented friction and wear. In the end, the savings of perhaps a few hundred dollars resulted in losses over thousands of dollars.

These are some questions you need to consider on the physical aspects:

◈ **What size is permitted on the shelves of the target retailers?** This size will drive the outer dimension of your retail package. You don't want to get into a situation where at the last minute you find out that your package cannot fit in the retailer's shelves and they (most national retailers) will not accept anything else.

◈ **How many units within a retail package?** This is a function of how much a retail package will cost the customer. Whether you include one, two, or multiple units in a package is a decision driven by your pricing strategy.

◈ **How many retail units can fit inside a master carton?** This has to do with how you maximize the storage space, minimize the freight cost, while abiding by OSHA's guidelines on occupations safety on lifting weight limits.

◈ **What is the size of the pallet to be used?** This has to do with how many master cartons can fit onto one and whether the size of the pallet can maximize a freight container's carrying capacity. Often, the size needs to be double-checked against warehousing rack sizes. The typical size is 48" x 40" x 5."

◈ **What is the size of the freight container?** Freight containers come in different lengths. Most of them are around 8 feet high by 8 feet wide, and about 20 feet or 40 feet long. Different sized containers cost differently and your decision has to do with how many pallets can fit into one at what cost.

20' Container has internal dimensions of:

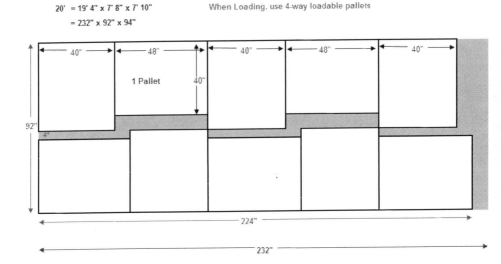

20' = 19' 4" x 7' 8" x 7' 10"   When Loading, use 4-way loadable pallets
     = 232" x 92" x 94"

◈ **What is the total freight cost of a single container?** You need to derive this answer in order to calculate the allocated cost per retail package. This cost is part of your direct cost and affects your profit margin.

◈ **What is the right type of material to use for the package?** The type of material can range from cardboard, vinyl bag, netting, to anything else. The decision has to do with appeal in both the material property as well as its message to the potential customer. You do not want to use plastic packaging for a product geared towards an environmentally sensitive target market. High end products should also not be wrapped in cheap coverings, etc.

◈ **Should the packaging be boxed or open?** This decision has to do with protection as well as appeal. A fully enclosed box depends on the artwork and design while a partially open box invites the interactivity.

◈ **What should its shape be?** This decision has to do with its ability to stack on a shelf and with its appeal at the same time. Packages in odd shapes that cannot stack up work against retailers who want to maximize their shelf display space. On the other hand, unique shapes draw attention. This comes down to a balancing act.

◈ **Should it have a display window?** This decision balances the need to protect and the need to attract. It may come down to cost since using a window will cost more than just a box.

◈ **Should the product be interactive (demo buttons etc.)?** It depends on whether the product stimulates the senses. If your product's main features include lights and sounds then not displaying it in an interactive mode would be a major mistake. If yours is an object that does not need to be touched, felt, or squeezed then you are better off protecting its surface.

◈ **How strong should it be?** This has to do with crushing weight when the products are stacked on top of each other. The packaging must withstand the total weight of at least the number of units expected to be stacked on top of each other during freight, warehousing, and shelf display.

◈ **Should it have a handle?** If the packaging is heavy and hard to carry, putting a handle on it for a few cents more is well worth it. If not, you should save this expense.

5.4.2 DISPLAY CONSIDERATIONS

The product's package or labeling display serves multiple purposes. Its main function is to attract, then to describe, and finally to comply with regulations.

The things you need to consider include the appropriateness of the images and messages. Is the information accurate besides being enticing? Are you using language that will get the message across, etc?

For example, if SnapIt! were designed primarily for men, then using pink or other feminine colors on the packaging obviously would be a turn off. And if the brushes were designed primarily for scrubbing sinks or other household surfaces where women tend to do more work, then neutral color or more feminine colors on the package would make the product's appearance more attractive.

Here are some the contents that need to be displayed:

◈ **Positioning** – This is perhaps the most important message your packaging needs to get across. The positioning statement and its insinuated perceptions should be displayed prominently. You will need to balance it against the other primary branding messages such as the product's name and the company logo.

- ❖ **Function** – Typically the function is fairly obvious given the name of the product. Sometimes when the product name has no affiliation with its function, you could use a subtitle as a functional statement for clarification.

- ❖ **Description** – Similar to function, if it's not obvious then a statement should be displayed on the package, but not necessarily in the most prominent position.

- ❖ **Instruction** – This is typically reserved for placement inside the box on a separately printed sheet or booklet. Sometimes to illustrate simplicity of usage (an appealing attribute), the instruction can be represented by images on the packaging.

- ❖ **Warning labels** – This is a requirement if your product contains anything that may cause injury or damages to the user. There are strict guidelines on warning labels and you should research for any industry-specific warning label requirements. Labels of similar products usually serve as a good reference.

- ❖ **UPC code** – This code needs to be printed (usually by the packaging printing entity, supplied by the manufacturer) so it can be scanned in a retail setting.

- ❖ **Country of manufacturing** – This information may be required on the packaging as well as the product. You should research for any industry-specific requirements.

- ❖ **Age guideline** – This is often a requirement for children's products. You will need to specify the appropriate age group based on their mental and physical developmental stage. This is particular important if your product will come in contact with young children who might be endangered by choking hazards, etc.

- ❖ **Color** – Color is part of the positioning strategy. Color has different connotations psychologically. You will need to choose the right color combinations for your target user group.

- ❖ **Choice of images** – The images should entice as well as project the primary value propositions of your product. If your product brings joy, then a joyful image depicting how it's used is appropriate. If it cleans well, then a sparking image may be more convincing.

5.4.3 TECHNIQUES

This section addresses ways to improve your packaging effectiveness besides the package design.

1   Using Surprises and Bonus as a Packaging Strategy

People love surprises and getting a little freebie here and there. Some marketing genius came up with the idea of putting miniature toys in cereal boxes some time ago. The incremental cost of those plastic toys was in fractions of a penny. Yet the resulting increase in sales over those of competitor's offerings was simply astounding. Who knows how many more boxes of cereal were sold because of this little application of the "expectations" paradigm. Regardless, the lesson can be applied in your own product packaging.

2   Value vs. Price as a Packaging Strategy

For relatively inexpensive consumer products, the technique of bundling often works well. Here is an example of how it works.

You have a useful product that costs less than a dollar to produce and can reasonably retail for up to $4.99. Your niche market is limited in size. At $4.99 per customer you're not sure if it's a business worth launching.

To get around this dilemma you realize that people might be interested in buying a pair of your product. The technique used to increase the perception of value in this case is to bundle three units in a pack and position it as a twin-pack at a slightly higher price (e.g. $12). In this case every purchase gives the customer an extra bonus as a backup unit. The perception is now shifted to buy two get one free.

The same technique is now used as a popular formula on home shopping channels where you can get a "bonus" product if you buy the product being sold.

There is another side of packaging that often eludes first time entrepreneurs of consumer products. As it turns out packaging descriptions also need to be sensitive to consumer psychology. The golden rule of ergonomics is to design with the user in mind. Likewise the description must align with the target user's capabilities.

A case in point, for a construction toy, a package that builds up to 3 structures would be easy to understand, but one that builds from 12 to 36 structures loses its meaning quickly. This is because few people can relate to 36 structures. Even though the package with more building possibilities brings more value, it is the package that is more familiar and meaningful to the potential buyer that gets sold.

LEGO learned this lesson and went from selling buckets of blocks (totally open ended) to specialized packages. They took it one step further and went down the licensing path where the structures took on meaning and relevance to the kids who could relate to the characters in movies and cartoons.

3 Licensing as a Packaging Strategy

Every year millions of kids' merchandises are sold because they have popular imprinting from the likes of Disney, Warners Brothers, and Hasbro characters. I remember, as a kid, distinctly asking for four different flavors of Welch's jelly glasses at the supermarket. I didn't even like peanut butter and jelly that much, but the tradeoff of eating four jars of jelly to get 4 drinking glasses with cartoon characters was well worth it. The lure of Bugs Bunny, Tweety Bird, Elmer Fudd, and Porky Pig on drinking glasses proved irresistible.

I've seen play tents that are otherwise indistinguishable from any others selling enviable number of units just because they have Disney characters imprinted.

Over years of watching products sold from tradeshows and shelves I have come to realize the power of the "herd mentality." Licensing is a good example of the masses following trends and fads. There are only a few trendsetters who can heavily influence whether something sells or not. The rest of the people tend to follow trends. Understanding the underlying dynamics can be helpful to your deciding on whether to license, what to license, and when to license.

A few observations on licensing... media promotions are expensive so only large companies can afford them. These production giants spend big money to create awareness and desire. Therefore to ride on the wave of such induced demand at a fraction of the cost is a worthy proposition. This is especially true if you know your market well and know which cultural icons or celebrities can influence buying behavior in your industry.

Licensing popular characters adds an incremental cost to your product, but if the target market is heavily influenced by the affiliation and endorsement, then it is a bona fide packaging strategy. The cost of such licensing varies, but if giving up (e.g.) 13 points on your profit margin can double or triple your unit sales, it is worth considering. In my experience a national retailer might be willing to require a 30% profit margin instead of 50% profit margin on popular licensed products.

Mathematically if your product is retailed at $100 and the national retailer would be willing to pay you $70 (30% margin requirement) for it instead of $50 (50% margin requirement), then the extra $20 can be used to pay for the $13 licensing fee per unit.

> Customers will judge your product's worth by looking at its packaging just as they will judge the content of a book by its cover.

Packaging Summary

Packaging is much more than meets the eye (both customer's and yours). Beyond the cardboard and plastic covering, the process requires a packaging strategy that is coherent with the rest of your positioning and promotional strategy.

To do the packaging correctly, you need to ask these high level questions:

1. Have you captured the perception that the marketing positioning statement is intended to invoke on your package design?

2. Is the packaging enticing enough to capture the customer's attention?

3. Is the product's function described on the packaging? The product's function would have been generated from a coordinated marketing and engineering effort.

4. What is the right size of the package? You need to consider the production costs of the package in addition to the pallet size, height of the freight container, and the freight/shipping cost.

5. Is the cost acceptable within your target profit margin? To calculate profit margin you need to know how to set the price.

6. What price point is acceptable and reasonable? To set the price you need to know the value and worth from the customer's perspective, including the prices of competitive products.

7. What is considered valuable and reasonable from your customer's perspective? To get all this information you need to know the customers.

8. What is the customer like? To identify their profile you need to do market research.

Once again this thinking process demonstrates that packaging should not be done in isolation; it should be a sub-strategy of the entire marketing strategy. This interconnected relationship is as important to realize as the actual business activities.

Evaluation Questions: Appendix 4 Section 2-1

- Is your packaging strategy coherent with your positioning and pricing strategies?

- Does your package design effectively communicate the product's value propositions at a glance?

- Does your package entice the customers to interact with it so they can experience it before buying?

HOW DID YOUR CONCEPT DO?

Ideally you will be able to create a package strategy in alignment with the other aspects of your marketing strategy. The package will entice, interact with, and sell itself to the customer. Your packaging will also comply with labeling requirements and occupational safety guidelines. The package design should also maximize the number of units per container while making sure the contents will not be damaged.

Potential Challenges and issues may include the inability to find a cost-effective packaging solution. The product may not fit onto the retail shelves because of its size or weight, or odd shape. The value propositions may not show through on the packaging. The package may not protect the contents during transit or storage. The package may not effectively reflect the value and worth of your merchandise.

5.5   PROMOTION

AN INSIDER'S INSIGHTS

Promotion is about telling the world what your invention or idea is, why they would care, and what they should do about it. This is a step within the overall marketing strategy that incorporates all the knowledge you have gained from earlier marketing research and analyses.

An effective promotional strategy takes the message content generated by the positioning strategy and delivers the message in the right presentation via the right channels to the target audience.

If you created the world's most amazing invention or business model but no one knows about it, is it still the most amazing or will something else take that distinction?

A promotional strategy lays the groundwork to prepare for the distribution and sale of your product. An inadequately implemented promotional effort will end up wasting not only the marketing campaign dollars but all the efforts that precede the promotional activities.

Promotion is an absolute necessity in a world full of noises vying for consumer attention. For every successful product, how many other just as useful and possibly more brilliantly designed products never get the recognition they deserve?

The same dynamic applies to celebrities and successful people. For every one of them, how many thousands of people could have done just as well or better if they had the right combination of circumstances, timing, and connections? A powerful promotional campaign can make the difference between a winner and an unknown. It does this by leveraging and sometimes creating the right circumstances, timing, and social relationships. Its significance in your pursuit of profitability cannot be overstated.

Let's start with the end in mind and *follow the thinking process behind the design of a promotional strategy.* When all is said and done, what is your objective for a promotional strategy for your product or service?

The good news is, if you have followed the prescribed marketing approach up to this point, most of the work has already been done.

5.5.1 THE PROMOTIONAL STRATEGY

There are four essential parts of the promotion strategy. Each one is expanded here with questions to help shape your own strategy:

    (1) Objective

    (2) Audience

    (3) Message

    (4) Delivery

1 Your Objective

❖ *Is your objective to create awareness, to announce the availability of a new development, or to induce sales? Say it another way, when people hear or know about your message, what actions do you want them to take?*

Defining your specific objective for a promotional event will help you focus on the right message, select the right audience, choose the right channel, and launch an effective campaign. If you don't define an objective you might end up wasting money on unrelated activities that generate little actual results.

❖ *What do you have to do to get the response you want?*

The answer is to identify the audience, the message, and the delivery mechanism.

2 The Audience

❖ *Who do you need to reach in order to accomplish your objective?*

If your objective is product announcement, then manufacturer's rep and subsequently distribution channel buyers would be your audience. If your intent is to sell, then consumers would be your audience. If your intent is to create a barrier of entry, then your competitors would be your audience. If your goal is to enhance your branding, then your fans would be your audience.

◈ *What are they like?*

This should already have been answered by the work done in competitive analysis (section 4.3) and customer profiling (section 4.4).

◈ *What do they care? What is of value to them?*

The answers lie within the work done for customer profiling (section 4.4) and positioning (section 5.2).

◈ *What language do they speak, what cultural influences exist?*

The answers come from work done for customer profiling (section 4.4).

3 The Message

◈ *What can I say or display that is of interest to them?*

This is a combination of your value proposition (section 5.2.2) and your pricing strategy (section 5.3). If you will be showing your packaging design as part of the promotional material then you can refer to work done in section 5.4.

◈ *Is my value proposition in alignment with theirs?*

Here we compare their value (section 4.4.5) and your product's or service's value proposition (section 5.2.2).

◈ *Why will people help me accomplish my goal? What's in it for them?*

This is slightly different from the customer's value proposition. In theory you would want to leverage word of mouth promotion as much as possible. The persons endorsing and helping to spread your message may not necessary have the same objective as a paying customer. Nevertheless the technique used in analyzing customer value can also be applied onto the endorsing party and messengers.

4 The Delivery Method and Media

◈ *Where do they hangout?*

This question deals more with physical locations. For example, if you are targeting teens and they hangout at the mall after school, then your promotional events and activities should include mall locations. If you are targeting potential licensees of your product, then a licensing convention is where you might consider advertising or setting up a tradeshow booth.

◆ *How can I reach them? (what channels)*

The answer needs to come from your customer profiling (section 4.4) where you would have identified their lifestyle preferences. Most groups have favorite "waterholes" where they gather. This might be a physical location or an online forum. In all likelihood you will score better if you take a mixed approach by looking both at social media sites and physical sites. To reach your target audience you will need to narrow down the time, space, and medium of their gatherings.

◆ *How do they prefer to communicate, to get their information?*

This answer should also have been analyzed in customer profile (section 4.4). Depending on your target audience, the media could include: blogs, forums, online or print catalogs, magazine ads, tradeshows, news, tweets, email campaign, press releases, online social networks, or texting.

For example, most school supplies continue to be sold via advertisement in school supply catalogs. If your promotion is aimed at the school segment then sending out a PR statement online would do you little good. If most of your target audiences get their information via online social networks or forums, then those would be your most effective communications channels. If your target audience is accustomed to getting their information by watching video clips online, then that's the type of delivery method you would use.

5.5.2 ADDITIONAL PROMOTIONAL INSIGHTS

Of the conventional 4Ps of marketing, promotion has undergone the most profound changes due to internet technology. With online purchases ever increasing, the preferred promotional channels have gone from mainstream broadcast media like TV, magazine ads, consumer tradeshows, store displays, and newspapers to websites, search engines ads, social networks, and tweets, etc.

We are now living in a transitional period of marketing spurred by advances in internet technology. It is an evolution moving from point A to Point B; it's not a revolution because the old is not completely obliterated and will not be for quite some time despite the hype that some people would like you to believe.

For now the right approach to promotion is a calculated mixture of the conventional and the online methods. To do this we all have to transition our thinking from conventional to the new paradigm as well as leverage the new online tools. As with anything in transition, it is not easy or straight forward. The intelligent marketer will reap the best of both worlds and apply the best channels for her purpose.

The following table lists promotional methods that you can use depending on your target audience's profile.

Objective	Conventional Method	Online Method
Methodology	Outbound marketing	Inbound marketing
Premise	Broadcast messages	Get found using content
Define user profiles	Library research Market research reports	Keyword searches on browsers
Get feedback	Focus groups	Online forums
Finding suppliers	Tradeshows	Online listings
Find distributors	Tradeshows	Use blogs to be found
Branding material	Print ads.	Keyword searches
	Brochures	Websites
	Packaging	Images and videos
Promoting	Word of mouth	Tweets, social networks
Build customer loyalty	Flyers, newsletters	Opt-in emails, RSS feed
	Market data analysis	Web analytics
Distribution	Brick and mortar stores	Online stores
Promotional expertise	Manufacturer reps PR companies	SEO expertise

Once you have identified all the potential avenues you can take to broadcast your new product or service to the world, you will need to prioritize them based on your resources. Just as collected information doesn't make an action plan, an action plan also doesn't make a strategy. A strategy is what you will need to make full use of the information you have gathered by analyzing it against your own time table and resources.

5.5.3   OTHER QUESTIONS TO CONSIDER

1   Should You Advertise or Not?

Product awareness is #1. People have very short spans of attention and memory at the same time the cost of constant and continuous promotion is too much for a small company with limited budget. One way to get around this is to leverage a sales channel's market presence and its promotional resources whenever possible.

Online advertising generally doesn't work well. This is because your image and message may not capture the attention given how quickly they are displayed online. A better way to capture a buyer's attention is to advertise with an industry journal where everyone goes to for the latest trends. Online advertising is like taking a shotgun approach while industry journal advertising is closer to a laser-focused approach since you know who will be reading your message.

Traditional outbound advertising channels and costs vary tremendously and are almost impossible to get a standard quote. Here are our actual costs and quotes listed here for comparison purposes:

◆ Magazine ads - $4000 for 3 issues of 2"x2" display

◆ Cable TV 30 second spots - $10,000 for 50 showings at off-prime time hours

◆ Direct mail - $14,000 for 20,000 leads

◆ Major newspaper ads - $120 depending on size and day of printing

◆ Local radio ads 30 second spot - $450, depending on station, seasonal factors.

◆ Internet ads (see Google or Yahoo pay-per-click current rates)

2 Should You Do Tradeshows?

Tradeshows make most sense when you target dealers and distributors. They are generally too expensive for direct to consumer sales. The typical cost elements of a tradeshow include booth rental and setup infrastructure, freight of your merchandise to and from the show, utilities rental fee, hotel, meals, and travel costs, advertising costs, and labor costs if you need help manning the booth. Your decision needs to be weighed against whether there is an easier and less expensive way to reach the people you need.

3 When Is The Right Time to Do Promotions?

Promotion should be a forethought, not an afterthought. Even as you shape your idea you need to be figuring out how to promote it. Depending on the medium you choose, leave about a 4-6 month timeframe at a minimum for preparations and strategizing. It might take even longer if you perform all the due diligence in terms of market search, competitive analysis, customer profiling, channel identification and analysis, etc. The more you put in the better your promotion will be.

4 Should You Hire a Marketing Agency?

Marketing agencies thrive on the relationships they have. They can help you generate events at locations that you would otherwise not be able to. The cost of hiring a marketing agency is not cheap so you'll have to weigh its benefit/cost for your own situation. Is that type of exposure what you really need at a particular point in time, and what will it do for you in terms of future dollars, etc.

You should know that press releases need to be highly focused like a laser beam onto the target; your money might provide some entertainment for others and some hope for yourself but the actual yield might not be justifiable. If this is a channel you believe you need, you can always emulate other press releases and go through online services where you can specify market segments as recipients. Be sure to consider your value proposition objective when writing your own PR.

 ### Can You Design Your Own Brochure?

Absolutely yes, if you have a good idea on your message and how to do graphics design. You can get your brochures printed fairly cheaply online. You should not have prices or fixed information that you might update within a year. It costs too much to redesign and reprint whenever you need to update your prices or product features and benefits. Instead, use a cut-out insert that fits nicely within the folded place to display current pricing information or any updated info.

5.5.4   A SAMPLE PROMOTION STRATEGY ACTION PLAN

Let's use SnapIt! to illustrate how the four parts (objective, audience, message, delivery) work together. A promotion strategy for this new product would probably be a multi-pronged approach with multiple objectives. In this case it involves 7 interdependent steps. All of them eventually lead to the goal of national distribution.

The steps are explained here. The objectives are bold-faced. See diagram on the following page for illustration.

1. **Launch a promotion with the objective to ascertain market acceptance and price ranges** – This is done both online and through local retailers such as small hardware and convenience stores.

2. **Find endorsement** – Get professionals or celebrities in the housewife/mom circle to try and provide endorsement.

3. **Get attention of wholesale distributors and manufacturer reps for targeted retailers** – Advertise in trade journals and exhibit at consumer goods shows geared towards business people (not consumers).

4. **Get the word out** – Join online forums and discussion groups of moms and housewives. Join inventor groups online and become an active participant in the discussion of household cleaning issues. Ask questions.

5. **Set up online reseller community** – Establish drop ship programs. Find resellers looking for new product and inventions to send them promotional package.

6. **Build sales traction** – Do this at the local level and keep track of results before getting in touch with home shopping networks.

7. **Establish national distribution channel networks** – Do this via distributors and large national chains as well as online resellers and possibly local brick and mortar stores.

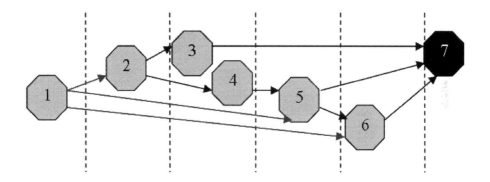

As you can see:

Step 1 leads to steps 2, 5, and 6.

Step 2 leads to steps 3 and 4.

Step 3 leads to the final goal of step 7.

Step 4 leads to step 5.

Step 5 leads to step 6 and 7.

Step 6 leads to step 7.

Some steps will naturally get out of sequence due to practical reasons, but each step brings knowledge that contributes to a coherent promotion strategy.

Evaluation Questions: Appendix 4 Section 2-1

- What is the primary purpose of your promotion?
- What promotional channels will be most effective for this type of product or service?
- What are the promotional media and their associated costs?
- What is the marketing budget percentage relative to your revenue?
- How important is advertising in your promotional plan?
- Is your promotional strategy in synch with the other marketing components?

HOW DID YOUR CONCEPT DO?

Ideally you would have started thinking about the promotional aspect of your concept just as you received validation on it. The promotional strategy should include all the marketing research and analyses you have already performed up to this point and incorporates them into a coherent action plan. You should also have a good idea of the available channels and their associated costs, including the reasons why or why you would not use them.

Potential Challenges and issues may include missing key information from your earlier research such as customer profile or even your value proposition. Your promotional strategy could be incoherent because you fail to consider the overall objective you are trying to achieve and instead take on a shotgun approach. You might also find that your strategy is not practical because you failed to account for the time required to prepare this strategy or that the cost of promotion is too high.

5.6   DISTRIBUTION & SALES

AN INSIDER'S INSIGHTS

Distribution is otherwise known as **placement**, the last P in the 6Ps of Marketing. In my experience, placement is more closely related to sales than it is to marketing; its strategic component is definitely a part of the overall marketing strategy while the implementation piece is distinctly sales oriented.

Placement of your product or service allows the target customers to have access to your product after they have become aware of it. A sale is the final transaction and goal of your entire product's existence. In this last section of the chapter we focus on insights as organized below to help with the placing and selling of your product or service:

5.6.1   Anatomy of the Distribution Network

(1) **Overview**

(2) **Impact on retail price**

(3) **Distributors**

(4) **Manufacturer's reps**

(5) **Retailers**

(6) **Placement Strategy**

5.6.2   Sales Insights

(1)   Know the piece parts of the puzzle

(2)   Work within their system

(3)   Buyer profiling

(4)   Sales management

If cash flow is the bloodline of any business, then distribution channels and sales channels create the flow that feeds your operation system. They are not only where exchanges of your offerings for payments take place but also where your customers' expectations are met. A failure to set up a distribution network to enable sale of your product or service in sufficient quantity is a guarantee of business loss.

One of the common mistakes shared by new entrepreneurs is trusting that they can sell successfully into the marketplace simply by relying on their product's strength in appeal. This could not be further from the truth.

A newcomer into a marketplace rarely has the necessary resources such as an established customer base, the best retail locations, brand loyalty, business operations efficiency, and promotional channels to capture market share on a large scale. An established distribution network can offer all that and more. In that sense wholesale distributors and retail channels are extremely valuable.

5.6.1   ANATOMY OF THE DISTRIBUTION NETWORK

 Overview

Once a product is ready for sale, it needs to be transported to a warehouse or retail location. The **distribution network** is what makes this possible every day. The network of ocean freight tankers, trains, trucks, warehouses, fulfillment centers, and retail stores are all part of the distribution network's physical transportation layer. The people who handle transactions at each of the nodes are part of the network's administrative layer. Beyond having produced the physical goods, a manufacturer needs such a network to distribute his goods to consumers. This network of infrastructures, systems, and people is where commerce really happens. Of particular interest to us are the hands that directly impact profit, namely the **distribution channels**.

For a consumer product, the distribution channels are made up of **wholesale distributors** and **retailers**. Retailers are further broken down into national retailers, local retailers, and online retailers. National retail chains typically work directly with a layer of middleman known as **manufacturer's representative** instead of with individual manufacturers.

In business, activities should either generate money or save money. Delays in sales transactions can cost money in different ways. Established distribution channels are therefore your best chances of selling your product or service expediently, before it naturally expires or is dethroned by competition.

It is in your best interest to thoroughly understand the distribution network for your concept as soon as possible. This includes knowing how the industry operates, especially knowing any special quirks or windows of opportunity, and who's who in the ecosystem. You can begin your research by benchmarking the nearest competitions and identify their distribution network and infrastructures.

2 Impact on Retail Price

Distribution networks differ from industry to industry. The most straight forward product ecosystem involves the factory, manufacturer, wholesale distributor, retailer, and the consumer. In this case every time a product passes hands its price doubles. This is based on an overly simplistic concept called keystone pricing that everyone seems to abide by. The idea is that everyone in the food chain makes 50% profit margin by doubling the price as the product moves up the chain.

For example, let's say the production cost of your product is $1 per unit. You as the manufacturer will sell it for $2 to the distributor, who then marks it up to $4 to sell to the retailer. The retailer then sells it for $8 to the consumer.

If you sold directly to retailers without a wholesale distributor, the retail price would be $4. Yet your potential sales volume would be severely limited if you rely on your own efforts to contact and convince each retailer directly.

There is tremendous cost involved in marketing directly to individual retailers if you do not have a relationship with them already. There is also time involved, which could eat into your product or service's estimated lifecycle. For example, if your product's lifecycle is 3 years and it takes 4 years to ramp up to the number of retailers you need in order to sell the quantities you need to break even, you should not even start the business.

This pricing scheme quickly escalates a product's retail price, or forces the product cost into ridiculous grounds with each added layer of distribution. Luckily distributors and national retail giants generally accept lower profit margins with larger quantities. For example, a national retail chain I worked with required 37.5% margin instead of the standard keystone 50% profit margin. Because of the mass market quantity involved, I was able to work within a 20%-25% profit margin instead of the industry standard 45% for my product. This was the only way to price the product at an affordable price point.

When each layer takes less, the retail price also lowers. On the other hand, I met a greedy distributor who specialized in selling to museum stores nationally yet demanded a 70% profit margin. Needless to say I was quite irritated with such unreasonable behavior and told her to take a hike and not come back.

3   Distributors - What You Need to Know

A distributor is basically a middleman. He may physically produce nothing, has a warehouse, buys from you and then doubles the price. Sounds quite unfair, and maybe it is, but the fact is that without the business relationships and infrastructure of a distributor, it would cost you much more time and money to promote and sell your product or service individually.

Distributors are your gateways to retailers. Their motivation in working with you may not be strictly making a profit from your product. Some distributors will accept your product in order to increase their range of selections for their customers (wholesaler or retailer). Some do it for differentiation reasons especially when they want exclusivity. Before signing up a deal with anyone you must examine their true motivation and their ability to help your sales.

A case in point, a UK-based children's furniture store was one of many international distributors who wanted exclusivity to distribute AeroBloks in the UK/European continent. After much back and forth communications I determined that they were not too concerned with bringing our product to their markets in a timely manner. Rather, they were waiting for the right time to synchronize the release with their other products. Apparently their intent was not at all to sell AeroBloks per se, but to use it to attract attention as a store display. Any incidental sale would be just a bonus. Even though at that point their profit margin requirement was the lowest amongst the other UK/ European distributors, their projection of unit sales was not genuine. I was under pressure to sign quickly or lose the deal. I walked away and was quite glad I did.

To find distributors for your product you can try where they congregate. A good place is industry tradeshows where some will set up booths and others will register and identify themselves as distributors.

Issuing press releases is another option. The more diligent distributors looking for newer products or services may contact you. Otherwise you might be wasting your money.

Another viable option is to go over trade magazines where some of them will put out advertisements to solicit new representations. Depending on your industry there may even be an online network of distributors.

On rare occasions a manufacturer will share his distributor's contact information with you. In doing so he takes a risk that the distributor could divert limited budget for new products towards your direction instead of his.

Manufacturer's Reps – What You Need to Know

If you decide to get into national distribution, your biggest challenge may be getting the attention and time from buyers of large retailers. The way to overcome this is to get referrals from someone who knows the buyer or to find manufacturer's reps who have a working relationship with your target buyer.

As discussed in Chapter 2 - *Who's Who in the Commerce Loop?* the manufacturer's rep plays a significant role in finding national sales channels. However you will need to balance out your portfolio of distributors and retailers so as not to become dependent, or at worst, blackmailed by a large national distributor or wholesalers who could bankrupt a small business with a single blow.

As far as hiring a manufacturer's rep is concerned, you would need to check a few things. First, identify product lines that he represents to ensure alignment with your type of product. Second, ask how they will go about pitching your product. Third, ask how long they have had the working relationship with your target market retailer.

In terms of compensation, in my experience one rep asked for commission at 5% of wholesale price. Another asked for 7% of wholesale. There were no differences in service other than the fact that the second rep company decided that since we were a small, relatively new company, additional money was needed to cover their risk. Depending on your own situation this may or may not be warranted.

The rep works on commission basis alone, so is as interested in selling volumes of your product as you are. Even though cash ends up flowing from you to him, yet you are not his customer. Without him or your product neither one of you would profit from the sales. The rep's value lies in his relationship with the buyer and his knowledge of the retailer's operating philosophies, unspoken rules, buyer's compensation structure (read: motivation factor) and product evaluation preferences, and most times ongoing trends in your industry.

The rep or rep company acts as a filter for the buyer on new products and will only recommend those that they believe will be profitable. Getting the attention of a manufacturer's rep takes the same path as that of a distributor.

Retailers – What You Need to Know

The types and levels of product-based distribution channels can be generalized here:

- ◆ **Small** – These are mostly online resellers, mom & pop retail stores, and merchants who take on your product as a sideline and not as a major product.

- ◆ **Medium** – These are stores with few locations but not yet at the national level.

- ◆ **National Chain** – Walmart, Target, and member clubs like Costco, etc.

- ◆ **International** – Country or region specific, often asks for exclusivity in return.

Another common mistake that first time entrepreneurs share is sending unsolicited samples or worst yet, prototypes to a retailer. You are just wasting money. At best they'll use it for themselves, give it away as presents, or just throw it away. At worst they could share your idea with others.

Retailers need finished packaging to help them visualize how the item will be displayed or sold. You'll be amazed at the level of ability for people to project something that's not there, it is shockingly low. This might be due to their unwillingness to take a risk without seeing the finished item as opposed to their lack of imagination.

It is understandable that when someone signs up a large distributor that they think they're all set. This unfortunately is also far from reality. In most cases buyers tend to want to wait and see what will sell before buying too much of any one thing. So the first order may be just a few cartons. Depending on how much promotion they put into your product, you may not see another order for a quite some time.

The important lesson to learn about retailers is that sales are built one unit at a time. Very few people get lucky breaks that catapult their sales quantity to a large level overnight.

6   Placement Strategy

A placement strategy involves the standard 5Ws + H questioning technique. The following questions will help you formulate a strategy that fits your product's or business operation's strengths and weaknesses:

- ◆ Are you able to create a profile of the potential distribution network and its infrastructure?

- ◆ Can you identify the profit margin requirements for each layer of the distribution infrastructure in order to assess whether your final retail price can be achieved?

◆ Have you determined which one of the distribution channels is the best fit for your product, your operational capability, your working capital, your manpower, and your package design?

◆ Do you have the working capital to engage a large wholesale distributor or a national retailer? This includes the required production quantity, the shipping timeframe, cash flow timeframe, and other distribution agreement terms.

◆ Would you be able to absorb clearance discounts and buy-backs from large retailers? Is this even the right strategy for your product?

◆ How difficult is it to find and grab the interest and attention of potential distributors and retailers?

◆ Do you have a clear understanding of why someone would distribute your product? Is there any synergy with their product strategy?

◆ Is your distribution and sales strategy realistic and based on attainable growth and cash flow?

5.6.2 SALES INSIGHTS

We sell every day, whether it's our ability, service, belief, or just an idea; selling your invention or innovation is no different.

Sales are the lifeline of any product. Without revenue, you will find very quickly that cash flow becomes an issue. When cash flow creates a debt situation, you'll find that any goodwill you have built will evaporate quickly. After all, how many employees and vendors will stick around if you stop paying them for their time and services?

Direct sales differ from distribution in that distribution broadens your sales reach like a web. Selling individually is limited by time and resources. Imagine having recruited an army to multiply your sales efforts. In effect it is what you do when you engage and utilize distribution networks with established processes and entrenched relationships. The hardest job about sales is building the trust within the relationship. That is where the true value of a distribution network comes in. They leverage their existing brand, trust, and accounts.

Before you engage distribution channels to sell your product or service, you also need to realize that there is a big difference in profit margin (assuming the retail price is unchanged), customer experience, resources requirement, and return management than if you were to handle sales yourself. There is less money, less control, but more volume if you farm out the sales aspect.

1 Know the Piece Parts of the Puzzle

Technology didn't just completely disrupt the conventional marketing approaches; it also took its closest ally (Sales) for a spin.

Take a look at the following diagram which shows a high level display of the piece parts of the sales ecosystem:

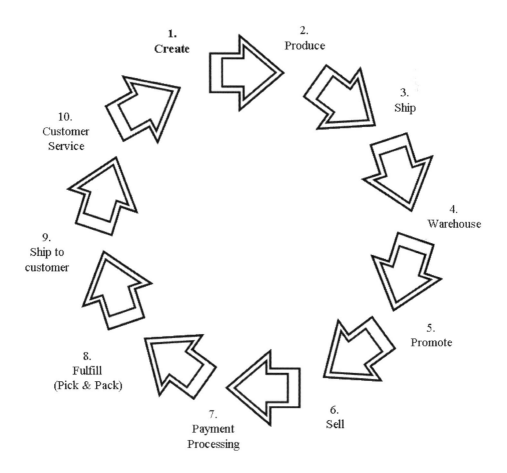

This diagram basically describes the movement of a product from idea to sales. Starting from the top, a product is created, produced, shipped to a warehouse, promoted, sold, money is exchanged, product is packaged and shipped, and any issues with the customer is addressed.

The conventional model is often handled by different parties serially. With technology it is now possible to "chop" this food chain into disparate pieces and reassembled.

For instance, there are several sales models that can be easily handled by technology today:

1. Direct Selling – If you were to sell directly to consumers you could end up managing every piece part of this chain or outsourcing some aspects such as production (manufacturing) and warehousing.

2. Consignment Sale – If you have a consignment sale agreement you will end up shipping your goods to a consignee's warehouse. The consignee will take over the rest of the steps and reconcile with you on an agreed upon timeframe.

3. Drop Ship Sale – If you work with drop shippers then the only pieces they handle are the promotion (their own), sale, and payment processing. You still need to handle the fulfillment and everything else beyond that. In theory the customer is their customer so you may not end up interfacing them.

4. Wholesale – If you work with wholesalers your responsibility basically ends with production. They will pay for shipping to their warehouse and take ownership of the goods from then on.

It is now easier than ever to mix these parts up. For example, Amazon offers different sales models for business owners to sell on its website. The Amazon Advantage program is basically a consignment sale agreement. The Amazon Marketplace program is basically a drop ship program. However Amazon also offers the ability to process payment for you to sell on your own web sites. Amazon can also handle the fulfillment aspect only. In any case not only Amazon but other established large online resellers can handle any piece of the chain for smaller businesses. The differences often come down to fees and commissions.

To handle such flexibility and potential confusion you will need to understand your options and the cost structures associated with each of the sales models.

The key point to understand is that the baseline process is the same regardless of who handles what portion. Technology has blurred the line between marketing and sales, between distributors and retailers, between fulfillment centers and customer service outfits. The list goes on.

With this understanding you can often demystify different sales models and pick the arrangement that suits your capabilities and budgets best. Regardless of technology and the changes of roles, the fundamental truth remains the same…you are still dealing with people and their systems and processes.

2   Work within Their System

When approaching a buyer you need to have respect for their processes or otherwise risk flat out rejection.

You need to be aware of inertia – the resistance to change and weariness of anything new (read: unproven). There is a paradox surrounding new products and innovations. People want it and they are afraid of it at the same time. Have you ever seen a child hesitant about touching something new even if he is mesmerized by it?

It takes a lot of work to evaluate a new product within an established corporate system. The same amount and probably number of steps of idea evaluation you would have to do before deciding to launch your company are similarly used to evaluate the market potential by the buyer's evaluation teams. The buyers are responsible for picking out products that meet their particular needs at the moment and ensuring profitability. After all, it is another business activity. The difference is that they would do the same evaluation work but minus your enthusiasm and emotional involvement.

The average sales cycle for developing a major channel can be 6 months to 2 years or more. There is always inertia to overcome when you try to open new doors to new channels. The larger the channel, the longer it typically takes.

Acquiring multiple large channels does not occur simultaneously even if you had a large team of well trained sales people. This process is not like landscaping where more hands equal less time. This process involves building trust and relationships which is what distribution channels and sales efforts are all about.

Even if there's money to be made, and your proposed case has obvious benefits to the distributors, you are effectively asking them to make changes to their status quo. Most people tend to avoid changes unless forced. Making money is a primary reason but may not be the only reason they have to consider. If carrying your product means bumping off someone else's product, then they must justify the move. There is more than what meets the eye the first time. By putting yourself in their position you gain a better position to help them overcome that inertia.

3   Buyer Profiling

Selling to a retail store's buyer is fundamentally the same as selling to a customer; you need to build a profile. However there are very different considerations.

A retail buyer's job is to find merchandise that can bring profit to her company. The process of evaluation typically involves teams of people whom the buyer would actually need to convince. The assumption is that the buyer decided to endorse your product but must also go through a team exercise. Rarely does a buyer make a unilateral decision on a new product.

To convince a buyer that she should become a champion of your product, you will need to understand several things, in particular what the business driver is. You can improve your odds of successful product placement with the buyer by asking the following questions:

1. *Where does she typically get information and news for new products on the market?*

   How would you know? Just ask. Ask to speak to someone in the purchasing department on how new products are brought in for review. Ask someone who has successfully placed his product with that distribution channel. If the answer is manufacturer's rep, then instead of using any PR agency or internet media to mass-blast your new product announcement, you should research this particular channel to get your message in front of her radar screen. This would prevent you from needlessly wasting your marketing dollars.

2. *What does she do when she has your business proposition?*

   This would identify her company's product review and approval process so you can set your expectations more realistically.

3. *When is the best time to approach your addressee?*

   This might shed light on any industry standard timeframes which directly govern your own product development and launch cycle. In some industries such windows of opportunity open up only once a year. Budgets are available only at the beginning of each fiscal year, for instance. Miss it and you would need to wait for another year to launch your product into their sales channels.

4. *Why would she be interested in your offering?*

   Here we look at the various motivational factors behind a person's decision making process. If you can correctly identify and manipulate any of them to your advantage then you would be much further ahead on your agenda.

   The reality is that with a full plate of already established and proven products, the buyer needs to justify the inclusion of any new entrant. The rationale for such inclusion may be to (1) beat the competition, (2) if not catch up to them with the newest and latest products, (3) diversify current product portfolio, (4) to find a lower cost replacement for an incumbent product, (5) to boost the company's own image, or anything in between.

   Sometimes the buyer simply is attracted to a new item but then faces the job of having to sell the new item internally to her review team.

If your product doesn't happen to fit into any of these preconceived categories, then your act of selling essentially boils down to an interruption, or intrusion to an established sales machine. In other words, you are not welcome.

5. *Buyer's responsibilities*

Contrary to public misconceptions, a buyer is not necessarily a product god. Her role is in determining the product mix that will optimize her organization's profit stream. If your product fits into her scheme, then you'll probably make it into her chosen pool. If not, then you won't. Presenting to a buyer for the first time is not like making a pilgrimage for the first time although emotionally it could feel like it. The buyer is your customer and deserves your proper attention. Understanding and meeting her job needs supersedes any other concerns. This is where the manufacturer's rep is invaluable.

Sales Management

Selling something to a business is a process that needs to be managed as a project. The goal is to establish a trusting relationship by fulfilling expectations each time. With a relationship, sales will hopefully become repeated and automatically replenished once your goods are in the system.

Beyond building a buyer profile, there are a few more items you will need to research. First, what is the typical lag time between buyer contact and the actual sale? Put it another way, how long is the sales cycle? Second, what is the anticipated timeframe to make final selections amongst different products? Third, what can you do to help in each step of their process?

You could always offer in-store trials, lab tests, demo units so they can get a feeling for the product and become familiar with it.

You will want to manage the sales process with a goal in mind. Set interim milestones and manage the sales process like a project plan. Communicate with the buyer when there is a milestone met or to be met.

These are a few insights that you can benefit from when selling to distributors:

1. **Clearance Discounts and Buy-Backs**

   Sometimes the initial sales quantity is not net sales but more like consignment sales. Some distributors will require that you take back unsold inventory. You should be weary of this practice. The reason is not so much aged inventory or even cash flow, both of which are serious concern, but the fact that in doing so the distributor no longer has a strong motivation to manage the sales effort if he can get refunds.

Once your inventory is in someone else's hands, and you have no control over their promotional or sales efforts, then you are taking a huge risk if you agree to take back your inventory.

Sometimes you may not have a choice but agree to the terms. Most times you need to consider the impact on your bottom line before you agree.

Another tactic is to require you to pay for a portion of any clearance discount on your product if the distributor or retailer cannot sell the inventory in a particular timeframe. In this case you will not be taking the inventory back but will be paying them back for any discount they offer to their customers. Once again this is a risky move.

2. The Quantity Game

Whereas factories always want to maximize the production quantity, distributors and retailers always want to minimize their inventory level. Your job is to find a balance where everyone is willing to meet that allows you to manage your cash flow. When possible you should test the market and sell to your channels with limited quantity first. Don't order large amounts of inventory until you have a real commitment in the form of a purchase order.

3. Business Relationships

Selling to businesses has to do with relationships, referrals, and credibility which may be considered more important than cost. If selling to consumers, it's all about the distribution channel.

4. Networking

Are you part of the "in" group or are you an outsider? It takes trust built upon previous successful transactions to break-in a new entrant. If you are not, can you prove that you are trustworthy to work with by having someone of relevance recommend you?

5. It's All About People

People can indeed make or break your business. If you are not aware of this unspoken rule then you must come to terms with it quickly or at least before you begin interacting with others in this intricate web.

The significance of business relationship is often not taught as a hardcore component of business management courses. This is unfortunate. All the number crunching on the spreadsheets and all the enticing promotions do not guarantee repeat sales. Understanding and being able to manipulate business relationships is the real key to running a business.

If you take the time to understand the motivations and dynamics behind each business transaction, you will be in a position of power to influence the outcome of your interaction with your business affiliates.

Evaluation Questions: Appendix 4 Section 2-2

- How well developed is your distribution strategy which identifies the distributors, manufacturer rep, and sales channels for your concept?

- What is the extent of your sales strategy which incorporates buyer motivation, buying process, and sales management techniques?

HOW DID YOUR CONCEPT DO?

Ideally you can determine the distribution network for your concept, including its channels and their profit margin requirements. You should also have a means to contact distributors or manufacturer's reps if your strategy is to sell into national distribution. You should be able to produce profiles of the corporate retail buyer and understand how to work within their systems and understand their true motivations behind looking at your product.

Potential Challenges and issues may occur if you fail to identify the distribution network and infrastructure of your concept. You might also be unable to make contact with anyone who can reach a corporate retail buyer. You may not be able to develop a distribution network and therefore are forced to sell directly to consumers.

A master salesperson is a master strategist. The envisioned objective is a sale but the planning is done with specific activities that have been proven to work time and again.

5.7   OVERALL STRATEGY

5.7.1   PRODUCT LIFECYCLE MANAGEMENT

AN INSIDER'S INSIGHTS

Product lifecycle management deals with a product from its conception to its end of life. There are various stages of a product's life that map to different business management issues.

Product commercialization is technically a part of product lifecycle management. The business issues of a product's lifecycle actually extend beyond bringing a product to market, which is where commercialization ends.

In terms of achieving profitability, bringing the concept to market is just the beginning. Managing the business aspects become a daily requirement. As market conditions change frequently, not paying attention to any aspect of the business could have serious consequences.

Even though bringing a concept to the market place is a significant achievement, the real test comes in during the next phase of business, which can either be profitable or not.

A new product introduced to the market will have a certain "honeymoon" period when it remains new. The newness fades away quickly; any shine will be dulled if another competitive product gets on the scene shortly after. There may be nothing wrong with your product, but people's taste changes and their insatiable quest for newer stimulations will make it obsolete sooner than you think.

In other words, no matter how good your product is, no product is in favor forever. Even best sellers need to be continuously improved. You will get to a point where the revenue doesn't justify the operation expenses anymore. That is the end of life for the product.

The following figure shows the various stages of a typical product's lifecycle:

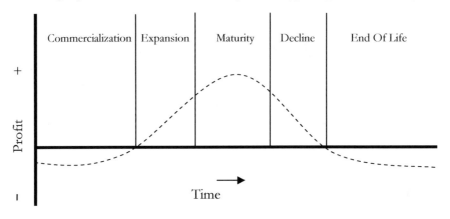

Market forces change everyday and can accelerate the stages of a product. Macroeconomic forces and regulatory changes in particular can suddenly kill a business before its planned obsolescence. These are just a couple of reasons to monitor the pulse of the business closely.

Key concepts to remember:

◈ Financial investment needs to match lifecycle.

◈ Short cycles tend to be for novelty items, fashion, fads.

◈ Use outsourced capabilities if the lifecycle is uncertain or short.

◈ Competitive products can shorten the lifecycle.

◈ Planning for end of life should begin at the first sign of decline in order to maximize existing inventory's value.

Evaluation Questions: Appendix 4 Section 2-1

● Is the projected product lifecycle in alignment with the profit expectation? In other words, will the product generate enough investment payback during its life time to justify setting up a company?

● How will your marketing strategy change as the product progresses through its lifecycle?

● Are there foreseeable market forces such as shifting trends, regulatory, testing requirements, and substitution technology that might impact the rollout or acceptance of your product?

HOW DID YOUR CONCEPT DO?

Ideally you have the management knowhow to handle the day-to-day business issues and challenges. Your product's lifecycle can be projected based on similar products in the market. By the same token, the length of its life exceeds that required to generate enough profit to pay back the financial investments. Likewise there are no foreseeable changes in the market trend, macroeconomics, and regulatory changes that might abruptly change your product's natural courses.

Potential Challenges and issues may be caused by the lack of product management competence. The product's lifecycle could be too short to make any significant amount of profit to justify launching a business. There could be issues that are either visible or potentially upcoming that could cut short your product's lifecycle.

> The sales process may begin with an idea but will always end up with people.

5.7.2 GO-TO-MARKET STRATEGY

AN INSIDER'S INSIGHTS

A go-to-market strategy deals with how you plan on approaching your market. It includes all the components of marketing leading to sales. As with any strategy, to do it correctly you will also need to balance it with the rest of your potential venture's operational capability and financial resources.

Even the best products cannot sell themselves without a deliberate marketing and sales strategy. If you proceed without a comprehensive strategy to penetrate the market and carve out a niche for your concept, then you risk tripping yourself with reworks at best, or completely wasting your time and resources at worst. Marketing and sales have evolved from an art form to virtually a science form; ignoring them is a sure way to fail.

First thing first...a strategy is a living tool; a framework with interdependencies that change as frequently as the market conditions. A direction, an objective, a culture, or an operating philosophy need to be steadfast, but not a living strategy. Don't make the mistake of thinking that once you've defined a strategy then it is set in stone.

The ultimate goal of a successful marketing campaign is to make selling a snap. If marketing is done correctly then sales come naturally. To successfully sell you will need to understand the underlying buying psychology and mental process.

Let's walk through an example to illustrate this point:

> Let us assume that your product is on a shelf of a retail store (successful **placement**). A prospective buyer (let's call her Jill) walks by and your product catches her eyes. The package intrigued her enough to take a closer look. If the content isn't obvious, she may just walk away or pick it up for a closer examination (**packaging**).
>
> Assuming Jill figures out what the product is based on its name (**positioning**), she may want to know more about what the product is designed to do (**product** function). If Jill believes that it is of interest (**expectation**), she continues to read, touch, or maneuver your product.
>
> Once she understands your value propositions (**value**), she then looks at the price and decides whether it's worth it or reasonable (**pricing**).

If at that point Jill still needs more information to help her decide, she may seek out a salesperson (assuming she **trusts** his opinion) or defer the purchase and find some reviews on it, video demos, etc. (**promotion**).

Assuming everything meets her expectations, Jill goes back to the store (good customer **relationship**) and buys your product (**sale**).

This entire episode may take an instant to a few minutes. This short window of opportunity is all you get. Yet to prepare for this encounter you will need to have a comprehensive marketing strategy that makes the buying decision a no-brainer and feels natural, maybe even satisfying. The amount of energy and effort that goes into this flawless marketing campaign could take months to expend.

If you perform a biopsy of the anatomy of this process you will see that every component of marketing and sales all roll up into a coherent go-to-market strategy. What's more fascinating is that there are actually three different processes involved in this simple transaction. You have just witnessed it from the **customer's buying process**.

Let's now take a look from a sale's perspectives:

The Sales Strategy Process

1. You identify the most natural place to sell your product - **Placement**

2. You determine how to get targeted customers to know about your product - **Promotion**

3. You designed the packaging to draw attention and entice selling – **Packaging**

4. You set a price that is attractive and profitable - **Pricing**

5. You figure out how best to describe your product - **Positioning**

6. You identify the product's benefits to hone your sales pitch - **Product**

As a sales person your highest priority would be to figure out location, location, and location (physical, online, partners) to maximize access to your product.

> The same event when viewed through three different lenses produces three distinctive sets of priorities.

The Go-to-Market Strategy Process

To put together a go-to-market plan, you will need to mesh both perspectives. The most powerful strategy is derived from a clear understanding of the marketing and sales objective while taking into consideration all the Ps of marketing and the product's potential. Together there are 14 steps in this strategy formulation process:

1	Evaluate concept
2	Industry analysis
3	Comparative analysis
4	Market segmentation
5	Customer profiling
6	Product strategy
7	Positioning strategy
8	Pricing strategy
9	Packaging strategy
10	Promotional strategy
11	Placement strategy
12	Set clear expectations
13	Build trusting relationship
14	Sell

This process will be explained in more detail in chapter 8 as part of the marketing management control mechanism.

Evaluation Questions: Appendix 4 Section 2-1

- Do you have a go-to-market strategy that covers the entire spectrum of marketing activities and coordinates with the business operations and financial activities?

- What will be the cost of marketing relative to your revenue? Does this product need a lot of promotion to the distribution channels?

HOW DID YOUR CONCEPT DO?

Ideally you will have developed a go-to-market strategy that encompasses all the critical elements in marketing management. Each element has been carefully considered and incorporated into its own strategy. All the strategies will roll up to the master strategy as a coherent whole. Meanwhile, the master marketing strategy is also in alignment with the business operations capability and financial resources. This ensures that nothing is prevented from being executed because of coordination problems or insufficient progress in other areas of the venture building process.

Potential Challenges and issues may be caused by the lack of coordinated efforts between the different elements of marketing. For example, packaging may not reflect the positioning statement, or that placement channels cannot work with the price range. In this case the entire project may fall apart or become incoherent at best. Even if it continues forward, it may be limping instead of going full speed ahead. Another potential problem is in the timing of a marketing campaign that does not synch up with operational readiness or the availability of money. In either case the effort could be wasted.

One does not begin with a strategy; one begins with a vision which then requires a strategy to fulfill.

Strategy is built from the bottom up just like every other infrastructure. First you identify the building blocks which are action steps. Then you organize and prioritize the steps into plans. Contingency planning involves the what-if scenarios. By following one set of plans and having backups you create a comprehensive strategy. When implemented, the piece parts of a strategy make the vision come true.

This is a universal process regardless of product types, services, industries, or company culture.

CHAPTER 5 ACTION ITEMS

Use the detailed questions and insights in Appendix 4 to help you tackle these action items.

1. Identify your product or service's functions and features in detail.

2. Establish your idea's best positioning statement as related to its primary target consumers or buyers.

3. Create your pricing strategy based on the most suitable model for your type of product or service.

4. Determine your packaging strategy.

5. Create your promotional strategy, laying out channels and how best to use each of them to reach your target audience.

6. Identify your distribution/placement channels and brainstorm on how you would acquire them.

7. Assemble your individual strategies and roll them into a coherent go-to-market strategy for your concept.

Chapter 6

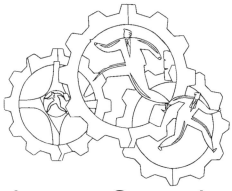

Company Infrastructures... Gears that Drive the Business Machine Forward

A great idea needs an amazing marketing and sales strategy on top of a dependable and capable business infrastructure to launch it into success. This last piece is like the engine under the hood of a high performance race car. When properly designed and tuned, teaming it with an experienced driver creates a formidable force to reckon with.

Alternatively a superb idea and a powerful marketing and sales campaign are a recipe for financial disaster if the execution of order fulfillment is poorly done. Efficiently fulfilling wrong orders can only lead to more problems. The role of business infrastructure may not be as glamorous and fun as the other business components, but it is no doubt a critical piece of a venture.

Beginning with this chapter and continuing onto the next, the contents will shift more towards measuring the profitability potential (commercialization viability) of a new venture instead of pure concept evaluation. Both are necessary to compile a comprehensive view of a concept's probability to commercial success.

Once a concept is deemed worthy to go to market, the next step is to form protections around it so that you can freely share details with others. Beyond that, the attention turns over to a company's ability to execute. A company is made up of physical infrastructures, systems, operational processes, procedures, and the people behind them. We will now examine each one of these components.

The contents have been organized into three sections. They are:

1. **Protecting your business and assets** (section 6.1)

   ◈ Intellectual property, legal, and insurance protections

2. **Managing service providers** (section 6.2)

   ◈ Factories and suppliers, vendors and service providers

3. **Business operations** (section 6.3)

   ◈ Designing business systems and business processes

In the **protection** section we will highlight the essence of intellectual property, legal agreements, and insurance protection. We will look at the questions of whether to protect, what to protect, and how to protect.

In the **service providers** section we will concentrate on insights pertaining to the people and entities that provide service in the commercialization ecosystem, specifically factories, vendors, and service providers which include employees.

In the **business operations** section we will draw attention to the underlying infrastructures that make everything possible, particularly systems and processes.

6.1 PROTECTING YOUR BUSINESS AND ASSETS

AN INSIDER'S INSIGHTS

Protection is about keeping what is rightfully yours from being exploited by others and reducing risks and potential harms to you and your investment.

Within this protection umbrella three sections are of particular importance to commercializing a concept. The first is intellectual property (IP). The next is legal protection. The final is insurance protection.

Without the proper protection you could end up with nothing despite all your hard work. Having the right amount of legal protection is often a pre-requisite to doing business with others. It also gives you the peace of mind to focus on developing and growing a business instead of worrying about idea theft or potential liabilities.

Intellectual property protection, legal agreements, and insurance have one goal in common, namely to protect you and your assets. Similarly, market research, product design, and user instruction also share a commonality to protect the intended users. Put the two sets of considerations together and you will develop an appreciation for the need to obtain protections before your innovation gets into the marketplace.

No one wants to work hard building up a business only to have unintended events or unscrupulous characters take it all away. The earlier you can anticipate such possibilities the less likely that financial or even legal troubles can dampen or even destroy your venture's profits.

It should be pointed out that each of these protections requires professional expertise and guidance that are beyond the scope of this book. The objective here is to identify them so that you can evaluate whether your idea warrants any or all of them.

6.1.1   INTELLECTUAL PROPERTY PROTECTION

We will look at six areas:

(1)   **Protection**

(2)   **Strategy**

(3)   **Enforcement**

(4)   **Infringement**

(5)   **How to get it**

(6)   **What you should also know**

1   Protection

Intellectual properties are literally one's brainchild; it takes tremendous amounts of mental energy, creativity, problem solving, and time to "make" a physical manifestation of your intellectual creation. Whether it is a refined idea, an analysis, knowledge, or wisdom that is placed into a book, a design, a movie, or a song, the reality is that it took a long time to procure. The process of creating an intellectual product is not very different from that of a physical product, but the brainwork behind it is often more intense and more involved. A physical product at least has manual labor involved; an intellectual property is all brainwork.

As such your intellectual property also has value and worth that are measured in the same way as a physical product. It goes without arguing that you need to take all the necessary steps to protect your intellectual property as you would any physical property that you labored over.

The three types of intellectual properties that an inventor or aspiring entrepreneur should become familiar with are: **patent**, **trademark**, and **copyright**.

The first question of protecting your intellectual property is whether or not it meets the criteria to receive legal protections. In other words, is your design patentable? Or if for a company or product name, can the name or logo get trademarked?

Intellectual property is a specialized branch of the law, and as such you should become much more familiar with any of the three types applicable to your situation than what is mentioned here. The US Patent and Trademark Office (USPTO) is the official government site of such information. Even if you hire an IP attorney to file your patent, trademark, or copyright applications, you should still browse through the USPTO website for some very helpful information www.uspto.gov.

Whereas patents protect your design, trademarks protect your brand, and copyrights protect your intellectual creation. Such legal protection helps promote creativity so that people are not worried about having their precious IP stolen. At the same time, however, it is not a silver bullet or an indicator of commercial viability. This last point often escapes the attention of inventors.

Patent

Patents are divided into two major classes: utility and design. In all likelihood the utility design is what is applicable when bringing an idea to market.

According to the USPTO:

*A **patent** gives an inventor the right to exclude all others from making, using, importing, selling or offering to sell the invention for up to 20 years without the inventor's permission. This gives the inventor the opportunity to produce and market the invention himself, or license others to do so, and to make a profit.*

Patent protection is 17 years if issued prior to 1995. It is 14 years for a design patent.

Trademark and Servicemark

As described in Chapter 5, a brand can be a powerful asset even as it is intangible. A company's name and logo, as well as its positioning statement can all be trademarked. Purchase decisions are often made on the basis of a company's brand, and trademarks enhance the company's brand recognition and familiarity.

It takes a long time and costs a lot of money to build up a customer base and sales. You would not want potential customers to get confused between your product and a competitive product, especially if the competitor is new to the scene.

If your product or service's name can be trademarked, you should by all means do so. It is a way of differentiating your offering from the competition, and also acts as a barrier to entry if you succeed in building a strong brand loyalty.

According to the USPTO:
http://www.uspto.gov/smallbusiness/trademarks/index_print.html

*A **trademark** includes any word, name, symbol, or device, or any combination used, or intended to be used, in commerce to identify and distinguish the goods of one manufacturer or seller from goods manufactured or sold by others, and to indicate the source of the goods. In short, a trademark is a brand name.*

*Trademarks which are used in interstate or foreign commerce may be **registered** with the USPTO.*

*A **service mark** is any word, name, symbol, device, or any combination, used, or intended to be used, in commerce, to identify and distinguish the services of one provider from the services provided by others, and to indicate the source of the services.*

Copyright

If your creation includes original work of writing or artwork that contributes to the value of your product or service, you should copyright them. The Copyright Office is a division of the Library of Congress www.copyright.gov.

According to the USPTO:

***Copyright** is a form of protection provided by U.S. law to the authors of "original works of authorship" fixed in any tangible medium of expression. The manner and medium of fixation are virtually unlimited. Creative expression may be captured in words, numbers, notes, sounds, pictures, or any other graphic or symbolic media. The subject matter of copyright is extremely broad, including literary, dramatic, musical, artistic, audiovisual, and architectural works. Copyright protection is available to both published and unpublished works.*

Another useful source of information on copyrights is the Copyright Clearance Center entity which also handles IP licensing www.copyright.com.

 Strategy

Not all inventions or designs should be patented. The central question should be whether it is justifiable to spend any money patenting, copyrighting, or trademarking your intellectual property.

This question seems counterintuitive at first to most first time inventors. However if you consider it as a business proposition, then the rationale becomes understandable.

There are several considerations surrounding this question. One that is often missed is whether a new concept's commercial shelf life can exceed the patent protection period. For household product inventions unfortunately the answer is often "No." For example, if a household invention's realistic profit-generating timeframe is five years, then will the product generate enough profit to justify the total patenting expense for that period? On the other hand, if the product does not have patent protection, will its commercial value invite knockoffs?

Another question is whether something similar to your concept has been launched successfully in the marketplace without patent protection. This could be an indicator of whether or not yours needs patenting. You should recall that there are many types of barriers to keep competition out and a patent is just one of them.

Likewise, is there an interested pool of potential licensees for your innovation, thereby warranting its IP protection?

These are all strategic questions that you must balance against your concept's commercial profit potential. Patenting has a dual function in this equation…it is both a competitive barrier (provided that the design and patent claims are strong enough) to ward off knockoffs and an intellectual asset that could generate licensing royalty. At the same time it could become a pure and unnecessary cost item if the product is not attractive enough to invite knockoffs (therefore no real threat) or will not generate enough profit during its shelf life to justify the often large expenditure of filing and maintaining the patent. This scenario is not uncommon amongst independent inventors of household items.

If you are simply testing the water and not entirely committed to commercializing an innovation and don't want to take the chance that someone else might beat you to filing, you can opt for the **provisional patent** application which allows you to claim a "patent pending" status for one year for about $110 (current rate). This helps you stake a claim as of the filing date on your design in case someone else is also working on something similar. However, until you file the non-provisional patent, or the legally enforceable formal version, you still are not officially protected if someone else files a full, formal patent before you.

Your decision to submit the **non-provisional** patent application should be driven only by validated market demand. In other words, having real customers willing to pay for your invention-based product or service should be a criterion. At that point you have a better than average chance of making back at least your patenting cost, and hopefully end up making profits from your concept.

I once had a patent attorney telling me to just apply for the non-provisional patent and skip the provisional patent application process. He was trying to help me save a couple of hundred dollars, but he didn't realize that the ramifications of the provisional patenting cost is nothing compared to the real cost of launching a venture. He also was not sensitive to the possibility of inducing a falsified sense of security from having applied or even received the non-provisional patent, both of which have no strong correlation to real commercial success.

Some people argue on whether products need to be patented at all, since the ratio of patents lawsuits are insignificant relative to the number of products in the market. Some products don't even have patent protection. But this argument misses the point. The reality is that for products that are truly commercially viable, patent protection is necessary, just like business liability insurance is necessary against unforeseen problems.

Once again the question points back to the central issue of whether a product idea should be patented at all. To not get legal protection for something that is clearly commercializable is taking a big risk against idea theft. To patent a product idea believing that the very act will guarantee commercial success is naïve. To weigh the likelihood of commercial acceptance before applying for patent protection is the right thing to do especially for consumer products with a limited shelf life.

For example, suppose SnapIt! is superior in function, power, and even usability. However it lacks the hardware distribution reach that an established hand tool manufacturer would have. Assuming you patented it and are able to get it into a handful of stores. Your total cost will probably not be as low as the incumbent models due to their mass production cost efficiency. Even if yours is priced lower, it doesn't have the market awareness or inherent brand loyalty. In that case whether you patent or not is almost immaterial. Your company may not survive long enough to reap the revenue to pay back your patent investment.

To patent or not to patent, that is the question.

This is one reason why experienced entrepreneurs will tell you that getting a patent is secondary to making sure marketing is on your side. For a profit driven business it makes most sense to assess the big picture before jumping in to get a patent.

On the other hand, if you don't have some sort of patent protection you may never even get to a licensing negotiation table. A reasonable compromise is to spend a few hundred dollars and get a provisional patent first. This will give you an exploratory opportunity for one year, which you could presumably also extend. If this applies to you then visiting the USPTO site is a must.

3 Enforcement

There are two other practical considerations you must evaluate when contemplating a patent application. First, how effective is the legal protection;

can you afford to fight any legal battle? Second, how easy could someone bypass your design and knock you off legally?

The answer to the first question depends on the quality and strength of the claims. This is why you will need an experienced patent attorney to write the claims.

The second question deals with the quality of your design. If you applied the KISS principle and ensured that your design is as efficient and cost effective as it can be, then knockoffs would not be as much of a threat.

4 Infringement

Let's not forget about the other side of the coin when patenting. Could your innovation be infringing on someone else's design? Similarly are you able to obtain trademarks or copyrights for any intellectual work you have produced without infringing on others' work?

You will need to do your due diligence and perform thorough patent searches and product searches online and in stores. Your ability to obtain registered trademark status depends on the originality of your name and logo. If there are competitive products with similar names then it becomes a challenge. This task should be completed well before you spend any money building up a brand.

5 How to Get It

Applying for trademarks and copyrights are straightforward and can be done fairly easily by you. A patent application gets a bit more complicated.

It is entirely reasonable to do your own patent search via the USPTO website or the Google Patents website www.google.com/patents. It is not unusual to peruse over thousands of patents before you can determine that your innovation is in fact unique. Assuming that you have completed your working prototype and are confident of its capabilities, you should protect your intellectual property by filing a patent if you believe it will lead to commercial applications.

The objective is to make sure that your design is unique, useful, and does not infringe on earlier designs known as prior arts. Researching the prior arts by yourself is actually an excellent idea as you can learn much from how the patent format, claims, drawings, and lingo work together. If you are adept at mechanical drawings you can also create your own patent drawings by following the guidelines on the USPTO website. You always have the option of hiring a patent drawing drafting service.

A patent attorney can help you determine whether your innovation is unique and useful and can be patented. He or she is also the one person who should represent your application and communications to and from the patent examination office of the USPTO.

No one wants to get into a patent war which could cost from hundreds of thousands to millions of dollars. So as soon as your design is finalized and you are sure that it is commercially viable then you should convert the provisional patent into the non-provisional patent. If you don't file a non-provisional patent before the one-year expiration date of the provisional patent application, you will lose the patent pending claim and any benefits associated with the earlier filing date.

Official patent examination takes time and is done in stages. As of this writing the traditional first action pendency is 24.5 months [7]. This is a response measurement put out by the USPTO for public information. It does not mean patent issuance by any stretch of imagination. Any issues with your claims on your patent will delay the process even further. Writing the claims should be a patent attorney's job; it is not for the do-it-yourselfers. The claims are the essence of your patent and the only part that is defensible in court. You can opt to do the patent search yourself, and do the descriptive parts or even the mechanical drawings if you are good enough, but definitely leave the claims and the submission to a patent attorney.

It is illegal to put "patented" status on your marketing material or product packaging until the patent is actually granted. I met a couple who submitted their patent application and then proceeded to tell everyone that they have patented their business software. This is a false claim; the practice is illegal. If your patent is not granted or has expired you should not claim it as in effect.

 ## What You Should Also Know

The patent examination and granting system was never intended to be a commercial viability evaluation and approval process. Inventors who mistake getting a patent as a validation that their concept will be commercially successful are making an unfounded huge mistake. The reality is that the number of inventions held by an inventor has no relevance to the inventor's ability to bring a product to market.

The U.S. patent system must be recognized for its intended purpose, which is to promote creativity within the confines of its own evaluation criteria. Patents hold commercial value ONLY IF the invention has been successfully commercialized. If the patent is never commercialized, it becomes a cost item, draining maintenance fees from the inventor every few years.

---

[7] USPTO monthly dashboard report on patent data http://www.uspto.gov/dashboards/patents/main.dashxml

So if you invented something and never commercialized it, to keep the patent protection "alive" you would have to pay periodic patent maintenance fees on top of the money already spent on attorney fees and patent examination fees. There are different fee structures for different types of patents and applicants. This is a sample maintenance fee schedule: $980 at the 3.5-year interval, $2,480 at the 7.5-year interval, and $4,110 at the 11.5-year interval[8]. All the while you could be paying real money for zero financial returns. Unless, of course, your goal is to pay all the fees in order to have bragging rights of being a patent holding inventor.

6.1.2 LEGAL PROTECTION

Beyond protecting your intellectual property and exploring the various aspects of a venture, once you begin to build a business you need to protect your company, your product, and especially yourself against frivolous lawsuits or legitimate damages.

There are many dimensions to protecting yourself and your business legally. Your objective is to establish a formal business entity that enjoys all the legal rights while protecting your personal assets. Business incorporation sets up a legal entity with rights and duties apart from your personal property.

This is an area where you will need to hire a small business attorney to cover all the grounds. There is also an abundance of free information online on incorporating your business and common business contracts and agreements. Developing a basic idea of what they are will help you carry on a more productive discussion with a small business attorney. At a minimum the baseline questions you need to consider include:

- Have you determined the appropriate type of business entity if you are to commercialize your concept?

- Are your personal assets protected in case of business related lawsuits?

- Are you able to get legal documents at a reasonable cost?

6.1.3 INSURANCE

There are a few things you need to think about relating to **General Business and Product Liability Insurance**:

- Are there health and safety concerns for your intended users from using your product, such as dangerous designs or toxic raw material, potential bodily injury, or property damage?

---

[8] Patent maintenance fee schedule http://www.uspto.gov/web/offices/ac/qs/ope/fee2009september15.htm#maintain

- Is your product liable to recalls?

- You will need to have sufficient general liability insurance in order to do business with most resellers. Many of them will require that you place them on your insurance riders.

- You might have difficulty obtaining mainstream general liability insurance and may have to work with surplus line insurance providers.

- Your insurance premium may offset any profit you make in the first few years.

The concept of liability covers two major areas: injury to body and damages to properties. There are other derivatives but we will focus on these two in the rest of this discussion.

General Business Insurance covers damages to users and to other people's facilities even if you happen to be doing a demonstration of your innovation. If your product contains flammable, volatile chemical, then you need to be extra diligent. If you are launching a service based on your innovation, you are still subject to the same property damage liability issues, not to mention business disruption to others.

Product Liability Insurance covers injuries and damages caused by your product. How much coverage you need is often driven by your distributor's requirement. For a consumer toy product ours was around $3M in combined coverage.

Notice that faulty product design is a big leading cause of product liability issues. Even if the design's faultiness is not immediately apparent, reasonably foreseeable injuries and damages from using the product is still a bona fide reason to punish the manufacturer.

If your innovation is a consumer product, then you need to pay serious attention to the consumer safety laws at the CPSC.gov web site. By the same token, one of the best resources you have (ironically) is the recall list and the reasons why some products were recalled. This list should serve as a warning in terms of the potential financial loss a company can suffer from a product liability perspective, and be used as a checklist for attributes your product should NOT have.

Designs that contain sharp edges, unstable bases, fragile material where it needed to be durable, etc. are all accidents waiting to happen. Non-ergonomic designs tend to create injuries to the body over time as people adjust themselves to awkward positions in order to operate or use products. Raw material needs to be checked to make sure it is not toxic or illegal. Another potential liability rises from false claims of the functions or inaccurate descriptions. If people get injured because a product is claimed to be safe when it is actually not, then you can expect personal injury lawsuits.

For example, even if the product's dimensions are designed for an older child, if it can be slipped into a choke tube, then warnings and other design considerations must be applied to prevent accidental choking death of children under the age of three.

Other types of insurance include employment insurance, health, and other employee benefits insurance. Some people may even opt for business interruption insurance. This topic is extensive and does not immediately concern a product's likelihood to become profitable so it will not be discussed. However if you proceed beyond product evaluation it is then essential that you look into them to get a sense of their impact on your financial projections.

Evaluation Questions: Appendix 4 Section 3-1, 3-2

Intellectual Property   section 3-1

- Is your innovation truly unique to warrant applying for a patent?
- Can your trade name and other intellectual creations be trademarked or copyrighted?
- Have you determined whether it makes strategic sense, not just legal sense, to patent your innovation?
- How effective are the legal claims on your patent application; how easily can someone bypass your legal protection?
- Will your innovation infringe on someone else's protected work?
- Do licensing arrangements exist for products similar to your concept?

Legal Protection   section 3-2

- Have you determined the appropriate type of business entity if you are to commercialize your concept?
- Are your personal assets protected in case of business related lawsuits?
- If you require legal documents are you able to obtain them at a reasonable cost?

Liability and Insurance Protection   section 3-2

- Does your concept design lead to potential bodily injury or property damage?
- What is the minimum amount of business liability insurance coverage required by your potential distribution channel?
- Will you be able to obtain business liability insurance for your type of product?
- Is the insurance premium justifiable from a profitability standpoint?

HOW DID YOUR CONCEPT DO?

Ideally you will have identified whether or not it makes sense to file for patent protection for your product, assuming your concept is patentable. You should also have the means to find legal assistance and insurance coverage sufficient for your type of venture.

Potential Challenges and issues may arise if your patent design is either suboptimal or too expensive to justify filing. Your legal expenses may also be too expensive. You may not be able to find insurance for your type of product due to its inherent property. You may find that patenting does not make sense yet you still have to spend tens of thousands to file because of the uncertainty involved.

6.2   MANAGING SERVICE PROVIDERS

AN INSIDER'S INSIGHTS

This section focuses on building the human side of the equation, which precedes issues surrounding the building of physical and logical sides of the equation.

High level questions have been grouped into four categories for consideration. They are: (1) identifying the capabilities, skills, and talents your venture needs, (2) evaluating the service and capabilities of service providers, (3) acquiring these services, and (4) managing these service providers.

Your venture's or a licensee's likelihood to achieve profitability is directly determined by the right mix of talents and capabilities. A business is necessarily multi-faceted and therefore outsourcing some aspects instead of building everything in-house can be a bona fide strategy. Your ability to acquire such talents and to effectively manage them is a critical factor to your venture's success.

Even as you might be just an inventor or the person behind a business idea, the world looks at you as the manufacturer or provider of your goods and services. If you decide to take on the monumental task of starting a business around your idea, you will also assume responsibilities to manage the entire commercialization process. If you instead are able to find licensees for your concept, you should still be aware of their talent pool and capabilities behind turning a concept into a finished product.

You need money to make money but people to manage systems and other people. Different types of talents are needed to provide the labor, skills, and management of tools, equipment, or facility. One way to make sense of such a large labor pool is to divide it into two segments which are **factories & suppliers**, and **vendors & service providers**.

If you intend on outsourcing the entire business to a licensee, in effect taking a hands-off approach, you should still understand how the licensee intends to fulfill the same set of responsibilities. You do this in order to assess whether they are a good fit for your concept. Keep in mind that a licensee may have a company but the company still needs to run optimally to generate your share of the profit.

6.2.1   FACTORIES AND SUPPLIERS

Factories physically turn out products and suppliers provide raw or finished material for your business' consumption. Since rarely does someone build a factory just because he has a great concept, the more typical scenario is to outsource the production capability to a factory that already produces similar products.

Suppliers, on the other hand, are more commonly utilized to procure your goods or services. Some examples of suppliers are office supply, tools and equipment, and loosely speaking infrastructure needed for operational systems. This is differentiated from vendors who provide services in the marketing and sales areas.

Listed below are high level questions that you should explore when dealing with factories and suppliers.

1   Identifying the Capabilities Needed

- ◈ **Outsourcing**
  - ▪ Have you determined what aspects of the business will be built internally or outsourced in order to cost effectively bring the innovation to market?

- ◈ **Types of suppliers**
  - ▪ What tools, equipment, and physical infrastructure do you need to produce and deliver your goods or services?
  - ▪ Which types of suppliers will you engage? Factory, freight, warehousing, order processing, fulfillment, web hosting, and/or eCommerce systems?

- ◈ **Balance of power**
  - ▪ Is the balance of power favorable for the innovator or for the suppliers of goods? Put it another way, is the industry growing with demand or are the suppliers willing to compete for business?

2   Evaluating Service and Capabilities of Factories and Suppliers

- ◈ **Technical considerations**
  - ▪ Can prospective suppliers fulfill the technical specifications of the product or service?

- Is this a breakthrough industry that requires years to perfect the manufacturing technology, such as was the case with Velcro®?

- Do they have the tools, equipment, manpower, and facility to handle your maximum production requirement?

◈ **Regulatory**

- Is the supplier industry subject to regulatory constraints that will in turn affect the innovation?

- Are they in compliance with local regulatory conditions and requirements such as work environmental safety issues and conditions?

◈ **Seasonal factors**

- Are there seasonal or industry specific timeframes that dictate the production schedule of products or services? Does this create any problem? For example, the entire China shuts down production for 2-3 weeks during the Chinese New Year holiday.

◈ **Supplier market conditions**

- Is the supplier's industry undergoing significant changes that could impact the innovation's time to market? Factors such as raw material shortage or supply/demand shifts play a major factor.

◈ **Cost of supply**

- Will the production costs match the quality of goods produced? In other words, will the suppliers try to find short cuts and material changes to meet their own cost reduction demands as so many Chinese factories were forced to do?

3   Acquiring These Capabilities

◈ **Do you have a good understanding of the supplier's motivational factors?**

◈ **Where will you find these resources?**

◈ **Are you prepared to negotiate business terms with them?**

4   Managing These Services

◈ **Supplier management**

- Will your venture or licensee be able to dictate the type of service, design specifications, and quality of work to be delivered by the suppliers?

- Will there be an agreed upon process and turnaround time, including the cost associated with revisions and mistakes?

Communications

- Will there be an established and proven method of communications with a factory or suppliers?

- Can information be transmitted in real time? Are time zone differences a major issue for your type of goods or services?

- Is there a potential for misunderstanding due to a language or cultural barrier?

All these questions pertain to the business engine and performance behind the concept. Since the capabilities are outsourced, they will need to be managed closely. When dealing with factories you will need to sign several agreements.

To begin, you will need a non-disclosure agreement to protect your IP. Next, you will need to execute a non-compete agreement or include it in the non-disclosure to protect your business. Then, you will need to have a pricing agreement which includes cost information and delivery information. Any quote on production cost must be honored within a specified period of time such as 90-180 days.

The factories you work with will also need to agree to periodic inspections by a third party company. Finally the factories need to have a warranty on their production quality, including successfully passing product tests also to be conducted by a third party entity.

These conditions need to be clearly spelled out especially if you are working with overseas factories where prosecution of violations may be extremely difficult and costly. The goal is to find factories that can cater to you at the minimum production quantity with the lowest cost and highest quality possible.

To find them you can do online keyword searches for manufacturers and service providers. The effort may include talking to professional trade associations or go to tradeshows where such service providers solicit their business. You will need to assess samples they send for quality and price quotes. If doing business overseas, you will need to learn about export control requirements, custom inspection process, warehousing, freight schedules, etc. or source a vendor who provides turnkey service for you.

These business considerations are almost impossible to gauge where there is only a concept, but absolutely necessary to explore if the decision is to go forth. The easiest way to do business is to establish a good and trusting relationship with your factories and suppliers. No one really has the time to be auditing everyone else but periodic checkups are the smart thing to do.

That said, never assume people will be responsible or diligent all the time for a long period of time. Things change, people adapt.

6.2.2   VENDORS & SERVICE PROVIDERS

Vendors are providers of goods or services to a business. Those who provide goods or services related to production or infrastructure are labeled as suppliers for the sake of differentiating from people who provide their expertise and services in marketing and sales activities. The latter group is often known as professionals, independent consultants, contractors, temporary, and even long term employees.

Professionals such as accountants, lawyers, webmasters, and business consultants are examples of vendors. People who are hired to do very specific tasks on a stint basis are usually considered contractors. There really isn't much difference and certainly no need to split hair about the differentiation. All are paid to provide needed expertise for particular areas.

In fact, the service provider category also includes employees who are paid in exchange for their services. Since job security and loyalty are pretty much anachronisms, employees are essentially service providers with benefits until they leave.

If you recall in Chapter 2 - *Who's Who in the Commerce Loop?* We identified a chart of players in the commercialization ecosystem. The information and questions raised here will help you manage different types of vendors and service providers identified on that chart.

Your objective is to be able to handle every business transaction professionally. You will need to manage every outsourced service supplier to ensure their work contributes to your business' goal. As your business is stabilized and begins to grow, you should develop a hiring strategy. You will need to determine whether to hire permanent or temporary employees and how to compensate them. You will also need to find expertise associated with employment law on benefits and tax reporting.

We will now look at high level questions and considerations that you should explore when dealing with vendors and service providers. The information is organized into four topics:

(1) **Identifying knowledge, experience, and skills**

(2) **Evaluating skills and capabilities**

(3) **Acquiring talents**

(4) **Managing talents**

1 Identifying the Knowledge, Experience, and Skills Needed

Given the importance of management expertise, you would think that most people would give it the utmost consideration. Unfortunately this is neither true nor consistently practiced.

Many first time entrepreneurs make the mistake of assuming that their "business advisors," specifically attorneys and accountants, should be tapped for business management advice. There are magazine articles that suggest taking this approach. It can be a dangerous practice.

New entrepreneurs tend to hire out of expediency and a sense of urgency. This is understandable with perceived time pressure and the need to get to market quickly. They tend to make a few classic mistakes in acquiring human resources. The list includes hiring family and friends, hiring casual referrals, trusting in people's positions in life and the implied expertise.

This last point was a trying lesson for the AeroBloks venture. Of course it was only in hindsight that the mistakes became clear. Here are a few of our own unexpected encounters:

Attorneys

Our first attorney claimed that he was a small business specialist and offered business advices. He happened to be a friend as well. In time I found that his business advice were in fact highly detrimental to our operation and presented unwarranted risks that only an amateur would take. Needless to say that relationship did not last too long. This should be a warning for anyone who is considering hiring someone you know (friends and relatives) just because of expediency instead of qualifications. It is a classic first time entrepreneurial mistake.

First of all, an attorney is trained in the field of law; not many of them earn an MBA in addition to their JD credentials. Their objective and perspective are not the same as an experienced business manager. In their course of dealing with business people (presumably many years), they may have witnessed business issues. But this is insufficient reason for anyone to place their business in the hands of a bystander. A football fan may know all the tricks of his favorite team but it does not mean that when he is on the field that he can perform any of them.

Attorneys need to stick to explaining and helping you determine the legal risks of your business dealings. If you end up paying attorney fees for business advice, then you need to blame yourself, not the other guy, for any faulty decision.

I also interacted with a patent attorney with an engineering background and had a habit of telling me stories about his engineering past at $300/hour, my cost. I had to point out that it was not right to be charging me for non-legal advice even if he thought it was good to mention.

Accountants

Accountants similarly are to be leveraged primarily for balancing your books. They may have witnessed cash-flow disasters that stranded or killed other businesses, but their advice similarly is at a high level. Anything beyond financial transactions and bookkeeping is not within their domain.

One accountant I interviewed proposed that he become my primary business advisor. He was probably no more than 26 years old and was just starting to build his own practice. One Friday afternoon he called to "chat" and asked how my business was going. After updating him on the business for about 30 minutes we hung up. The next thing I knew was receiving an invoice of $100 for a 30 minutes "consultation." Not only did he not mention a single accounting advice but I actually did all the talking. Needless to say I promptly ended the relationship.

Another accountant I interviewed strongly urged that he become a member of my board because his vocation may be accounting but his avocation was marketing. His initial free consultation turned into an hour of rambling on how he would go about doing advertising and how the brochure should be designed, etc. I never called back his office.

I believe my decision was quite right as later events proved that neither was worthy in their own specialty, never mind my business management.

The School Market Expert

While I was looking to expand into the childcare segment via direct marketing, I met an entrenched industry veteran whose business was to analyze market data and sell sales leads. While in his opinion the childcare market was exactly where AeroBloks needed to be, he offered no substantial insights as to why.

While rushing to meet the new budget season of most childcare centers I made the decision to hire his business on a turnkey level. What this also meant was that I was to hire his wife as a design specialist for the brochures based on his recommendation. Purely by affiliation I thought that she must also be an expert at designing (which was told to me explicitly by him) since they had been in business for a long time. The brochure turned out to be a failure from a design perspective. Once I saw the finalized layout I immediately realized that the quality was amateurish. By that time it was too late for any modifications.

This direct mail campaign became my worst promotional effort ever. It cost almost three times as much as a tradeshow with virtually no return on investment. This was and still remains a haunting experience about the perception of experience by professional position and by pure affiliation. What I should have done in hindsight was to ask for design samples even if she was positioned as a marketing and design expert.

◈ **Knowledge & experience**

- What type of knowledge and experience does the venture need in the areas of product development, technical, marketing, operational, financial, and product management?

- Do you have these skill sets or do you need to hire someone who does?

◈ **Organization planning**

- What type of business experience does the management team have? Do the experiences complement each other and cover the entire spectrum of skills or do some overlap?

- What is the employment break down for each phase of the product lifecycle (see section 5.7.1)? That is, full time, part time, managerial staff, support staff, production/service labor?

- What is the anticipated need in the immediate future? Can you justify the reason for each hire?

2 Evaluating Skills and Capabilities of Service Providers

There is a very good reason why some venture capitalists make their investment decisions with more emphasis on the management team than on the concept, or put it another way…betting on the jockey instead of the horse. You may have a world-class facility and a great concept, but if the management lacks the vision and talent to leverage such assets, the business will not prosper. It would be like putting an amateur jockey on a champion race horse.

Before you hire executives or license your concept to someone else, you need to carefully consider the skills and experience offered by potential candidates.

People who manage financial investments understand that there is a tiered approach to measuring a financial instrument's potential worth.

Shaped like an hour-glass, the tiered analysis begins with looking at global forces that will have the greatest impact on an investment, including its competition and the industry. There is a popular saying that when the tide comes in all boats rise. This is what essentially happens when a global force such as the recent rise of the Chinese economic power drives up the costs of raw materials.

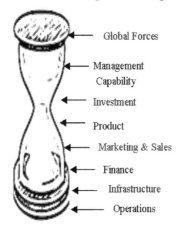

Global Forces

Management Capability

Investment

Product

Marketing & Sales

Finance

Infrastructure

Operations

They next look at the management team of a company, measuring such criteria as insider selling, year to year operations margin, and different financial ratios designed to expose the operational strength of a company.

Bringing your innovation to market is a financial investment. Global forces tend to equate to timing, opportunities, and threats but management capability is unmistakably tied to the expertise you pay for.

◈ **Critical skills**

▪ Is the labor force primarily skilled or unskilled workers?

◈ **Filling the void**

▪ What void in skills and capabilities would hiring or outsourcing fill?

▪ Do they need to be employed full time or part time?

▪ What specific functions and goals will they accomplish? Do you have a detailed job description including set goals and timeframe?

▪ Does the cost of outsourcing justify not hiring employees?

3 Acquiring Talents

Hiring people should be a step-wise process. Most bootstrapping entrepreneurs start with just one or two people working full time until the business starts to show stability. At that point hiring someone is a sign of growth. On the other hand many people also make the mistake of immediately hiring an entire team without any proven traction.

The right approach is to consider the process as a spectrum. As the amount of workload increases your own efficiency will invariably decrease. You should start with identifying what needs you have, and how hiring a person would meet that specific need. You will need to quantify the results against the cost. Next you should determine whether this is on a long term basis or just a short term stint. That information will help you determine whether to hire contractors, temp agencies, outsourcing to specific companies (e.g. payroll processing companies), or to hire a long term employee as well as making full or part time decisions.

You will need to research employment laws and employment tax laws at the federal level and state level (i.e. where you incorporate). There may also be taxation at the local level (e.g. city sales license). Employment taxes such as social security, 401K contribution, medical and dental insurance, unemployment insurance, etc. all come with hiring employees. Once you have the entire scope in mind and know what you need to do, you can then layout a stepwise action plan and get going.

- ◈ **Hiring**
  - Can you acquire these resources within a reasonable amount of time and effort?
  - What is the cost of hiring each person and is it within budget and justified by the projected additional revenue or cost savings for the business?
  - How will you ensure that different personalities will work together coherently and not let work politics get in the way of progress?

- ◈ **Payroll and benefits**
  - Do you have payroll and other benefits administration expertise?
  - Will you be able to afford full time help including paying for attractive benefits?
  - What is the cost of training a new hire, is it included in the total employment cost projection?

- ◈ **Employment law**
  - How prepared are you to comply with employment law expertise, including firing?

- ◈ **Union**
  - Does the type of business involve hiring union-based labor? If so is there a proven expertise in dealing with union issues?

4   Managing Talents

Management of people has much to do with leadership, which is also a topic that has been extensively written about. These sample questions are most relevant to a new venture and therefore have been added here to stimulate your thinking.

◆ **Vision**

- Is your business objective easy to understand and capable of being carried out?

- Do you have a centralized vision for the company, the product, and for short term accomplishments in concrete terms and projected timeframes?

- Will your organizational design collaborate with your vision or will different responsibilities clash?

◆ **Motivation**

- Can the team accomplish the job outlined in the business plan?

- Are the team members proven achievers?

- What incentives do people have in joining the company? Is it straight pay, stock option, or company ownership?

- How will you keep them motivated to accomplish the objectives?

Evaluation Questions: Appendix 4 Section 4-1, 4-2

Factories and Suppliers   section 4-1

- Do you have a clear idea on what capabilities are needed to commercialize your concept?

- Do you have the means to evaluate providers of such capabilities including how to acquire their services?

- Is there a plan on how to communicate and manage factories and suppliers?

Vendors and Service Providers   section 4-2

- How well can you identify the skill sets and experiences needed to manage the company behind your concept?

- How prepared are you to evaluate potential vendors and suppliers?

- Do you have the resources to hire and manage contractors and employees, including meeting employment law compliance?

HOW DID YOUR CONCEPT DO?

Ideally you will have a good understanding of the talents and skill sets you need to run a business around your concept. Likewise if you license it out you will know how to evaluate a potential licensee's capabilities. You should also know what criteria to consider when evaluating a potential factory, vendor, or service supplier. Lastly if you have to hire employees you should be familiar with employment laws or have the expertise in someone you can hire.

Potential Challenges and issues may arise when you are not sure what skills and experiences your concept will need to become commercialized. You could also have learned that to hire all the necessary talents and infrastructure will cost much more than you anticipate or can afford. Finally you could potentially make the same set of classic mistakes as most new entrepreneurs by hiring wrong, too soon, or too little.

6.3 BUSINESS SYSTEMS & PROCESSES

AN INSIDER'S INSIGHTS

Business infrastructure is the combined set of information technology software and hardware systems and their related processes. It takes an integrated approach to ensure that information flows seamlessly from one end of the company to the other. The best example is reflected by a customer's purchase experience.

Business operations and systems are where the rubber hits the road, or the moment of truth. It is here that a customer's expectations are either fulfilled or not. It is also here that a business can continue to earn customer loyalty or turn them away. All the marketing and sales activities may get a sale but if the operational support systems and processes don't support the customers, the hard-earned sales will fly away in no time.

In this section we will look at the underlying business systems and point out insights pertaining to designing them. There is also a list of questions to be considered when evaluating the business processes.

Even the greatest ideas with the best strategy and action plans will go nowhere without successful implementation. Your ability to execute flawlessly has much to do with how your company's infrastructure is set up. Of particular importance is its ability to meet the company's goal on cost efficiently.

A correctly set up infrastructure with its systems and processes will create an efficient and effective operation which in turn saves money and makes money. A poorly designed or incoherent infrastructure is a recipe for disasters and emergencies both of which can cost the company to lose businesses in many ways.

Taking a customer-centric approach to managing your business has always been regarded as a smart move. But for a small business or a new venture it has become more imperative than ever.

There are two reasons for this:

1. Small businesses rely on word-of-mouth marketing in a disproportionately higher level than large businesses. This reality is a double-edged sword in the sense that good services may get mentioned sometimes but a bad service experience can spread like wildfire online. A customer-centric approach limits such bad presses.

2. Whereas large businesses have a hard time reinventing or realigning their existing processes, small businesses and startups have an opportunity to begin with a clean slate to designing the various components of the company's infrastructure. Each component can be designed to work with the others in proportion and synchronization.

If designed correctly, a company's infrastructure design can optimize its operational efficiency which in turn contributes to better operational profitability. In this scenario it becomes a competitive advantage and a barrier to entry for the competition.

6.3.1   DESIGNING BUSINESS SYSTEMS

Designing with a clean slate allows you to apply two guidelines:

 Model the Company's Systems and Processes on a Sale Order

A sale order is what a customer cares about most. From the moment they place an order to the time the order is fulfilled and the product or service delivered, there is a sequence of events that must happen. These events are enabled by operational systems and driven by operational processes. By mapping out what happens to a sale order at each step you will be able to identify the system capabilities and the information needed from A to Z.

In order to produce the capabilities you will need various systems. For example, in order to accept an online order and process it for credit you will need the shopping cart module of an eCommerce system.

The type of information needed to be passed along the systems will help you create processes. For example, if your order fulfillment policy is within one day, then the customer and order information need to move from the eCommerce module to the fulfillment system within one day and still allow time for shipping pickup. The process that governs such movement of information will need to be written and understood by the people who manage the systems. In doing so you create an infrastructure that is manageable, controllable, predictable, and easy to troubleshoot.

Within each process are detailed procedures that people will follow to ensure the process is implemented consistently. When you run a tight ship in the operations area you are more likely to be in control of the customer experience and your costs.

The most critical piece for building systems, processes, and procedures is seamless communications among them. In this example it is all about getting the right data flowing downstream to shipping and tracking. Anyone familiar with Enterprise Resource Planning systems (ERP) should readily appreciate this approach.

The customer interface piece of the infrastructure is often referred to as frontend, as in the storefront. Production, inventory control, warehousing, fulfillment, eCommerce, and accounting systems are all backend systems. They all need to work seamlessly together to provide a smooth buying experience. The flowchart below shows a very high level example:

For example, how much warehouse space you will need is linked to how many orders you expect per month. That in turn is tied to your marketing campaign

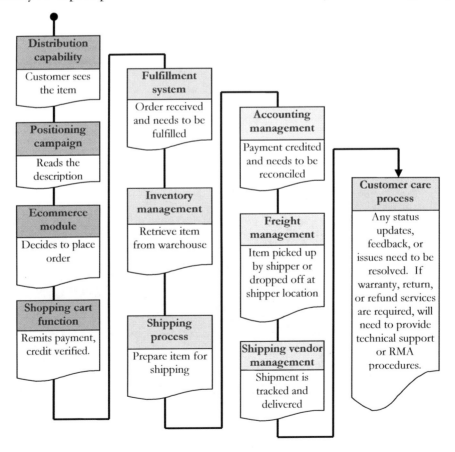

level and expected sales units. The quality of your product and the expected defect/return rate should dictate your customer service's capacity.

Think of the business infrastructure as a residential house. A house is designed with a certain number of occupants in mind first. The capacity of its HVAC systems are then designed to match the amount of expected usage. You would not want to put a 100 gallon hot water heater for a house meant for four occupants; it would be a waste of energy most of the time.

2 Design Scalable Systems and Processes in Proportion to the Overall Business Scope and Company Size

When it comes to capital-intensive investments like buying IT systems and equipment, or renting office spaces and warehouses, you always want to think two steps ahead but work on the here and now.

Business infrastructure is about having strategy and systems working together. How profitable a business might become could be somewhat predicted based on how well systems are aligned to the business strategy.

It is said that as people age with experience, their views of the world becomes more shades of grey instead of the absolutes of black and white. As business is a part of life, it should come as no surprise that the understanding of how a company works likewise incorporates more shades of grey with experience instead of the absolute ends of a spectrum.

The following figure illustrates the concept that as a company grows, its various components also need to grow in synchronization:

If your venture or a licensee's company is in the mid-size range (X), then each and every one of the infrastructure components should be in alignment with each

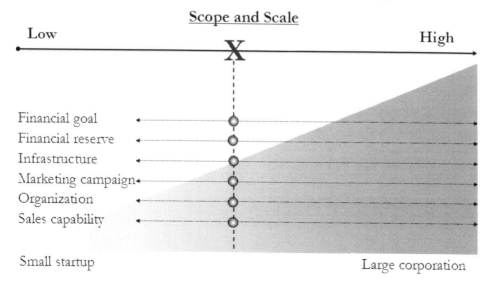

other in capability or capacity. They should also be scalable to match potential growth. Otherwise you can expect operational issues such as over or under capacity, inability to deliver as promised, underutilized resources, etc.

To read this figure you would slide a ruler across the spectrum. Scalability means that as you move from left to right on the spectrum the company's scope and size increase. Synchronization is depicted by the small spheres where X intersects each component. As you move up and down the various company infrastructure components the spheres should align. If you understand this paradigm then you will be better able to scale your business design up or down while making sure everything works proportionally and in synch for now and future.

For example, the annual sales goal of a small startup may be $500K and a corporation may need to make $500M. Their respective cost structures and gross profit margins are also different; the larger entity would need a higher revenue and profit margin to pay for its larger operation. In this case the intersecting spheres would be closer to the right side on the financial goal and reserve lines.

The financial reserve of a typical small company will limit its infrastructure capability. For a small business or a typical startup you would not want to set up an infrastructure meant for a large operation only to find that the revenue could not sustain the operational costs because your marketing budget is limited. Similarly you would not want to hire as many employees as a mid-size company while your backend system is only geared for a small operation. Such discrepancies in capacity cause operational tension in the system. Imagine a company's infrastructure as a gearbox. If the gears are not in the right ratio, then the box would not work as designed. Designing a company's infrastructure is no different than this basic principle. Everything must be designed to work in tandem to prevent dysfunction.

By the way, the most important thing about launching a business and managing it successfully is not about efficiency (to the dismay of process-oriented people). It is certainly not because you had a great idea (sorry, inventors). It cannot be wholly attributed to the execution (great project managers are not the only reason). It also cannot be attributed to the perception created around the product/service (although marketers and spin doctors would like to believe so). Many would say that it's all about distribution (only partially correct, although not to the business development person). Finally it's not even due to timing (what good would timing be if everything else is not). The true reason is a synthesized view and approach that keeps everything in balance and in check at all times to ensure success.

A real life example of strategic misalignment is in the year 2001 when home grocery delivery was thought to be the next groundbreaking business model. A well known case at the time was Webvan[9] which had nearly $8 billion of market capitalization and made zero profits. They spent $1.2 billion of that cash reserve building a state-of-the-art distribution center in Oakland, California. This was during the early days of commercialized web technology which enabled online food shopping.

This was one company who took the next seemingly logical step of ramping up its distribution facility with robotic technology, thinking that superiority in technology was the key to dominating the market. Not long after the facility was completed the company went bankrupt.

The reason was simple. Changing people's habits and lifestyles with technology takes time. And few orders a day simply could not pay for the capital expenditure and operational costs of something so gigantic. In this case the operations facility and systems were in alignment with the strategy, but the strategy was faulty because it failed to consider technology adoption rate, a phenomenon that was well studied for years. The end result was a financial disaster.

Technology or innovative products are enablers, not drivers, of a business. They are certainly no substitution for a well defined business strategy that takes the human dimension into account.

6.3.2 BUSINESS PROCESSES

Whereas designing operational systems is about matching business components with the overall strategy, creating business processes is about aligning systems with people.

Matching the best race car with an inexperienced driver equals potential disaster. This is equivalent to implementing the best systems but man them with poorly qualified or mismatched human operators. One way to rectify such a situation is to provide training to suitable operators while producing business processes that clearly illustrate the flow of the business.

If you take the business process creation a step further, you could pinpoint methods and procedures that spell out every step in an operational environment for the human operators. This applies to experienced as well as new employees. Well documented processes with clearly written methods and procedures help cut down confusion as well as new employee training time. It is a task that is well worth doing. If nothing else it will allow you to delegate certain duties to others knowing that they have guidelines to follow and be accountable to.

---

[9] There are quite a few case studies and background information on Webvan on the internet. One such source is Wikipedia®. Wikipedia® is a registered trademark of the Wikimedia Foundation, Inc., a non-profit organization.

Business Infrastructure Questions to Consider

This list of questions is by no means comprehensive in covering all systems and processes concerns. Its purpose is to help stimulate your own set of questions pertaining to your own business situation. Whether you intend on launching a business or rely on a licensee to commercialize your concept, asking these questions can help to clarify the picture and to make right decisions.

- ◈ **Facility**
    - What is the capacity of your business facility needed to be fully operational?
    - Does the facility require up-to-date technology in order to compete on an equal footing?
    - What are the yearly maintenance costs of capital equipment and systems?
    - Do your competitors have an advantage because of their systems and equipment?
    - Have you determined whether to lease, own, or outsource your operations?
    - Is the cost to own or lease the facility acceptable and in alignment with the product's life cycle expectations?
    - Is your business facility scalable relative to potential growth?

- ◈ **Technology**
    - What are the functions and features of a technology under consideration? Is it necessary or just helpful?
    - What is the total cost of the technology to purchase, implement, provide training, and maintenance (including making changes)?
    - How proprietary is the technology behind the required operations systems? In other words, what is the penalty for switching to others?
    - How do advances in technology affect your product and business?

- ◈ **Systems**
    - Are the required systems for business operations readily available, or do they need to be built from scratch?
    - A sample listing of business systems:
        - Data and communications systems

- Frontend customer interface technology
- Customer relationship management
- Order and payment processing
- Inventory management
- Warehousing management
- Shipping and freight management
- Supplier management
- Management reporting
- Accounting & tax reporting

Customer interfacing

- What is the level of customer interface required for the business transaction?

- Does the customer interface system or process address support functions on order processing, questions, feedback, and return issues?

- Does the customer interface system or process entice customer good will, loyalty, up-sell, viral promotions, or repeat business?

- How difficult is it to define and cultivate the desired customer service culture and processes?

- What is the level of training required for the customer facing staff?

Information flow

- Are you able to create business processes required to integrate disparate operations systems?

- How difficult will it be to implement the processes, including publishing the methods and procedures for each job function?

Integration

- What is the level of integration between the frontend customer interfacing system and the backend order fulfillment systems?

- Are the internal business processes and operating procedures in alignment with the business growth strategy?

- Are the internal business processes and operating procedures compatible with the corresponding counterparts of suppliers, service providers, regulators, and business customers?

Evaluation Questions: Appendix 4 Section 4-3, 4-4

Business Systems   section 4-3

● Do you or a licensee have a business infrastructure strategy that incorporates customer-centric systems, processes, and methods and procedures?

● Will you or a licensee be able to identify and implement all the necessary infrastructures and systems based on their costs?

Business Processes   section 4-4

● Will a licensee's or your system and processes align to the current company size and business scope while being scalable for potential growth scenarios?

● Is there a process map that captures the entire customer experience, including both frontend and backend processes and procedures?

HOW DID YOUR CONCEPT DO?

Ideally you will have developed a clear understanding of your company's objective and resources. With that information you will identify a process by which you can create customer satisfying experiences and promote your business. In order to do this you will have mapped the entire process in a flowchart, and then identify the necessary information technology systems needed to perform each step. Within each step you will also be able to identify the processes involved in the movement of goods, services, and information. You should be able to write down specific methods and procedures for each process so that an employee or contractor can competently perform the required duties.   All this should be done with you looking ahead to potential growth and understanding that all of your systems and processes need to grow with the company, or in other words, be scalable.

Potential Challenges and issues include not thoroughly understanding the company's vision, financial goals, and resources in order to map out the necessary infrastructure needs. This is a challenging task to say the least. You may run into cost issues when you realize that the systems you need are too expensive. You may also make the mistake of purchasing software or hardware only to find that they are not scalable. One possible scenario is that you could choose the wrong vendor and become stuck with their product and services even as you try to leave. The cost of migration might be too great.

> A well designed business process takes the guesswork out in the future.

CHAPTER 6 ACTION ITEMS

1. Identify the necessary types of intellectual property protection your concept needs.

2. Formulate a protection strategy that includes acquisition and enforcement.

3. Research legal protection for your intellectual assets and physical assets. Obtain them as you build your concept and business infrastructures.

4. Research insurance protection for your product and business, acquire them if you will be going into business.

5. Identify service providers and vendors. Research each and determine how to work with them.

6. Design your business operating systems and processes as if you will be going into business with your concept. Otherwise understand what it takes to deliver the product or service even if done by someone else. This will help with negotiating licensing royalty.

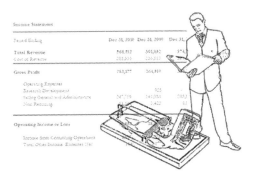

Chapter 7

Financial Considerations... Is It Worth Doing?

The final and most important piece of the evaluation process looks at the financials. After all, doesn't everyone ask whether their idea will make money?

To do a thorough job of assessing a concept's commercial viability you need to perform both **qualitative** and **quantitative** analyses. While marketing-centric questions are more qualitative in nature, financial questions provide the quantitative analyses that validate the preceding marketing presumptions. It is here that the numbers either make sense for your concept to go to market or will stop it in its track. For the typical inventor money is much harder to earn than to spend; moving forward carries major financial implications and should be backed by a substantiated decision.

I remember selling lemonades with neighborhood kids at the heart of Harvard Square, across the street from Harvard University. We correctly assumed that people would be thirsty walking around and would not mind buying lemonade from a bunch of kids in the midst of a hot summer afternoon. We didn't quite know how much to charge per cup so we arbitrarily set it at 50¢. Meanwhile the costs of sugar, bottled water, and lemons from the convenience store next door were quickly adding up. After six hours of hard work we each walked away with a (very slight) profit. Looking back, that afternoon of fun and work taught us a very practical lesson which was that cost must be considered before launching a business.

Managing business finances is a critical task that should be handled by someone with such expertise. Although evaluating invention commercialization shares some common steps as that of a new product introduction process in corporations, the differences lie in rigor and depth. Aspiring entrepreneurs tend not to have the resources or professional expertise to handle every aspect of the process as professional teams of managers do. We will similarly not explore financial management in depth here but will instead focus on profitability potential and the ability of a concept to attract capital investment.

The topics in this chapter provide background information to the questions in Section 5 of the evaluation list. The examples use numbers from Appendix 5 sample financial statements. We will focus on costs, revenue generation, profitability, financial projections, breakeven analysis, cash flow, capital requirement, ROI, funding strategy, and royalty.

If launching a business or licensing your concept proves out to be a viable option, I would strongly urge you to read up and understand the basic managerial financial control principles in much more depth. Besides financial books there is free information from government and non-profit sites on financial asset management.

7.1   COST

AN INSIDER'S INSIGHTS

Of the number crunching you will do, identifying cost factors is the first step. It allows you to calculate a product's retail price, wholesale revenue, and profit margin. Collectively these four key figures provide the central basis in determining the go/no go decision for your concept.

There are many types of costs involved with bringing a concept to market. The initial development and modeling costs familiar to inventors are almost always miniscule when compared to the subsequent costs of establishing a company and running a business. You need to pay attention to two particular classes of costs. The first is Cost of Goods Sold (**COGS**) and the other is Sales, General and Administrative (**SG&A**) expenses.

Business activities also generate other secondary costs such as the cost of financing, capital equipment acquisition, and income taxes, etc. For the specific purpose of profitability assessment we will focus on COGS and SG&A.

COST OF GOODS SOLD

The term COGS essentially applies to all the direct costs incurred from making a finished product to a point where it is ready to be shipped to distributors or retail customers. They include:

- ◈ Production costs (material and labor)
- ◈ Testing and inspection costs
- ◈ Freight cost, including customs inspection if applicable
- ◈ Packaging cost as part of a shelf-ready product
- ◈ Insurance cost on the inventory
- ◈ Warehousing and fulfillment costs

In some cases some of these costs are not capitalized as part of the inventory cost. This is where an accountant can help with determining the accounting structure.

At this point it is a good place to differentiate cost from price as they are sometimes used interchangeably but erroneously. Your cost is someone else's price if you pay him or her. For example, a factory quotes you $10/piece, which is your cost and their price. Conversely your price is someone else's cost if they pay you (e.g. your selling to distributors or consumers). This clarification is necessary in order to understand the financial perspectives of each person in the distribution food chain when looking at their profit margin requirements.

The base number you will use the most is the unit cost. Unit cost is calculated by dividing the <u>total cost incurred in making the product available for sale</u> by the quantity of units made. Here is a numerical example:

Let's say we need to produce 10,000 units of SnapIt! to meet the minimum quantity dictated by the factory. Your cost is:

$4 per unit for production material and labor

$2 per unit for packaging material and allocated art designs

$2000 for testing and inspection by a 3rd party

$5000 for ocean freight

$500 for customs inspection and trucking to the warehouse

$2.18 per unit for warehousing and fulfillment

Your COGS would be 4 + 2 + [(2000+5000+500)/10,000] +2.18 which comes out to be $8.93 per unit.

Sometimes you will hear people say that your product's price needs to be at least 4x or 5x of your cost. This is the cost they are referring to. By that scheme your retail price would be $35.72 to $44.65 respectively. However, as you will soon see, this is a rule of thumb approximation only.

SALES, GENERAL AND ADMINISTRATIVE

SG&A costs associated with running the business are not used in establishing a baseline for the retail price. These other costs are not directly related to the product and therefore reflect more about the company's management efficiency.

In fact the SG&A number is used to calculate operations profit which is a financial indicator of a business's operational effectiveness and efficiency. A positive quarter to quarter increase in the operations profit shows that a company is getting better at generating profits without tweaking the direct costs. This will make more sense in the profitability section where different profit margins are looked at.

SG&A expenses consist of these components:

- Selling: Cost of marketing and sales, which includes promotional expenses, sales salaries and commissions, and all expenses and taxes directly related to selling the product/service.

- General: Operating expenses that are related to the general business and operation activities not accounted for within the other two categories. They include insurance, rent, and miscellaneous costs.

- Administrative: Non-sales salaries and benefits related to managing the business.

These expenses are typically not allocated at a per unit basis although some accounting practices do recommend measuring and allocating such expenses from general business activities to product lines, even down to a per unit basis. For the purpose of evaluation it's more important for you to be able to identify SG&A costs than to get into their role in accounting.

HOW CAN YOU TELL IF COSTS WILL INCREASE?

The biggest culprit that wrecked havoc in the AeroBloks venture was cost. There were many simultaneous cost increases for the AeroBloks product. The largest increase was in the raw material, which was vinyl. Vinyl is a direct byproduct of petroleum. The oil price crises from 2004-2008 created unprecedented cost control headaches in almost every aspect of business cost management for us.

There are telling signs of potential cost increases even if you don't have a crystal ball. Check out Yahoo Finance and do an industry research for your concept. You may find stock analyses that discuss trends in raw material. In our example the hypothetical hand tool SnapIt! invention belongs to the small tools & accessories industry, in the Industrial Goods sector.

You can also do primary research to call and ask factories or factory reps if they anticipate any cost increases. You will need to determine whether any projected increase is an isolated situation or if the entire industry is anticipating the same. For example, in 2008 ocean freight cost was projected to increase by 50% from 2007 since the price was reset annually. In that case no matter whom you ship your goods with, the cost increase would be universal.

Granted, hindsight is 20/20 and no one could have foreseen the oil crises development, there is still a lesson to be learned. If the raw material of your product (e.g. steel for the SnapIt! tool) is subject to global demand and political influx, the so called "geo-political" influences, then you need to find out more about what could potentially happen to the cost of your raw material.

Evaluation Questions: Appendix 4 Section 5-1

- Do you have sufficient data to identify the total cost per unit for your product or service?

- Are the cost elements for the product likely to remain stable or will they fluctuate/increase?

HOW DID YOUR CONCEPT DO?

Ideally your concept will have this set of conditions to work with: stable costs, not rising, low demand on raw material (domestic as well as global markets), steady labor supply, fixed compensation, and non-unionized work force.

Potential Challenges can exist in many forms. Unpredictable and simultaneous increases in labor and material costs can greatly stress a business' financial state. Sharp increases in advertising costs, travel costs, selling expenses, and operations costs are some categories that increase with inflation. Another cost factor is currency exchange rate. If you import/export then the money you pay to your suppliers or money you receive from your customers could have less value if currency exchange is not in your favor.

One less known cost factor to new entrepreneurs is the cost of doing business with distributors. Some large distributors will require inventory build-up before agreeing to buy; this is to ensure that they don't run out of stock to sell. If they don't do a good job selling, the inventory may end up back on your books. If the quantity is significant then such arrangements could bankrupt a small operation.

Another issue is with minimum production quantity. Factories will often dictate a minimum quantity in order to quote you the production cost you need. This quantity may exceed your capacity to warehouse or distribute for quite some time. For inventory with limited sales cycle this could be problematic.

In answering the evaluation questions you should consider the product's industry and a typical company's capability in that industry to control their costs. When the tide comes in all boats will rise, but the wave will rock the smaller boats more violently. So if yours will be a small business to start, you should weigh the considerably higher impacts and the lack of a financial cushion to absorb unforeseen cost increases.

All these situations present cost variables often ignored in the initial profit calculations, which is all the more reason why the costs need to be clearly identified.

7.2   REVENUE GENERATION

AN INSIDER'S INSIGHTS

What revenue is...sometimes called the top line; it is more accurately referred to as **sales revenue**. (See Appendix 5 Income Statement)

Revenue is not income. It does not include any other source of income such as those from investment or rental activities, etc. It is money paid by customers for goods and/or services rendered. The net remainder after paying out expenses is income or profit.

Revenue is calculated by multiplying units sold x price. It is earned one unit at a time if you sell directly to consumers and one account at a time if you sell to distribution channels. When selling directly to consumers, simply multiply the quantity of units sold by the retail price you charge. In most cases, however, businesses rarely succeed without relying on other distribution and sales channels.

From a revenue perspective, the retail price of a product is "eroded" with each additional layer of middlemen. Your revenue is what is paid to you by a wholesale distributor or a retailer/reseller next to you in the food chain.

Let's use the SnapIt! example to clarify:

> Revenue for the year 2010 is **$568,512**
>
> This is from sales of the product, and excludes any other income. This revenue is calculated by the wholesale price ($16.23) x units sold (35,020).
>
> Whereas if the product were sold directly to consumers, then it would be the retail price ($49.95) x 35,020 units = **$1,749,249**

Who wouldn't want to reap the higher revenue? But the reality is that without distribution channels and middlemen, the number of units sold would quickly dwindle. Distribution channel plays an essential role in raising product awareness and putting it where consumers can easily make the purchase.

Within the framework of a food chain, even if you outsource everything and never physically create a product, when you are the source of the product's creation you are considered the manufacturer.

Based on its COGS, the retail price of SnapIt! needs to be at a minimum $49.95 (see 7.3 Profitability section in this chapter on how this number is derived). But as a manufacturer who sells to a distributor which in turn sells to a retailer, you will only see a fraction of that retail money from the consumer's pocket. Recalling that the COGS is $8.93 per unit, in this case your share would be $16.23 per unit at a profit margin of 45%.

Assuming also that you have a distribution network of 1750 stores selling on average of 20 units per year (a reasonable assumption), your annual revenue would be $568,512. Whereas the retailer's collective revenue would be $1.75M.

Keep in mind, however, that this scenario uses the bare minimum floor pricing of $49.95, which is calculated using a cost-plus approach. This approach defines what the lowest retail price needs to be after each player in the food chain is fed with his profit margin requirement.

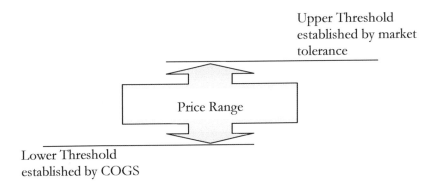

Meanwhile, as suggested in the marketing and sales sections in Chapter 5, pricing is an art and not a mechanical approach. A price range needs to be established with the lowest and the highest thresholds. The low end in this case is $49.95, and the high end is based on competitive pricing and perceived value statements.

Many factors affect a product's revenue generation capability. Amongst them three stand out. They are: product's seasonality, its ability to maintain market demand, and whether it entices repeat, affiliated, or accessories sales.

Seasonal products have limited windows of opportunity to generate revenue. Meanwhile, a build up in inventory costs money. Discounting merchandise that should have generated full revenue also hurts the bottom line. This type of product would require much better timing and planning.

Maintaining demand is harder than one thinks. Constant competitive pressure and substitution products vie for the consumer and therefore the distributor's attention. If a product cannot be evolved or improved with new features or add-ons, it risks being outdated quickly.

Cost of customer acquisition is a major factor in a company's profitability makeup. If a product is a onetime sale type of transaction without any accessories, and is especially built well, then to generate another sale would require more marketing and sales dollars. Products that entice repeat sales, such as modular units, reduce such revenue generation cost. Products that encourage affiliated sales such as separate attachments and extra batteries or waterproof pouch as in the case of SnapIt! can generate much more revenue beyond a single sales event.

Evaluation Question: Appendix 4 Section 5-1

- Can you determine the retail price range and the product's/service's revenue?
- If your product is seasonal, can the business be maintained year round?
- Does the product generate repeat sales or revenue from accessories?

HOW DID YOUR CONCEPT DO?

Ideally revenue should be predictable based on planned marketing strategy and controlled sales efforts. If price sensitivity is low, then raising prices would be relatively easier. Revenue would preferably be a constant stream from repeat sales and generated without much human interactions (think about how credit card companies can process millions of transactions without human interventions).

Potential Challenges and issues include inconsistent revenue stream and amount, as well as any cyclical or seasonal nature of the demand for your product/service. For example, if your goods/services are designed for the winter months, then cash inflow could create a problem for other seasons. Other problems include demand fluctuations, fading demands, and substitution or knockoff products that siphon away your revenue. Lastly, if your product is built to be indestructible and has no potential for add-on sales or repeat sales, then you might be looking at limited revenue per customer or sale.

> Revenue is directly tied to pricing, but don't make the mistake of pricing based on target revenue. It would be like designing a pair of gloves then trying to find the right hands to fit them.

7.3   PROFITABILITY

AN INSIDER'S INSIGHTS

Profit is the most important factor you need to consider even if it is not the first thought that crosses your mind when you initially develop an exciting idea.

Running a company's finances shares the same bottom line principles as managing personal finance; you want to make more than you spend. The key to doing this is to understand the basic terminologies and how to manage them.

RELATIONSHIP BETWEEN COST, REVENUE, AND PROFIT

Calculating profit is fairly simple and straightforward, but managing the relationship of these three elements is anything but straightforward. Take a look at this diagram below. Each element is dynamic, and can move up or down (increase or decrease) at anytime.

As cost increases, if revenue is fixed because of a price ceiling, then your profit gets squeezed. To maintain profit margin, companies raise prices in times of inflation.

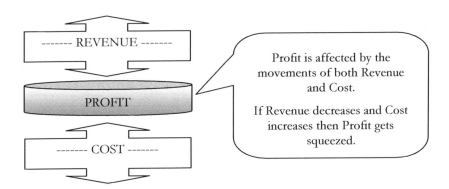

Toys and luxury products, especially non-essential entertainment (some people would rather starve than to give up their cable service) tend to be the most vulnerable to inflation, recession, and other economic swings.

The key point is that you must understand where your product lies relative to the need vs. want and essential vs. non-essential scale. You also must look out for any foreseeable cost increases in its production cycle and possibly sales cycle. Having awareness allows you to be better prepared when your profit margin is reduced even if it does not insulate you from the impacts.

Some Definitions

It is a fairly common practice to use a product's gross profit margin (**GM**) to assess whether it is a good business to be in, and how well it is positioned amongst other products in its industry sector.

To calculate gross profit margin you will need to know the gross profit, which is calculated with this formula:

Gross Profit = Revenue – COGS

For SnapIt! the 2010 gross profit is $255,831, which equals to revenue ($568,512) minus COGS ($312,681).

Contrast the gross profit to net profit (net income), which is $13,504. Net profit is gross profit minus all the other expenses and adding all other income, then subtracting any interest expenses and taxes owed. This figure is the true profit for the business. It is the amount that is equivalent to the money put into a personal savings account after all the bills have been paid.

Gross profit margin is gross profit expressed as a percentage of revenue.

GM = gross profit / revenue

In this case it is 45% (255,831 as a percentage of 568,512)

This is not to be confused with the other two types of accounting profit margins, namely operating margin and net profit margin. For the purpose of this evaluation we will focus on using the gross profit margin to assess the health of a potential concept turned business. If you are curious about the other two types, one good source of explanations is www.investopedia.com.

How Gross Margin Affects Pricing

Here is a table that illustrates how an item's cost is marked up through the food chain. It includes the gross margins of the players and how they in turn affect the retail price. The cost information corresponds to the sample income statement in Appendix 5.

	COGS	Cost %	Price	Profit	GM
consumer	$ 49.95	-	-	-	-
retailer	$ 24.98	50%	$ 49.95	$ 24.98	50%
distributor	$ 16.23	65%	$ 24.98	$ 8.74	35%
manufacturer	$ 8.93	55%	$ 16.23	$ 7.31	45%
factory	$ 6.25	70%	$ 8.93	$ 2.68	30%

In this example, using the SnapIt! financial data, you can see that a consumer pays $49.95 for a SnapIt! hand tool set. The hardware store (retailer) paid $24.98 for the unit to the wholesale distributor, making a 50% GM (a common practice known as keystoning).

The distributor needs to maintain a 35% GM for his business, so he paid $16.23 to you the manufacturer. As the manufacturer you need to maintain a 45% margin which is at par with the rest of your industry. You paid $8.93 to the factory per unit. The factory in turn had COGS of $6.25 that it paid to its labor force and raw material suppliers.

All in all, something that costs $6.25 to produce and $8.93 to be ready for pick up costs $49.95 to the consumer.

This structure is quite common for household goods and other everyday inventions. So if you took the $8.93 (manufacturer's COGS) and divide into the retail price of $49.95 you will get approximately 18%, which is pretty close to the 20% (5x) rule of thumb on pricing.

Here's another view from the manufacturer's perspective:

Manufacturer's perspective		
Revenue/unit	$	16.23
COGS/unit	$	8.93
Profit/unit	$	7.31
Profit margin		45%
Annual units		35,020
Revenue	$	568,512
COGS	$	312,682
Profit	$	255,830
GM		45%

What Is A Profitable Business?

A positive net profit shows that a business generated positive income after all the expenses have been paid. Notice that profitability is not measured by the amount of revenue. If you earned $1M of revenue but spent $1.5M to get it, you would have been better off spending that $500,000 loss at a beach resort for two years!

Once again we look to the Income Statement in Appendix 5 and see that the business launched around the SnapIt! invention was profitable three years in a row. If you do the gross margin analysis you will see that its GM went from 56% to 53% to 45%, which tells a slightly different story. However the analysis is far from complete if the rest of the companies in the same industry are not used for comparison. The moral of the story is that a company must be profitable year to year, and its GM must be in alignment with its industry if not doing better to be considered a good investment.

Period Ending	31-Dec-10	31-Dec-09	31-Dec-08
Total Revenue	568,512	501,032	574,724
Cost of Goods Sold	312,681	235,485	252,878
Gross Profit	**255,831**	**265,547**	**321,846**
GM	45%	53%	56%

The gross margin is a useful number to gauge the relative health of a business because it measures ratios between revenue and cost. A profit margin of 45% indicates a cost margin of 55% relative to the revenue. If cost increases, then to maintain the gross margin it would necessitate either a corresponding increase in revenue or finding some ways to counter the cost. As the gross margin fluctuates it provides information on how the product's sales revenue is doing relative to the cost of producing the goods. At the same time it functions like a barometer in showing how the company is doing relative to other companies in the same industry.

Where can one find the margin information for the industry? The US Census Bureau has gross margin as a percentage of sales data on retail businesses. They can be found here www.census.gov/retail. Another possible source is an accountant who is familiar with your type of business.

For example, in 2008 these select industries have gross margins of:

INDUSTRY	GM
Motor vehicle and parts dealers	17.8
Furniture and home furnishings stores	45.3
Electronics and appliance stores	24.8
Building mat. and garden equip. and supplies dealers	31.8
Food and beverage stores	29.0
Health and personal care stores	30.4
Gasoline stations	14.6
Clothing and clothing access. stores	43.8
Sporting goods, hobby, book, and music stores	37.8
General merchandise stores	26.1
Miscellaneous store retailers	44.3

When I started the AeroBloks business I was not aware of the toy industry's gross margin structure and its particular impact on retail price. I made the classic mistake of not factoring the margin requirements of a distributor and accounted for just the straight manufacturing cost, which didn't include packaging design and box, crate, freight, customs, storage, handling, etc. By the time the total cost was identified, we were forced to sell direct, not wholesale, since there were not enough margins built into the equation for everyone in the food chain. This initial mistake severely limited our market visibility and distribution for quite some time.

Evaluation Question: Appendix 4 Section 5-1

● Do you have enough information to do a profit analysis for your concept?

● Is your concept's projected profit margin in alignment with the industry's norm?

● At a very high level, will your concept have the potential to be profitable?

HOW DID YOUR CONCEPT DO?

Ideally a profitable business will generate positive profits consistently and increase them quarterly or annually.

A solid business will have a gross margin that is higher than its competitors in the same industry sector.

A good business will consistently generate future profits even if the first couple of years end up in losses. This is expected for most businesses because the initial developmental expenditure plus the infrastructure building, and the eventually marketing and sales expenses all add up quickly before the first dollar is earned.

A healthy business will have sufficient gross margin to buffer against downturns in sales for a period of time. Its GM will also be maintained even as cost increases because of its ability to raise prices correspondingly.

Potential Challenges and issues often rise from external operating environments. Or put it another way, unexpected things often happen outside of your planning.

Lots of things can impact a company's ability to earn profits. Rising costs, competition that drives away business, economic conditions (e.g. decrease in the demand of the product or service), loss of marketing and sales channels, and operational inefficiency over time all negatively impact the bottom line.

Sometimes an entire industry is hit with unforeseen disasters such as the toy industry in the great recession of 2007. In that case only those with deep pockets or higher than most gross margins will be able to weather the storm.

7.4   FINANCIAL PROJECTIONS

AN INSIDER'S INSIGHTS

Financial projections are essential tools used to simulate financial outcomes of a business operation ahead of time. Sometimes called a budgeting tool or a pro forma profit and loss projection, the purpose is to crunch the numbers and see if there are issues that can be spotted ahead of time. As pertained to the evaluation process, it is used to project profitability as well as capital requirements.

This is an exercise that cannot be dismissed. Beyond seeing whether and when the bottom line (net income) is positive, in the process it will help you identify all the cost elements and see where the income is coming from and where the expenses are spent.

If done correctly (as realistically as possible), it can be used for budgeting and capital acquisition. If not done at all or done poorly, it could mislead you into thinking about the earning potential of your concept when it may not even exist, or worse yet, that it would cost you financial losses.

HOW TO DO PROJECTIONS

Most people use a financial spreadsheet like Microsoft Excel® or an accounting system like QuickBooks® to plug in data and run the calculations. The cost information should be as realistic as possible while the revenue projections should be as down-to-earth as possible.

Typically the assumptions used to project the income and expenses are grouped into three categories. There should be a conservative model, a realistic model, and an aggressive growth model to simulate the what-if scenarios when your concept is launched as a business. Conservative assumptions naturally assume lower revenue and higher costs than the realistic model assumptions. Aggressive assumptions would be the other way around.

There are at least a couple of guidelines to begin with. First you will need to create an income statement-like structure where revenue and expenses are separated. Next you will want to identify revenue sources and as many possible types of expenditure that the business would incur.

Sales revenue is the most straight-forward. Simply use the revenue equation described earlier. However, simplicity does not mean easy. Many newbies make the mistake of projecting revenue based on a certain percentage of the market size. I made the same mistake as well. If you were a large established company that has mature sales tools and forecasting tools, this might be the right approach. However, for someone with limited market-influencing ability, the right approach is from a bottom-up process.

Whereas pricing should be a top down approach based on value and market tolerance, sales projection needs to be counted one unit or one account at a time from zero. You can do this with primary research. One way is to ask a retailer directly about his interest in selling your concept/prototype at your suggested price. You should also determine the number of units they are willing to buy each time, and the frequency per year. If multiple local retailers share the same enthusiasm and projection, then you can comfortably use the quantity and price information in your realistic projection model.

> Sales revenue is counted one unit at a time!

If, on the other hand, the responses of your potential sales channel is at best lukewarm or the quantity they are willing to carry is minimum, then you need to rethink about your revenue projection as well as the marketing and sales dollars you may have budgeted earlier.

To do a reality check, let's assume that the industry size is $2B, and you modestly assume that you just need to take 1% of its revenue. That figure comes out to be $20M. Sounds reasonable right? How many units will that equate to? In the case of SnapIt! it would be 1,232,286 wholesale units. If a retail store is willing and able to sell 20 units a year, you would need 61,614 stores. How will you reach and sell to this number of stores? It should be obvious by now that this approach is a pie-in-the-sky approach even if it sounds reasonable!

Setting Up the Projection Format

There are three sections of data to crunch. The first section, revenue calculation, begins with sale revenue per unit, followed by the quantity of units expected to be sold. Multiplying revenue per unit by the quantity yields the expected revenue. If you sell through national chain stores, you might be expected to contribute to a clearance discount for inventory not sold within a particular period. In that case you would reserve a percentage (e.g. 15%) of the product at (e.g. 30%) discount as an assumption.

	Conservative	Realistic	Aggressive
Sales revenue per unit	$15.00	$16.23	$17.50
Units sold	20,000	35,020	45,000
Clearance discount	($13,500)*	($25.577)	($35,438)
Total sale revenue	$286,500	$542,797	$752,062

* 15% of 20,000 is 3000 units. Each unit would receive 30% less revenue as part of the "contribution" to clearance or promotional expenses of a national retailer. Therefore 3000 units x 30% of $15 = $13,500 that you might have to give back, out of a potential $300,000.

Notice that as the assumptions change, so do the revenue projections. This same 3-column format should be used to project costs and therefore generate the net incomes.

The second section contains **COGS** per unit, multiplied by the number of units sold to yield the total gross profit. With that information you should also calculate the gross margin.

The third section should capture as many of the **SG&A expenses** as you can identify. They may include:

◈ Administrative salary

◈ Marketing costs

◈ Sales costs

◈ Systems costs

◈ Operations expenses

◈ Capital expenditures

◈ Interests paid on borrowed capital

◈ Income tax rate

In the end you will calculate the net income by subtracting the SG&A expenses and any interest payment and/or tax liability from the gross profit. If your gross profit is sufficient to pay for all the necessary expenses and still generates a net profit, then it's a good scenario to start with.

A PIECE OF PIE

How would you know what the appropriate percentage of each cost element is within the total SG&A expenses account? How do you know if you are spending too much or too little in a particular business area? One way to tell is to look at another company's income statement and do a percentage of expense analysis. Public companies are required to file their financial statements and they are available online at Yahoo Finance or Google Finance.

Keep in mind, however, that the income statements of these companies are from established operations. At best they serve as a guideline to where you want your product based business to be once it is on track but not necessarily how you should allocate your current spending.

In most cases if you are in a startup situation most of your expenditure will go towards concept development and then marketing and sales. Not only would you have to prove your product/service but you would also need to prove your business to the world.

Here is an example of the expenses allocation from the AeroBloks venture captured during a moment in time:

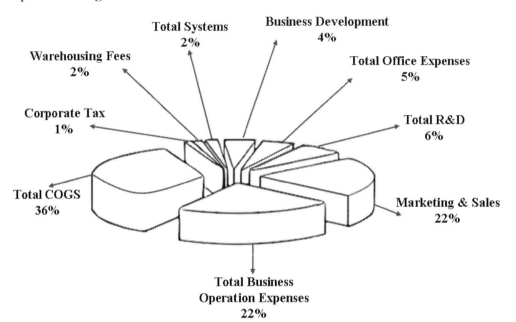

Another thing to keep in mind is that the proportion of the expenditures shifts within the total budget as a company grows. It is necessary and natural for a new entrant to spend a lot more money on marketing in order to establish brand awareness. It is also natural for a company to work on the next iteration of product after the first two years of introduction, thereby spending less on R&D during those first two years.

Pro forma statements or financial projections are best guesses. It may be a good idea to project on a quarterly basis when first starting. Once the business follows a particular pattern then you can project on an annual basis.

Evaluation Questions: Appendix 4 Section 5-1

- Do you have enough information to run financial projections on three scenarios for your concept?

- Are your projection assumptions backed with solid research?

- Does your projection allow for unforeseen developments or significant changes in the data values?

- Do you know the typical expenses allocation scheme for your type of product based business?

HOW DID YOUR CONCEPT DO?

Ideally you should have revenue numbers based on verified sales channels and not based on vague assumptions like % of market share. Cost information is accurate and stable. Profit is generated in all three scenarios. The percent of expense allocation is similar to established companies, meaning that the new operation can be as efficiently run as the more established operations.

Potential Challenges and issues include faulty projections due to incorrect or overly naïve assumptions. This can be caused by a lack of in-depth understanding of the target market, or a failure in gathering sufficient and realistic cost data. A failure to account for cost increases or substitution products that erode sales revenue in time can also generate a false picture.

For AeroBloks, we were content with the then-current cost information which would skyrocket within a year of launch. What we missed was the oil industry and material cost projections produced by market research firms. These reports had early warning signs that global demand for oil was projected to rise quickly. Due primarily to the cost of these reports (in the thousands), we opted not to subscribe to them. That turned out to be a costly mistake.

Even if the projection is calculated correctly, the result can show that a new venture's gross margins are nowhere close to the industry's average margin. In this case it is an indicator that the venture's cost basis may be too high, price is too low, or operations is inefficient, or the barrier to entry to the target market is too high and expensive (a reflection of marketing and sales efforts).

7.5 BREAKEVEN

AN INSIDER'S INSIGHTS

Breakeven is a concept that simply asks the question of when you will make zero profit, or stop making a loss. The calculation is useful in helping you get a sense of the sales quantity required to reach that time.

Theoretically, once you hit that breakeven number, making money will be a lot easier because fixed expenses have already been spent and now will begin to be recouped. Variable expenses such as salary and per unit sales costs will then constitute the primary cost of business which should in turn boost your profit margin.

To calculate the breakeven point, take a look at these two scenarios below using this equation:

PROFIT   = **REVENUE** – **COGS** – **SG&A** (ignoring tax for now)

                 = (unit price x qty) – (unit COGS x qty) – SG&A

                 = qty (price-COGS) – SG&A

<u>**Scenario 1** (assumption is 20,000 units sold, data taken from Appendix 5)</u>

Profit   = 20,000 ($16.23-$8.93) - $220,413

           = **($74,413)**

<u>**Scenario 2** (assumption is 50,000 units sold, data taken from Appendix 5)</u>

Profit   = 50,000 ($16.23-$8.93) - $220,413

           = **$144,587**

Therefore if you sold only 20,000 units in 2010, you would have incurred a loss of $74,413 instead of a profit of $144,587 if you sold 50,000 units.

To calculate the breakeven quantity, simply recognize that any gross profit generated from the sales must also pay for the corresponding SG&A. Set them equal to find the quantity required.

         Units (price-COGS) = SG&A

       Units ($16.23 - $8.93) = $220,413

               Units = $220,413/ ($16.23 - $8.93)

               Units = **30,194**

You will have reached breakeven or incurred zero profit or loss if you sold 30,194 units for the year.

Evaluation Question: Appendix 4 Section 5-1

● How many units do you have to sell to breakeven?

● When will you breakeven, and is the timeframe within the product's expected shelf life?

HOW DID YOUR CONCEPT DO?

Ideally the business operation will hit the breakeven point as planned.   Beyond breakeven it can begin to reap cost efficiencies from scaled operations. This is predicated upon the accuracy of the projected cash flow, assuming that there is a high confidence level behind the data and the company's ability to achieve its target.

Potential Challenges and issues can be caused by any of the components. Amongst them sales volume could be much less than required to achieve the breakeven point in the time projected. In this case the business incurs a loss. Other problems can be due to cost increases, price caps, inefficient operations, or external forces that impede the business operations.

If your calculation yields a unit count that cannot be realistically achieved within the timeframe required (product shelf life, expected timeframe from investors), then you need to rate the concept/business lower and seriously reconsider launching the venture.

7.6   CASH FLOW

AN INSIDER'S INSIGHTS

Cash flow is a financial concept used to describe the movements between revenue and expenses. Calculating cash flow can be somewhat complex in accounting terms when some account (e.g. depreciation) is used to reduce taxable income but does not contribute to the free flowing cash, or liquidity, available for payments. For the purpose of concept evaluation we will stay with the more conventional usage of the term to mean managing the available and/or incoming revenue so that you will not get caught in an insolvent situation when payments are due.

There are two major levers in cash flow management, which are time and liquidity. Making sure that there will be sufficient cash on hand to make payments when they are due has to do with coordinating the time of cash coming in and going out. Liquidity is a measure of whether you can convert your assets into cash in a jiffy. Buildings and heavy equipment are not liquid, in the sense that if you have a big bill due immediately, you could not convert them to cash to pay your bills or debt without some delay or financial loss (discounted value).

CASH FLOW IS YOUR NUMBER ONE CONCERN

Everyday that your business is operating or even just existing, money flows out like water from a faucet. This happens even if you do absolutely no work.

This is because fixed expenses like rent, utilities, tax & licenses, full time salary, and insurance etc. continue to drain money from your company's bank account even if you don't make a single sale. The point is that you need to be cognizant of the cash flow. Imagine looking at a meter running for insurance, one for salary, etc., and you'll soon realize that revenue must continuously come in otherwise you would run out of cash very quickly.

If your type of business is product based, then your fixed expenditures would be much higher than those of a service-based business.

If you intend on mass producing then you will have a very significant capital investment which requires correspondingly large initial investments as well as subsequent expenditures such as warehousing, backend office systems for inventory control etc.

The spreadsheet below shows an example of a two-year cash flow analysis/projection broken down on a quarterly basis. You will see that the initial $200,000 seeding money is insufficient. It takes another $300,600 (sum of the encircled negative ending cash balance) to make it to a cash flow positive state in Q2 second year.

SnapIt!
Quarterly Cash Flow Projection

	Q1	Q2	Q3	Q4	Q1	Q2	Q3	Q4
Cash								
Beginning Cash	$ 200,000	$ 8,500	$ (57,000)	$ (149,800)	$ (88,700)	$ (5,100)	$ 112,500	$ 239,100
Cash Received	$ -	$ -	$ 98,000	$ 127,000	$ 165,000	$ 183,000	$ 192,000	$ 182,000
Adjustments	$ -	$ -	$ -	$ -	$ -	$ -	$ -	$ -
Total Cash	$ 200,000	$ 8,500	$ 41,000	$ (22,800)	$ 76,300	$ 177,900	$ 304,500	$ 421,100
Business Expenses								
Utilities	$ 1,000	$ 1,000	$ 1,000	$ 1,000	$ 1,000	$ 1,000	$ 1,000	$ 1,000
Rent	$ 8,000	$ 8,000	$ 8,000	$ 8,000	$ 8,000	$ 8,000	$ 8,000	$ 8,000
Salary & Benefits	$ 54,000	$ 54,000	$ 54,000	$ 54,000	$ 54,000	$ 54,000	$ 54,000	$ 54,000
COGS	$ 125,000	$ -	$ 125,000	$ -	$ 16,000	$ -	$ -	$ -
Adjustments	$ -	$ -	$ -	$ -	$ -	$ -	$ -	$ -
Total Expenses	$ 188,000	$ 63,000	$ 188,000	$ 63,000	$ 79,000	$ 63,000	$ 63,000	$ 63,000
Accounts Payable								
Vendor 1	$ 2,000	$ 2,000	$ 2,000	$ 2,000	$ 2,000	$ 2,000	$ 2,000	$ 2,000
Vendor 2	$ 1,200	$ 400	$ 600	$ 800	$ 300	$ 300	$ 300	$ 300
Vendor 3	$ 300	$ 100	$ 200	$ 100	$ 100	$ 100	$ 100	$ 100
Total A/P	$ 3,500	$ 2,500	$ 2,800	$ 2,900	$ 2,400	$ 2,400	$ 2,400	$ 2,400
Ending Cash Balance	$ 8,500	$ (57,000)	$ (149,800)	$ (88,700)	$ (5,100)	$ 112,500	$ 239,100	$ 355,700

Many small businesses go under not because they were not generating revenue or didn't hold significant assets, but because they were insolvent and could not pay their bills on time. Imagine what would happen if employees were not paid and suppliers withhold key components because you couldn't pay them on time. Similar to forced foreclosure of a house, the mortgagee owns the house but is forced to foreclose because he cannot produce the mortgage; an illiquid situation can force bankruptcy on small businesses quickly despite their owning any significant long term assets.

Before deciding whether or not to introduce a new product, corporations typically go through a capital budgeting process. A new business based on an invention requires the same discipline and approach. Determining cash flow for the project is a necessary component of the capital budgeting exercise. The ability of the management team to do this accurately can make or break the new business venture.

Cash flow management is a measurement more on the entrepreneur or the team behind the venture than on the concept or invention. Nonetheless some classes of products are more susceptible to cash flow issues than others. Products that generate large revenues in lumps with long periods in between while having to pay fixed expenses fall into this category. Jewelry stores do not have to sell a lot of jewelry because their profit margin is very high; their sales quantity is also fewer than everyday items. When a jewelry store has one big sale worth tens of thousands of dollars but does not have the cash reserve to pay for the ongoing SG&A expenses before the second big sales comes in, the business goes into insolvency.

One other potential scenario where cash flow gets a company in trouble is when a business gets involved in too large a sale without the capital reserve. Imagine a situation where a household product manufacturer secures an order worth five million dollars from a national chain store. The stipulation is that the order must be delivered to the US warehouse of the chain store by July for Christmas sales. In order to make this happen the product needs to be ready for shipment from China by May. The production cycle for such a large quantity is four months, which means production needs to begin in January. For the production to begin the manufacturer needs to have a firm order in the form of a Purchase Order (PO) from the buyer. The issue comes in when the buyer states that payment will not be rendered until the goods have cleared customs and in their warehouses. Furthermore the payment term is net 90 days after receipt, and not upon the issuance of the PO.

Whether this large order is a blessing or curse depends on the manufacturer's cash reserve. Let us assume that gross margin is 25%, which means the turnkey production cost is 75%, or $3,750,000. The factory requires a 40/40/20 payment schedule which says 40% of payment is due upon receiving a PO from the manufacturer, 40% is due at the shipping port, and 20% is due upon customs inspection at the US warehouse. Given this payment schedule, the manufacturer would have to pay $1.5M in January, another $1.5M in May, and finally $750,000 in July. Meanwhile, the manufacturer would not get paid the $5M until October. This translates into an out-of-pocket expense of $3.75M cash for 10 months. If the manufacturer has to borrow this amount of money, he would be paying interest for the duration on the whole amount.

A lot of things can go wrong in the interim; the manufacturer faces a potential risk of the inventory not made to the buyer's specifications, thereby canceling the order. The buyer could change the quantity in midstream and cause financial issues. The testing and inspection could fail. Customs could hold up the shipment for prolonged inspection, etc. and the list goes on.

Meanwhile, the manufacturer is still operating a business and paying all of its fixed expense. If the payment from the buyer is in anyway reduced, delayed, or cancelled, that could spell the death of the business.

Evaluation Question: Appendix 4 Section 5-1

● Are you able to perform a cash flow analysis with accurate revenue for a venture based on your concept?

● Is your type of product/service more susceptible to cash flow issues?

HOW DID YOUR CONCEPT DO?

Ideally the revenue projection is accurate and income is largely predictable. The future business operation has a large cash reserve, guaranteed good paying customers, low accounts receivables, favorable payment terms from factory, an ability to get revolving line-of-credit loans, and an accounting system for regular monitoring of cash flow.

Managing cash flow is not rocket science; all you need is a good accounting system and the knowledge of the elements that contribute to cash flow. However you do need to have financial management understanding even if only at a rudimentary level. Either you or your management team should have the financial expertise to accurately produce a cash flow projection. A more difficult task is in determining whether your product would produce the type of cash flow problems described here. If the sales projection calls for increased revenue then the matching cost of sales must go up. If your product is a low margin, high quantity type of goods, then your account receivables must be prompt. If your product is a high margin, low quantity type, then you must have a large cash reserve or assets that can be converted to cash quickly to pay for daily operating expenses.

Potential Challenges and issues are diverse. A few common causes of cash flow issues are:

1. A mismatch between accounts receivable and accounts payable. In other words, the money you expect to receive does not come in time to pay for the bills you expect to pay.

2. Unfavorable payment terms from powerful buyers.

3. Delays or non-payment from your customers.

4. Long production cycle which lengthens the time between down payments paid to the factory and payment to be received from the buyer.

5. Tied-up cash in inventory, capital equipment, or building etc. that are not producing revenue.

6. Over leveraging of business capability, as in the example given above.

7. Inaccurate revenue forecasts or pricing that reduces revenue.

8. Unexpected large cost increases in both COGS and SG&A.

7.7   CAPITAL REQUIREMENTS

AN INSIDER'S INSIGHTS

Nowhere does the adage "you need money to make money" exposed more clearly than in a capital budgeting process. Capital budgeting is the quantitative approach of the go or no go decision that companies of all sizes make with existing or new products. The exercise can get quite intensive and technical and should be prepared by someone with financial analysis background and expertise.

For the purpose of concept evaluation, we will focus on two types of measurements. The first is the easiest but does not generate lots of detailed return on investment data. It is called the payback period analysis.

PAYBACK PERIOD AS A DECISION CRITERION

Payback is essentially a concept that tells you how long before the capital investment can begin to be recouped. It is somewhat similar to the break-even analysis in that you are looking for a point in time where loss equals zero and begins to turn into profit. If this period is too long or is beyond the shelf life of the product, then obviously the venture should not be pursued.

To calculate payback you will need to do the cash flow projection with best guess revenues and costs. You will also need to know the amount of initial capital (a.k.a. seeding money) you need.

Let's look at the hypothetical cash flow projection in section 7-6 of this chapter. You will see that in the first quarter of year 1, an initial amount of $200,000 was injected to begin the venture. There was no revenue since there was no production and no sales, yet expenses began with equipment purchase, utilities, salaries, and professional fees that generated a negative cash flow until Q2 of the second year.

In order to cover the negative cash in the sum of $300,600 from Q2 year 1 to Q1 year 2 , the venture needed more cash infusion in that amount. This additional amount plus the initial investment of $200,000 is the total capital required until the business can begin to sustain itself with positive cash flow. The sum of $500,600 would be the total capital investment required in this hypothetical projection.

In terms of payback period, the way to think about it is to ask how long it would take to make back the total investment of $500,600 from the venture's operations. As it turns out, it is some time between Q3 and Q4 of year two. The calculation involves taking the initial investment of $200,000 and subtracting the negative cash flow number until the result turns positive. Since there is still $8,500 left in Q1 year 1, the amount actually spent was $191,500.

Visually it is easier to understand if you set up a table that shows how the cash amount accumulates and at which point becomes positive:

	Q1	Q2	Q3	Q4	Q1	Q2	Q3	Q4
Quarterly Cash Flow	$ (191,500)	$ (57,000)	$ (149,800)	$ (88,700)	$ (5,100)	$ 112,500	$ 239,100	$ 355,700
Cumulative Cash Flow	$ (191,500)	$ (248,500)	$ (398,300)	$ (487,000)	$ (492,100)	$ (379,600)	$ (140,500)	$ 215,200

Some time between Q3 and Q4 of the second year the cumulative cash flow turns positive. To calculate the exact time, you would see that as of Q3 year 2 the cumulative cash flow is a loss of $140,500. By Q4 year 2 the cumulative cash flow is a positive $215,200. This means that a portion of the $215, 200 is used to pay down the negative $140, 500 with a remainder of $74,700. Assuming Q4 year 2 cash flow comes in evenly, then the $74,700 is divided into the Q4 cash flow which equals 35% (74.7/215.2). The amount of time is therefore approximately 1/3 of a quarter or just one month. The exact moment of payback is then 1 year 3 quarters and 1 month, or 22 months.

NET PRESENT VALUE (NPV) AS A DECISION CRITERION

Using cash flow to calculate capital requirement and the time it takes to recoup the investment is a form of **return on investment (ROI)** calculation. The family of ROI calculation methods consists of many variations using different components of a company. For instance, there is **return on assets (ROA)**, **return on equity (ROE)**, and a whole slew of other measurements designed to measure a company's financial performance and payback.

Larger companies tend to use the net present value method to decide whether to launch a new product. This is a much more sophisticated approach and requires an understanding of the cost of acquiring capital from investors. The concept is essentially to apply a discounted cash flow analysis that calculates future income stream at today's value using a discount rate known as the cost of capital rate.

Small companies and private companies tend not to have that type of ROI calculations because they do not have common stocks issued as a form of equity funding. Instead, they rely on a mix of loans and private equity for their capital infusion needs.

The fact that they don't have a public equity-based cost of capital rate does not necessarily prevent them from performing the more sophisticated **net present value (NPV)** calculation. Net present value is used to ascertain whether a project is worth pursuing. The theory is that a project/venture is worth pursuing if during the course of its lifespan it produces a positive return for the company, after paying all expenses and debts.

> **Net present value measures what the combined future earnings will be in today's dollar**

To do this, the future cash flow stream is discounted by a rate that represents the cost of borrowing/acquiring the capital investment over the product's lifespan (number of years) to arrive at the present value in cash. The total sum of this discounted cash flow stream in today's money value is then compared to the total capital investment. If the NPV of the total cash to be earned is more than the investment, then it makes quantitative sense to go with the venture. If not, then the venture will generate a loss overall and should be discarded.

NPV calculation requires the cost of capital rate, which is synonymous to borrowing rate in a basic sense. Depending on the source of the capital investment, there are different rates. For example, there is the cost of debt rate (debt), the cost of preferred and common stock rates (equity), cost from the issuance of bond, and finally the **weighted average cost of capital (WACC)** approach that takes the different rates and assigns each the appropriate weight based on the total investment portfolio.

For a small company or private company, the closest thing would be the interest rate plus any processing costs. Borrowing from banks, credit card companies, etc. will result in different cost of capital rates. Using such rates to discount future cash inflow to the present value is a workable substitution of the other cost of capital rates typically used by publicly held companies.

Using Microsoft Excel® built-in NPV function, the projected cash flow for the first two years is:

NPV calculation

	Q1	Q2	Q3	Q4	Q1	Q2	Q3	Q4
Quarterly Cash Flow	$ (191,500)	$ (57,000)	$ (149,800)	$ (88,700)	$ (5,100)	$ 112,500	$ 239,100	$ 355,700

Annual rate	12%
Quarterly rate	3%

NPV of cash flow	$304,258 (calculated using 3% quarterly rate)
Project Earning	$112,758 (NPV minus initial investment)

Here we see that the projected cash flow over the two year period (assume is less than product shelf life) discounted with the cost of capital rate of 12% annually yields a present cash value of $112,758 after subtracting the initial effective investment of $191,500. This means the project will be positive and generate $112,758 net profit in two years. Since this is within the expected shelf life timeframe, it is a go decision. Of course the time horizon would typically be longer but for the purpose of a sample illustration we will assume the future cash flow will be large and positive by year 2 of operation.

Evaluation Question: Appendix 4 Section 5-1

- How much capital do you need to run the business until it becomes self-financing?
- How long is the payback period for the capital investment?
- What is the cost of capital for the project?
- What is the Net Present Value for the project?
- Is the venture worth doing from a quantitative perspective?

HOW DID YOUR CONCEPT DO?

Ideally the project will have a low cost of capital, easy access to capital, generates positive cash flows almost immediately, has a short payback timeframe, and a positive net present value of future cash flows.

Potential Challenges and issues will center on the quality of the calculations and their underlying assumptions. The accuracy of the results can be far from reality if any element is off target. To do the return on investment assessments here you will need to have a reasonably accurate financial projection complete with realistic cash flow numbers.

Even if the payback period is acceptable, the actual projection beyond payback may be iffy at best due to unforeseen developments. Keep in mind that quantitative measurements are only a part of the decision process; qualitative assessment based on experience and knowledge might be even better for small businesses who don't have an army to do this type of calculation.

If the cost of capital is too high, then even with the best idea in the world, the venture would not be able to make back the investment money; the decision would be to stop altogether.

The lack of understanding on the return of investment on part of the entrepreneur needs to be addressed. Launching ahead without this type of quantitative analysis could potentially be devastating.

7.8 FUNDING STRATEGY

AN INSIDER'S INSIGHTS

Once you know the amount of capital infusion your venture needs, the next logical step is to determine how much funding you need and where to get it.

When it comes to acquiring the investment needed to launch a venture, most people naturally default to VCs as their first choice. This isn't necessary the right approach for every type of business. It really depends on the type of invention, product, or business concept.

The right approach considers a few factors. The type of concept, the amount required, your preference for risk and rewards, and the available funding sources all play a role in coming up with a funding strategy that spells out the 5Ws + H details.

WHERE CAN YOU FIND THE MONEY?

There are essentially three sources of funding: self funding, debt funding, and equity funding.

Self funding is by far the easiest since there is no need to pour over a business plan in order to justify why someone else might see your proposed business as a good investment. Not everyone has the deep pocket to launch a business, or for that matter, a capital-intensive business that is typically associated with everyday products. Some people dip into their retirement funds, which is considered a very risky move and not advised by most financial advisors.

Debt financing sources include credit cards, bank loans, and small business loans from institutions. Credit cards carry the highest interest rates and are subject to compounding. Bank loans usually require collaterals and may be just as risky; betting one's primary residence in pursuit of a highly uncertain outcome is indeed risky. Small business loans from the SBA and other government agencies likewise may require collaterals for secured loans or an excellent credit rating for unsecured small business loans in smaller amounts. All loans have to be repaid whether your business succeeds or not.

Equity financing is an exchange of your company's ownership (in stocks) for cash. This can happen sometimes if the factory making your product has the interest to do a joint venture with co-ownership. They may produce the products in exchange for ownership in stocks. VCs tend to invest in high tech companies with promises of large returns. In 2010 the national average of VC investment was allocated to the software industry at 18%, biotechnology at 17%, and in contrast consumer products and services only at 2%[10]. Angel investors operate at a lower level per se and are more willing to invest in a variety of industries. Both will require much higher returns on their investment than the everyday investment vehicles like stocks and bonds.

Credit card interest rates can be up to 20% compounded monthly. As of this writing small business loans average about 8% for amounts less than $100,000. This rate obviously will fluctuate daily and is used only as a rough reference here. VCs like to see investments that return ten times or more, which is 1000%. A $50,000 investment would ideally return $500,000 to the VCs when they either cash out their shares at an IPO or when the venture is sold. Contrast this with the forecasted return on stocks (S&P 500) of 7% that stock market investors can expect in 2011 by the Federal Reserve Bank of Philadelphia, [11] a $50,000 investment would generate $53,500 in one year from the stock market.

MATCH MAKING

Let's use SnapIt! to illustrate a reality check. Suppose you need funding for the entire capital requirement of $500,000. If a venture capitalist invests that sum for 50% of the company, then in 5 years time (give or take) he would expect his share to grow to $5M for 50% of the company. This means the company will need to

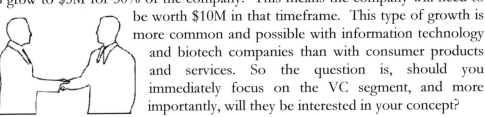

be worth $10M in that timeframe. This type of growth is more common and possible with information technology and biotech companies than with consumer products and services. So the question is, should you immediately focus on the VC segment, and more importantly, will they be interested in your concept?

Getting funding is typically not an all-or-nothing ordeal. More likely there will be a mix of the funding sources. In fact funding tends to be done in stages such as seeding, early stage, growth, and later stage (before IPO or sale of company). To maximize your share you will need to have a funding strategy.

Different investors have different risk tolerance and returns expectations. If you opt for equity investment you will need to research your target investor and match their preference for the type of companies to invest versus yours. Otherwise you might be wasting your time and money while barking up the wrong tree.

The following table provides a bird's eye view of the funding sources and risks:

---

[10] NVCA Venture Capital Investments Q4-2010 – MoneyTree Results - National Data

[11] Federal Reserve Bank of Philadelphia 10-year forecasted return rate for S&P 500

Venture Type	Probability of Failure	Funding Type	Funding Source	Impact on Founder's Finance
Startups	High	Loan	Credit card	Highest
			Bank lines of credit	
			Small business loans	
True Innovations	Extremely high	Self	Savings	Mid
			Retirement funds	
		Equity	Vendor financing	Lowest
			Angels	
			VCs	

Startups by nature are a high risk investment. If your concept is truly innovative, it may add yet another layer of risk on top. Innovations take time to break into a market. Truly innovative products or concepts require a learning curve and acceptance timeframe from the market place. As such it may burn more money than you anticipate while paying for marketing mistakes that pave the way for later entrants who first watch on the sideline then take over the market shares.

Your risk tolerance and objective for payback will dictate how you fund your venture. Unless you are able and willing to lose all of your investment in exchange for 100% of the potential payback, otherwise you should remember that 5% of something is always better than 100% of nothing. This simple logic applies in both the amount of equity you are willing to exchange for funding as well as your willingness to take a backseat and get royalty in return for licensing your concept.

Where you want to be is well capitalized, but not to the extent of getting excess investment. Initial projections are almost always unrealistically optimistic. Surprises and events that derail your original plans are almost a guarantee in real life. Being well funded gives you a substantial competitive advantage over others especially in a downturn.

Conversely you don't want to be underfunded. The investment money is in every sense a war chest. When you launch an entrepreneurial venture in an established industry, it can feel very much like fighting against large armies with an arsenal of your guerrilla entity. Although you may pinch and save in every way, eventually your smaller chest will run out sooner than an established profit center that gets replenished with cash. Plan carefully with more cash than you think you need is the safer approach.

Matching the funding sources with your needs is important. Think of the process as irrigating a plot of farmland where you will grow your crop. Imagine the cash infusion as the water source. If all goes well you will produce, sell, and make a handsome profit for you and the person providing the water. Depending on the size of land, the amount of water needed should be matched with the water source. You don't want to irrigate your small plot with downpours from a dam, or watering your crop one bucket at a time. Both end up in wastes (financial losses).

GETTING FUNDING WITH A BUSINESS PLAN

If you are planning on getting equity financing, there is no escape from preparing a business plan. In fact, some small business loans will also require this document.

There's a very good chance that preparing a business plan is something you loathe, as do most people starting a business. Just the thought of doing a ton of research, analyses, planning, and pulling-hair strategizing before putting all the information together in a professional presentation is enough to daunt even the most seasoned business person.

However, by the time you follow through the commercialization blueprint and arrive at the end of Phase II, you should already have all the major work completed. All that's left is a matter of organizing and presenting to your intended audience.

Developing a rough first draft of an outline where you can decidedly process the information in a systematic way is a good start. You can overcome the initial inertia often by simply tackling the smallest steps.

Points to consider when writing a business plan:

◆ Prioritize your content for your target audience. If finance is their primary concern, then put the financial analysis section first.

◆ What level of details is needed? Too much or too little have the same undesirable effects.

❖ What research is needed, how to get it, who will do it?

❖ What strategies are needed, who will work on it, who makes final decisions?

❖ Who will write and put it together?

❖ A business plan is a dynamic culmination of research, analyses, strategic formulation & projections, not just a fixed document. It can be used for future strategy revisions.

Business plans can in fact serve as another funding source by being entered in business plan contests. Granted, the awards money is most likely insufficient to launch any real business, it is nevertheless free money, if you can get it.

Evaluation Question: Appendix 4 Section 5-1

● Have you determined the most appropriate types of funding for commercializing your concept?

● Can your concept attract the amount of investment money required to launch a business?

● Do you have a funding strategy (5Ws + H)?

● Will you have a business plan ready for funding purposes?

HOW DID YOUR CONCEPT DO?

Ideally you can find the right match between funding sources and a business based on your concept. This can happen when you know who the right kind of investors is for the type of product/industry. This also assumes that you are connected to the community of investors, thereby have easy access to meetings and be able to make your presentations.

You will also have a business plan ready with all the marketing and financial analyses plus realistic ROI projections. Furthermore the economic condition is favorable where investors are flush with money, interest, and motivation for your type of concept.

Potential Challenges and issues can be caused by factors within and outside of your control. Your concept could be worth much less than you anticipate; the projected return from your business does not reach the amount of payback that investors require. You might have spent all the time preparing a great business plan but wasted all the time chasing down the wrong type of investors. Your financial projections, cash flow, and capital requirement may not match the risk tolerance level of your investors. You may not know the right people to pitch your ideas. The economy may not be conducive to investing in high risk startups.

7.9   LICENSING AND ROYALTY

AN INSIDER'S INSIGHTS

If you have proven that your idea is highly profitable, legally protectable, and meets a solid need of a target market segment, you should consider launching a business around it.

At the same time, you would need the money, talent, experience, and other resources to make it happen. If you happen to be that special individual with all these capabilities (or at least can afford them) then you have better odds of success than most people. Yet again, commercial viability and profitability are largely dependent on timing, circumstances, and luck. If you go alone you may garner all the profit but also risk all the potential losses. This is a very serious consideration unless you can afford to lose the investment in time, money, and quality of life.

YOUR OPTIONS

One option is to partner up with someone who has complementary skills or the resources you lack. A commercial partner such as a factory or even a venture capitalist may dramatically increase your capabilities. Both of these entities have the money, network, skills, or know-how to help commercialize your innovation. It is true that you will have to give up something, whether it is ownership shares and/or  control. However, 100% of a loss is much worse than 10% of a gain. Many aspiring entrepreneurs falter on the fault of being too greedy.

Another viable option is to let someone else who is better prepared to do the commercialization. You can sell the patent (not the idea), leave it to a product commercialization company and take a small percentage of royalty, or license it out directly.

It would be difficult to sell the patent without doing some research and finding the right buyers. This is not a simple and straight forward process. There are patent brokers you can find online but they require the same level of due diligence checking to ensure they have your interest in mind. Some product commercialization companies will help you launch the product into a business while others' business model is to prepare your concept to a point where they can then find licensees and split the royalty with you.

Licensing is typically difficult for the inventor of a patented product who has no industry relationships to speak of. As most first time inventors are unaware of the intricacies of the product development and promotional process, they tend to ask for too much money upfront. Many also make the classic mistake of thinking that their patents are commercially viable when in fact a company making similar products could readily determine that they are not. The first step is to do your homework and determine what the commercial worth is for your idea. This requires all the due diligence steps in the commercialization blueprint all the way to writing a business plan.

The point is that unless you know or can convince the potential licensee by demonstrating your knowledge of and projection of the market size, why should someone else spend anytime with you? They are potential investors of your innovation who will reap rewards by commercializing the product or service. They are not interested in anything that cannot already be substantiated. Your homework would be necessary whether you use it to justify funding or licensing.

By the way, most inventors call their inventions their "baby." In many ways the analogy works well. A concept needs to be nurtured every step of the way just like a child. Nobody wants to leave the parenting to someone else if they can help it. To license out your invention is essentially giving it up for adoption. Before you do that, would you not want to make sure that the adoptive parent is qualified? Product re-launches are rare and can get very expensive. You may only have one chance to get the "adoption" done correctly. This is all the more reason why you need to do your due diligence.

Depending on the type of product the royalty could be anywhere from 1% to 10% of the licensee's **sales revenue** (not the product's retail price), or 5% to 15% of their **net profit.** It is important to differentiate the two arrangements.

For example, if a product's retail price is $100, the licensee's revenue may be $60 wholesale, and his profit may be $10 after subtracting the direct and indirect costs including tax. A 7% payoff on his revenue is $4.20 in your pocket. Compare this to 15% of his profit which is only $1.50. Be sure to understand the financial projections carefully before agreeing to the percentage.

Retail	$100
Wholesale	$60
Profit	$10

What is a reasonable royalty for your product? That depends on many factors. Readiness and market demand will largely dictate what a licensee is willing to pay you, after deducting his expenses. There is no definitive answer to this question but inventors looking for such information can find a collection of sample licensing arrangements on the invention statistics website.[12]

---

[12] See http://www.inventionstatistics.com/ for a sampling of royalty fees paid in different scenarios.

Because ideas are essentially "worthless," production costs money, marketing effort payback is unknown, and actual sales volume may depend on a slew of factors, a 5% licensing royalty fee is actually quite reasonable. From a licensee's perspective, it is a fixed expense equivalent to his development costs if he had come up with the idea and patented it himself. A licensee would not be interested in your idea unless he can make money from it during the product's foreseeable lifecycle.

Time is a major factor. The longer the lifecycle the better it is for an inventor who wants to license out his invention. As the inventor your concept development cost may be recouped in a couple of years by royalty payments. Any payment you receive beyond this payback period is purely a bonus. Yet a licensee is required to continue to pay for the equivalent of the development cost for the duration of your agreement. So the lesson here is that no one likes a short product lifecycle but in the end the inventor makes more if the lifecycle is long.

According to the Idaho Small Business Development Center, the original inventors of companies that became publicly traded on average retain about three percent of ownership.[13] Let's take a look at what this translates to in terms of the worth of ownership verses that of royalty payment.

Scenario 1 – public corporation

Sales revenue is $500,000

Assuming the industry's multiplier for business valuation is 2x sales revenue, so company is worth $1M

Inventor's **ownership** is 3% of a company; 3% of 1M = **$30,000**

Whereas royalty would be:

Assume 5% of revenue = $500,000 x 5% = **$25,000/year**

Clearly it is better to be taking royalty in this situation. However, you should realize that this scenario is not realistic as most public companies generate revenues in the millions, not hundreds of thousands. Nevertheless the calculation methodology is the same.

For a company with sales revenue of $50M, valuation of $100M, the ownership would be $3M while royalty would be $2.5M/year. It would still be a better deal to license than to venture.

---

[13] Small Business Development Center of Idaho – Commercialization Planning

Scenario 2 – small private company

For small private companies the ownership may be up to 50% if you choose to launch the venture yourself with funding. In this case the **ownership** would be worth $1M x 50% = **$500,000**.

If you license it out, let's assume a 5-year agreement, the royalty payment would be $25k/year x 5 years = $125,000.

Before you decide that ownership is better, remember that the **royalty** payment of **$125,000** is for doing no work in production, marketing, or operations on your part. It is pure gravy.

Software products can command much higher royalty precisely because there isn't much production cost per se other than the physical packaging. Therefore if your product is software based, you can perform this calculation using a much higher (up to 50%) royalty payment to justify ownership or licensing.

When you are ready to negotiate the royalty %, you should be aware that the final figure depends on several factors. They are:

◆ Royalty range is typically 1-10% of sales during life of agreement

◆ The product's value proposition to intended users

◆ Sales potential/market size

◆ Costs associated with production

◆ Newness of invention (innovation) relative to its adoption curve

◆ IP protection strength and the barrier to entry (difficulty to knockoff)

◆ Readiness of invention, whether it is shelf ready or requires refinement

◆ The product's ability to enter the existing market, especially if the industry is capital intensive and well established

◆ Financial considerations: GM, revenue, cost

◆ Terms of agreement: duration, shelf life, exclusivity

Evaluation Question: Appendix 4 Section 5-1

● Is it worthwhile to pursue a venture or is royalty payment a more practical approach for you?

HOW DID YOUR CONCEPT DO?

Ideally you will find several conditions when you are tackling this question:

Your calculations result in a clear, quantitative comparison of the future cash flows between the licensing vs. venture scenarios.

Multiple reputable licensees with resources and distribution channels share the interest in your concept, and determine that it makes better sense to license it from you than to develop one internally.

Licensing terms are fair and equitable. Any exclusivity is countered by guaranteed minimum quantity, well defined territories, and payment schedules.

Your cost information is confirmed by potential licensees to be accurate.

Potential Challenges and issues begin with inaccurate or missing assumptions and cost information. Such mistakes distort the comparison and make the exercise not meaningful.

Furthermore your concept does not have a high market demand. Potential licensees may already have developed similar products or do not see the need to license when they can develop it internally.

You may also find that limited potential revenue makes licensing not worthwhile for both sides of the negotiation table.

Another likelihood may be that a licensee locks in on a contract but fails to pay and does not provide the means to audit their sales revenue. Worse yet, the licensee may have an ulterior motive such as to license and kill/wither your product by intent.

CHAPTER 7 ACTION ITEMS

1. Understand the financial terms and their inter-relatedness for your product or service.

2. Identify all the cost factors.

3. Research and determine a price range for your product or service.

4. Make financial projections and determine whether your business will be profitable.

5. Determine the amount of capital your venture will require.

6. Identify funding options and develop a strategy to get funding.

7. Research licensing options as needed.

Part IV

PUTTING THE C2C SYSTEM INTO ACTION

"Vision without action is a daydream. Action without vision is a nightmare."

Japanese proverb

Chapter 8

The C2C Progress Monitoring Framework… Staying In Control

In a nutshell, this was the simple exchange between a friend's question and my answer, a few years after the launch of our venture.

8.1 WORKING WITH THE PROCESS

There is the right way and the wrong way when it comes to commercializing a concept;   it may be "wrong" in the sense that the path taken could have been shortened and not be as costly.

It is common knowledge that experienced entrepreneurs stress that it's not the product that determines how successful your idea will be, but the marketing strategy behind it. The right approach is to develop an idea, research the market to see if there is a need, do some preliminary financial analysis, and if you get green lights all the way, then work on the prototype. The wrong approach would be to take an idea and immediately spend thousands of dollars on prototyping and patenting, and then try to define or even create a market to sell it and hopefully make money.

So if this is fairly common knowledge then why do most inventors continue to go about the "wrong" way? The answer lies in the word "experience," which is more accurately stated as business experience.

For someone lacking the exposure on how products actually move through the market, the "wrong" way may be the only logical way she knows to go about discovering the path. People in the engineering and hardcore science disciplines tend to fall victim most to this predicament. This is not a fault per se but a deficiency. Someone may be a genius in the sciences, a prolific inventor, or a master mechanic, but may be poorly equipped to tackle a very different type of intelligence. Products created in controlled environments can only go so far into the world of business without expertise in the more fluid and chaotic interactive ecosystems of commerce. Folks in marketing and sales by comparison understand the rhythm and reality of commerce and therefore have an easier time doing it the "right" way.

I know of two inventors who exemplify this explanation. Donna[14] is a marketing person who has come up with a pet product idea. She understands that no matter how great she thinks her idea may be, the market may tell her a completely different story. Her first step was to research that particular industry sector to see if it was growing. Next she did a segmentation analysis and discovered that her idea could be sold in some of the market segments. She then built profiles of her most probable customers using demographics and usage data. With that data she turned to professional designers to help her build a working prototype, which she then used for refining her design, marketing messages, and funding pitches. She is fairly confident based on her online research and surveys via social network groups that she has a ready pool of potential customers.

Laura is a chemical engineer in a multi-billion dollar corporation. She has come up with a kitchen product idea that she's sure would be a hit. She had not seen it in the stores she's familiar with and had asked a few neighbors and friends if they thought the idea was good. Based on the limited positive feedback she proceeded to have a professional prototype made. On the verge of filing a patent she discovered that a similar product was already on a store shelf she had not visited. On further research she realized that the idea was not unique and in fact several products have been commercialized and are sold online exclusively. Now she faces the dilemma of whether to continue or not. If she continues she does not know how to compete against the entrenched companies. If she forfeits then she would have lost several thousand dollars to date. The decision is a daunting one because she has no solid information to act on. Both inventors are working professionals, well-educated, and smart. Whose predicament would you rather be in?

---

[14] All names and concept types changed

It's easy to pick Donna's path and follow suit, however most people will run into a familiar conundrum quickly. If the prototype is not to be made until the market research and financial analysis give a GO signal, how then do you conduct any evaluation or get feedback without the prototype? This makes Laura's approach seem much more logical.

The answer is not obvious which explains why most people end up making prototypes first, then getting the market feedback later. In this way spending money making the prototype is almost inescapable. In reality the answer to the conundrum lies literally in shades of gray as with most everything in life. The path you take and the progress you make are a function of the information available to you at a particular point in time. This dynamic will now be illustrated.

By now you have been exposed to the blueprint that details each step of the concept commercialization process. You have been introduced to the different players in a typical ecosystem. You have witnesses the detailed and involved exploration and rigorous analyses required to substantiate a go or no-go decision. And you have read the supplemental business insights to help you make a determination. These are all tools and components of the C2C system. What you need is a way to ensure that if you pursue the commercialization path, that you have a mechanism to monitor and keep all of your activities in synch, which is what business management is mostly about. That is the purpose of the framework to be described in this chapter.

8.2 COMPONENTS OF THE FRAMEWORK

This concept to commercialization progression framework has been designed for two objectives: (1) to be used primarily as a tracking and monitoring tool and (2) to provide insights into how well orchestrated and synchronized your activities are.

There are four parallel tracks depicting four concurrent business areas and their activities over time. Each track is shown as cone-shaped shades which denote the amount as well as intensity over time, much like the sound waves that propagate out of a bullhorn. The shaded regions represent major phases in the concept to commercialization process. Within each phase are steps in logical sequence.

1. **Product Track** – Represents the progression from concept to its finished commercial product form, including functional prototyping in midstream.

2. **Market Track** – Represents the progression from initial market exploration to full blown marketing campaign, including strategic planning in midstream.

3. **Operations Track** – Represents the progression from identifying preliminary resource requirements to company operational readiness,

including implementation of underlying infrastructures and related methods, processes, and procedures.

4. **Finance Track** – Represents the progression from disposal income spending to significant business spending, including funding in midstream.

8.3 HOW TO USE THIS FRAMEWORK

In theory, you begin your project where each business area is at its earliest timeline, therefore expending the least amount of activities, expenses, costs, or potential losses. In this case you will draw four dots, one per track, all aligned under step 1 of Phase I. As you take on each step of the process, you will consider all four tracks at the same time, weighing the collective information you obtain and deciding whether you should proceed to the next step.

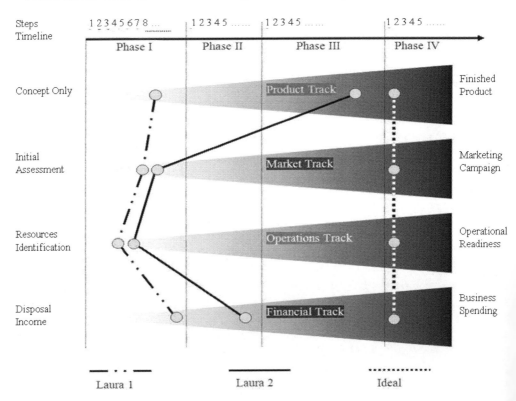

Concept to Commercialization Progress Monitoring Framework

In an animated version of the framework, the four dots on the tracks would travel serially from left to right over time if all the steps (activities) have been performed. A snapshot in time will capture their concurrent positions. A line connecting the four dots will show the relative synchronicity of their movement. <u>Ideally</u>

zigzagging is minimized. Skipping steps is not recommended since it often results in reworks in the future.

Here is one potential scenario:

In the beginning, you would have just the concept (*Product Track*), minimum market information (*Market Track*), a vague idea of the type of talents and resources you might need (*Operations Track*), and have spent next to zero dollars (*Financial Track*) on your progress.

In the next steps you discover that your target market is growing (*Market Track*), and you have identified that you will need technical help in building a website with eCommerce capabilities (*Operations Track*), but to get feedback you will need some rough modeling (*Product Track*) which requires spending only disposable income on raw material (*Financial Track*). A snapshot at this point will show a relatively straight line connecting the four tracking dots within phase I.

At some point in time you have acquired solid feedback and the decision is a go based on market research (*Market Track*). You need to tweak your model (*Product* Track) with professional looking prototyping material (a full functional one is not yet needed) to do the online video demo for potential distributors. At the same time you need to submit a non-provisional patent application (*Operations Track*). Both of these activities will now cost you in the hundreds of dollars (*Financial Track*). Given the progress to date and the information you have, this spending is justifiable.

Closer to the third phase you realize that getting funding is the next big thing (*Financial Track*) since you've done all your planning on marketing and infrastructure (*Operations Track*). At this point making the functional prototype (*Product Track*) will require several thousand dollars. Sending out samples to prospective distribution channels (*Market Track*) will cost upwards to tens of thousands of dollars. You need outside funding and proceed to prepare the business plan.

At the final stage you have secured funding (*Financial Track*) and acquired the necessary human and other resources (*Operations Track*). You have also fine-tuned your prototype several times based on buyer feedback and are now ready for actual production (*Product Track*). From this point onward you have a real business to run (*Market Track*) and will focus on the day-to-day product lifecycle management activities. The line that depicts this situation in phase IV on the graph is shown as (**Line – Ideal**).

Of course real life is never ideal, and most likely your actual progress will zigzag across steps on the timeline for each of the tracks. For example:

You might find yourself in Laura's situation where you cannot get real meaningful feedback until you produce a fully functional prototype (e.g. a kitchen product may need to work before people will commit to a serious interest). However, to get to that point you need to assess the market to make sure that all else indicate that the market segment you are after is healthy and growing, and that the demand exists for similar products.

As of now you are not sure that you want to start a company considering all the resources and infrastructures needed to bring it to market.

Meanwhile, the cost of the prototype is $300 for a real rough, non-aesthetic model, or $4000 for a fully functional, multi-colored and contoured model. You decide that since you don't yet have substantiated feedback that you should gamble no more than $300. This makes sense since you can also supplement it with either Photoshop images or in-person illustrations with props showing before and after images to produce a video that can get you the feedback you need.

At this point that would be a wise decision as no outside funding is needed, and the provisional patent costs only $110. Even if you later discover that market feedback discourages any further development, you would have only invested a few hundred dollars.

The progress line in this case will not be straight up and down; it will zigzag more on the product track, less on the marketing track, almost at the first step on the operations track, and maybe a couple of steps on the financial track (see **Line – Laura 1** on the framework).

If, however, you decide that you must develop the fully functional prototype and risk the financial loss, then your line will zigzag even more since you will have crossed into a darker shaded region (phase III) on the product track and likewise phase II on the financial track while keeping your marketing and operations progression relatively unchanged (see **Line – Laura 2** on the framework).

The goal is obviously to synchronize movements along each track as closely as possible. This would minimize risks while allowing you to obtain sufficient information to move systematically to the next steps and phases.

But in real life everyone knows that no business building ever goes smoothly; zigzagging is naturally expected. However, using this system will give you a visual cue on how well coordinated your activities are. If the zigzagging is overtly exaggerated, it becomes a warning signal that you are overstretching yourself or underperforming in one or more of the major business areas.

If you are not daunted by complexity, you might even enjoy taking this system to the next level, which is to shift the tracks to accurately depict your venture. In other words, the four tracks don't necessarily have to align as they are shown on the framework. For example, your particular situation may call for a much deferred infrastructure track because you have all the skills you need and are able to leverage existing plant and equipment, systems, and processes, etc. In that case your infrastructure track would be shifted more to the right (later in time).

8.4 DISSECTING THE FOUR SPECTRUMS

I hear the phrases **"proof of concept"** and **"proof of market"** tossed around loosely and often by people who do not fully understand the contents of either. Some people mistake proof of concept as showing that a prototype works while others mistake proof of market as getting positive feedback from a few people. This is very unfortunate. There are brilliant inventions that sit idly and "waste away" while the dream of commercializing them never materializes; it's a loss not only for the inventor but for the rest of us. What is actually missing from the equation is not just the marketing piece as most aspiring entrepreneurs have come to conclude, but an understanding and an approach to coordinating the various business aspects of the entire venture.

Some people may see the commercialization of a concept as a dual-track approach which contains product and business activities. This is a good start but insufficient. Let's look deeper and identify the four tracks and their components.

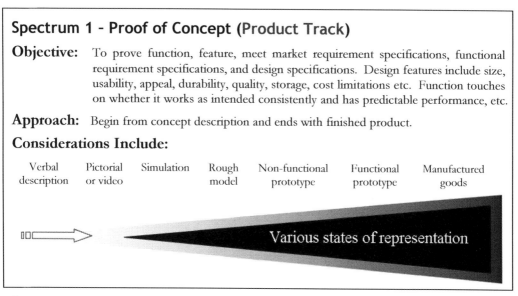

Spectrum 1 – Proof of Concept (Product Track)

Objective: To prove function, feature, meet market requirement specifications, functional requirement specifications, and design specifications. Design features include size, usability, appeal, durability, quality, storage, cost limitations etc. Function touches on whether it works as intended consistently and has predictable performance, etc.

Approach: Begin from concept description and ends with finished product.

Considerations Include:

| Verbal description | Pictorial or video | Simulation | Rough model | Non-functional prototype | Functional prototype | Manufactured goods |

Various states of representation

Spectrum 1- Here we see that proof of concept involves successfully meeting various expectations and can be represented in various states; some can be achieved without spending a lot of money. It is certainly not just about function.

Spectrum 2 - Market Validation (Market Track)

Objective: To prove that the market will buy and distribute the quantity needed to meet the financial goal.

Approach: Begin with preliminary high level research and analysis and resulting in detailed planning, strategy, and execution.

Considerations Include:

| Industry analysis | Segmentation study | Comparative research | Custom profiling | Strategy formulation | Marketing campaign | Distribution strategy |

Level of work and intensity

Spectrum 2 - Proving the market involves repeating a range of activities at every phase. Over time the nature of the work does not change but the intensity and analysis do. In other words, you will need to perform just about all the activities listed here in the preliminary phase as well as the final phase, but you will begin with a cursory stance and progressively perform deeper research and analysis along each phase of the entire process.

Spectrum 3 - Resources Spectrum (Operations Track)

Objective: To identify and obtain IP protection, required technology, skills, and financial resources. This includes systems, methods and procedures, equipment and plants, human resources, and legal/insurance protection.

Approach: Begin with preliminary high level assumptions and resulting in detailed planning, strategy, and execution.

Considerations Include:

| IP protection | Vendors and suppliers | Technology & systems | Plant & equipment | Methods & procedures | Legal & insurance | Human resources |

Level of work and intensity

Spectrum 3 - The infrastructure that supports a business's ability to operate is critical in reaching profitability. This is why some people stress that it's all in the execution. Inefficient and ineffective infrastructure will prevent even the most promising inventions from ever making a profit. The work involved begins with basic assumptions which are either proven or revised along the timeline until an implementation strategy is devised. Work performed in each phase is used to refine the research in subsequent phases.

Spectrum 4 - Financial Spectrum (Financial Track)

Objective: To spend money only when necessary. Figure out the amount of funding needed and manage company finances to ensure that financial objectives such as gross margin and return on investment are achieved.

Approach: Begin with high level estimates of cost, price, and gross margin. Refine financial projections with more substantiated data as time goes on. Get to the point where financial management roadmap is laid out.

Considerations Include:

| Cost analysis | Revenue projection | Profit margin calculation | Breakeven analysis | Cash flow projection | Capital requirements | Licensing evaluation |

Level of work and intensity

Spectrum 4 - Financial analysis should also be performed by the level of work and intensity over time. When beginning, it will be sufficient to estimate the production cost, and use assumptions on retail price ranges based on competitive study. However, if the decision is to commercialize the concept, then actual cost and gross margin data must be used. The integrity of data moves from reasonable assumptions to actual data as you progress through the phases.

8.5 WHAT THIS MEANS TO YOU

The different levels of activities suggest that progress should be made sequentially and purposefully. This is to ensure systematic and incremental improvements in the quality of research and the usefulness of information. Doing so helps to ensure that nothing important is lost and efforts are not repeated. You don't want to skip around or pick out activities out of sequence for the same reason that you would not want to install a brand new carpet in a half completed house without a roof.

By researching an industry first you are able to dissect it into market segments and furthermore into profiles with which you can use to build your marketing strategy. If you skip a step here and there you might end up missing a potential segment or launching the product with the wrong strategy because the industry data was inaccurate. In either case you lose.

It's not uncommon for inventors to make such mistakes. There are plenty of cases where an inventor spends several thousands of dollars making a functional prototype before the market is proven. This is a classic example of doing the activities out of sequence. They may prove the function but certainly not the concept. There is much more to proof of concept than just its function; product appeal is certainly one of them and a critical component of selling the invention eventually. In this case if the market assumptions are shown to be false later, the inventor risks losing all the money he or she has already invested.

Another example of tackling a concept out of sequence is when someone spends months making a functional prototype without ensuring that the technology exists for mass producing it. In this scenario even if market research (specifically focus group feedback) indicates that people want and may even need the invention, the concept cannot be produced for years to come until the production technology is ready. Miniaturization falls squarely in this scenario; just because you can make a prototype work with existing components doesn't mean production technology can make it in the size and cost it needs to be commercialized.

All said, it's much more prudent if you take the time to understand a product, its associated business components, and the process that unites them all instead of aimlessly tackling anything that comes across first. Once again knowledge is power.

The path to commercial success can be aptly described as a road race. Imagine participating in an ironman race where only the fittest will complete. Now imagine that instead of running, swimming, and biking grueling distances you will:

1. Run a marathon

2. Climb Mt. Everest

3. Cross miles of a suspension bridge over a canyon

4. Then reach the beach where you will swim amongst the sharks across the strait to reach "treasure island."

Clearly, nothing is as simple as it appears when it comes to transforming a mere idea into reality. In the next chapter we will focus on the complementary side of the management and control aspects, namely the arch business principles that help guide the progression so as to enable better management of the entire process.

CHAPTER 8 ACTION ITEMS

1. Develop an overall project management approach to bringing your idea to market.

2. Identify the components within the four tracks of the framework as they pertain to your concept development and deployment efforts.

3. For each of the four spectrums, identify your concept's movement from beginning to end.

4. Create your own framework and analyze for synchronicity amongst your activities.

Chapter 9

The Ten Commandments... Business Arch Principles and Rules to Apply

Fascinating stories are always filled with interesting characters weaving in and out of the ever twisting plot. Every new adventure is filled with unfamiliar places, events, and takes on a life of its own.

The good news is, launching your venture from your own creation promises to be such a story. The bad news is, it's the same as the good news.

PARADIGM SHIFTS

The concept to commercialization system transforms more than an idea; it has the potential to transform the person behind the idea as well.

Aspiring entrepreneurs come from all walks of life. I have met people who dreamed of working for themselves but have never come up with a "good enough" business idea. Others filled their spare moments with creative ideas but never seem to get beyond the initial ideation stage.

Then there are those inventors who created some version of their "inventions" yet never succeeded in crossing the line from inventor to entrepreneur. Thomas Edison was said to have been called "too stupid to succeed" by a teacher and subsequently failed over 1000 attempts before he succeeded with inventing the light bulb. His world was certainly transformed after he began commercializing his inventions.

There are lots of reasons why people cannot launch a business from their everyday ideas. Some of these are practical matters such as the lack of time, finances, and a solid idea. Sometimes the barrier is more psychological because of the seemingly overwhelming challenges and the unspoken fear of failure. Regardless of their differences, there is the commonality of ever wishing but never crossing that divisive line. If you wish to cross that line, then you must be aware that what you are familiar with may be completely altered by a new set of culture and hidden operating protocols also known as a paradigm.

Shift #1 - From Consumer to Producer

For me it was exactly a paradigm shift. No amount of prior product management experience and business education could have prepared me fully for the challenges ahead once I embarked on the new path.

Instead of being a member of the corporate army, by changing industry and relying on my own two hands I had transformed myself into the equivalency of a guerrilla fighter. As a rank-and-file professional and a regular consumer, the adjustment for me was sudden and far-reaching.

As a guerrilla fighter with limited resources fighting many battles against establishments of all sizes and shapes, my game plan had to be drastically changed. All the previous rules of engagement were scratched. In their place was now a live-or-die mentality, an instant fight-or-flight stance, a succinct "what's in it for you" communications style, and a cleared-eye understanding that each mistake could be fatal and no backups or safety nets existed anymore.

Shift #2 – From Proprietary to Collaborative

If you have never been in the position of commercializing something, or being a producer instead of a consumer in the commercial ecosystem, and happen to have an idea that you want to explore, then there's another paradigm shift to reconcile with.

This second paradigm has everything to do with the technological advancements in data communications today. Specifically it is caused by the ever evolving social media that surrounds us.

For people who use social media for its original intent the end is to socialize. But for people who are interested in leveraging its commercial applicability the social media is a means to the end. In fact, it is probably THE means to the end for niche products, the end being promotional activities.

The obvious usage of social media as a commercial vehicle is word-of-mouth advertising. The not so obvious but equally important usage extends beyond marketing and sales activities and straight into product design, possibly even operational design.

How is this possible? The key word here is collaborative vs. proprietary environment. The conventional approach to commercializing a product is to create, design, produce, promote, and sell within a closed environment. The customer doesn't get involved until the sales stage. Historically for a company to involve the customer in the earlier stages of this process was more of an exception.

Not anymore! Social media has turned the world upside for many people in many ways. In today's environment it is entirely advocated that you involve potential customers in each aspect of the concept to commercialization process if possible. The paradigm shift is not only in thinking but in actual mechanics as well.

Companies that involved customers in their product design processes before the dawning of the socials media mechanism had a shift in their thinking, but the mechanics were still of yesterday. They asked for customer opinions via feedbacks and surveys then incorporate them into the product's design as appropriate.

The shift today involves both mental and mechanical means. With social media it is now entirely possible to involve potential customers in every step of the commercialization process, including ideation. When you open up your idea to others (within control of course) you can gather different opinions and improve your idea. This same pattern can repeat across product design, production, promotion, pricing, and packaging, etc. The process no longer is done by a closed team of people but can be completed as a collaborative project with outsiders that no one ever would have dreamt of.

The advantage is that once produced, the goods or services will have a ready pool of clients who have vested interest in the product that they helped produced. At the same time they become more willing to help promote the goods or services because of the virtual ownership. This new business model completely changes the way a concept is transformed into commercialized goods or services.

The rewards are obvious, but the tricky part is in balancing how much control to retain and how much information to share in a public forum. In essence the focus group has grown national or even international and becomes a part of the company, without additional expenses.

For niche products this is an avenue that should not be ignored. Even as the first paradigm shift has been compounded by this complexity, it literally pays to think through the double shifts (from consumer to producer, and also from conventional to social media capabilities) and take action.

These paradigm shifts do not necessarily change time-tested business principles. Rather they become a different platform to apply such principles. Remember, the technology may have changed, but you are still dealing with human beings in every aspect of your potential business venture.

The impact of the paradigm shifts has been profound; I now see the world differently and understand much more than what meets the eyes. What helps me retain such experiences now is a set of "commandments" that I recite regularly.

There are plenty of business insights, guidelines, principles, shortcuts, etc. spread across the pages of this book. Nestled amongst them are three arch principles and seven cardinal rules of business management that I hope you can take with you if nothing else. An arch principle is similar to a doctrine that encompasses every aspect of business management and does not pertain to just any one of them. The cardinal rules are just as powerful but are more specific in their applications. Together they make up the "*Ten Commandments*" that will help you keep your eyes on the goal and your feet firmly grounded as you tackle a very complex business endeavor.

9.1   ARCH PRINCIPLES OF COMMERCIALIZATION

A skilled artisan can carve master pieces out of an ordinary object such as clay or a tree trunk without much agonizing. A master technician can troubleshoot your car's mechanical issues simply by listening to the hum of the engine.

What these people have in common is their mastery of skills pertaining to their trade, practiced over long periods of time. They are able to operate seemingly effortlessly in various situations. They have the confidence and the ability to address challenges even if they had not encountered a specific one before. What they have is a commanding view that transcends all aspects of their trade.

In a similar fashion the arch principles described here are applicable to not just a particular business area. These principles need to be understood, practiced, and adopted as a set of master skills in a new paradigm you may be thinking of entering. This is like the general but essential advice that someone who has lived to tell the story from surviving the Wild West gives to the newly bright eyed, bushy-tailed, and hopeful new wagon of pioneers.

There are three arch principles that we will look at in this chapter:

    (1) Creative vs. critical thinking

    (2) The K.I.S.S. of life and death

    (3) Timing, luck, and macroeconomics

(1) Creative vs. Critical Thinking

When preparing yourself for a paradigm shift, the first thing to recognize is a major transition in your thinking pattern. The concept to commercialization process requires both creative and critical thinking skills.

In the early stages of the process, tinkerers and inventors tend to exercise predominantly their creative thinking abilities to come up with something new, something improved, or just something. The mental energy tends to focus on tweaking and more tweaking until their idea becomes something tangible. Once achieved, the feeling at that point can only be described as euphoric. Of course the potential for making lots of money certainly helps to fan the flame of imagination.

On the other hand, entrepreneurs need to exercise proportionally much more of their critical thinking skills.

There is a huge difference between the two. The difference can eventually translate to either a lifetime of tinkering only or attempts that end in success vs. failure.

Critical thinking skills begin with my favorite "5Ws + H" equation. By asking the What, Who, When, Where, and Why questions as well as the How question, most nagging business issues can be eventually figured out.

$$5Ws + H = \text{Critical Thinking}$$

Through my experiences I've discovered that, in most cases, there is a sequential order to asking these questions. Begin the first step by asking the "What" question to identify the exact issue followed by exploring the relationships with the "Who" question within the same context.

The next step is to explore the "When," followed by the "Where," and "Why." Once the scope is clear, wrap up by asking the "How" set of questions to determine necessary actions.

For example:

What exactly am I dealing with here?

Ask yourself about the subject, identify it and describe it as much as you can.

Who is involved?

Here is the mother of all questions that needs to be examined up-and-down and inside-and-out. Who gets involved and why, particularly what's in it for whoever is involved. This question is so crucial that an entire Chapter 2 is devoted to it.

When will significant events happen?

The question of "When" has a lot to do with opportunities and timing, both equally crucial in your success. Yet the "When" questions should be considered primarily relative to the "What" and "Who" questions so as to help you stay focused on the scope of the issues.

Where will events take place?

Examples of this include tradeshows, factory locations, etc. Such questions help to explore earlier questions in more depth. Tradeshow locations are important after you've determined to host a show. Factory locations are necessary if you decide to go into production, etc.

Why should it matter?

Such questions serve more as an analysis to the rationale of your judgment or decisions. This helps you determine whether your understanding of a situation is clear-eyed and makes sense.

How does it happen?

This set of questions has to do with devising an actionable plan to achieve an envisioned goal. The "How" questions often come up first in conversations, but if the end goal is not clearly spelled out, such questions tend to go around in circles. Begin with the end in mind then work backwards by filling in the missing pieces. In answering your own questions on how things happen you'll identify the necessary steps to make them happen.

In essence, this is the thinking process and technique behind business analysis that is absolutely critical in your entrepreneurial endeavor. When flying solo, or mostly without the vast resources of corporate backing, you are often working many times harder while having to be much more vigilant. There is no one else to double-check your assumptions for free.

By employing this technique, you can generate a list of critical thinking questions that sharpen your understanding of the issues at hand and how best to tackle them. With a list organized by business functional areas, you will be better prepared to prioritize them in the order of importance as well as determine which activities require priority and which ones can be processed in parallel or are dependent on prerequisites. An excellent tool for that is project management software to help you visualize your plan of attack.

(2) The K.I.S.S. of Life and Death

I can still see even with my eyes closed…"Keep It Simple, Stupid." Those were the giant welcoming words I saw on my college engineering 101 course blackboard. This has proven to be one of the most life-impacting adages I have come to appreciate and live by.

The premise is rather simple…if you can make something simple instead of complex, by all means do it. There is much beauty in simplicity.

It turns out that simplicity has its tremendous value and strength in other aspects besides engineering. From a product design perspective, a simple design requires fewer parts, which results in fewer interactions between parts, and becomes easier to operate, manage, and fix.

From a financial perspective, less parts means less production cost, lower maintenance cost, and less chance of breakage purely from a statistical measure.

From a marketing perspective, simple means more concise communications of the user benefits. Direct value statements that can be demonstrated with a simple product have more power than the inverse.

I have heard from inventors who falsely assumed that in order to protect their patent design from knock-offs, it was better to make the design more complex. This is in fact a potentially costly mistake especially if complexity had been engineered into the design. The market reality dictates that all else being equal, the product with the lower cost stands a better chance at becoming successful.

A lowered cost product that delivers the same functionality with similar aesthetic features has more leeway and pricing flexibility than a comparable one that does not. Its retail pricing can be lower than the competitor's while maintaining the same or better profit margin. When necessary, more wholesale discounts can also be given to those buyers who absolutely require it before agreeing to distribute the product.

The same principle applies to an existing design as well. If and when possible, existing designs should be relooked at to see if it can be simplified. Simplification can happen in terms of the design, the raw material, the manufacturing process, or the assembly process.

In my own case, it was the simplification of the product design that led the way to reduced manufacturing steps. Labor cost had always been the Achilles' heel for the AeroBloks product line due to the triple-durability design behind the paired latches. It was not until I revisited the original design and simplified it down from 12 manufacturing steps to 6 steps per latch that I was finally able to reach the production cost requirement for our mass market line. If the original cost per latch assembly was $0.40, I was able to reduce it down to about $0.30 per piece.

The $0.10 difference may seem insignificant at first. However, once you multiply the $0.10 savings by 16 connectors per block, and 22 blocks per package, the per retail package saving amounted to $35.20. Multiply this by 4 and the savings in retail price was $140.80. That from a 22-piece play set with an original retail price of $299 is roughly 50% lower. This was an incredibly huge reduction that enabled me to introduce a brand new line that met the stringent mass market pricing requirement. It was only possible because of simplification amongst other cost saving measures I took.

Clearly, if I had learned about this lesson and took action much earlier, our venture could have acquired a very significant market share through lots of distribution channel from the very beginning. If only I had known! But you do now.

(3)   Timing, Luck, and Macroeconomics

The AeroBloks venture could have ended on a high note with about $6M of revenue per year had the recession not hit when it did in 2007. This was quite unfortunate in one sense but fortunate in another. As it turned out I was right in anticipating a massive slaughter of the toy industry due to several coinciding factors. Amongst them were rising oil costs, labor costs, devalued currency exchange, a foreseeable drop in demands for classic toys, and a prolonged economic downturn that casts an ugly shadow for non-necessities.

Of all the factors I analyzed that led to my decision to end the venture, one that overwhelms every other is timing. The right timing is necessary for all the conditions to collide and the ensuing success to happen. The wrong timing will sink even the most promising ideas and strongest team with the right preparation, strategy, and execution.

This is because timing is largely not controllable. Those who can anticipate correctly reap rewards that most others cannot. Look at the Great Recession of 2007, which has its lingering effects even until today and for the foreseeable near future. Most people lost great amounts of earnings, lifetime savings, along with their dreams and plans. The few that were in the financial market and foresaw suspicious warning signs from market indices had to make a choice of either to continue marching with the crowd or act in a contrarian way and bet against the ongoing tides. Not all contrarians are right all the time, but the very few that bet against this recession early on made off handsomely and are set for life.

Even these folks did not control the events that unfolded. Their timing was simply very good. Their judgment and gamble paid off this time.

In business, as in life, timing is everything. This adage itself survives the test of time. Even though timing cannot always be controlled and circumstances cannot be choreographed in real life, there is still something that can be done to ensure a better than random probability.

History is a good indicator but not a perfect predictor of the future. It is a good indicator because human nature and tendencies have largely remained unchanged throughout history. Business drivers are simple when compared against life in general; most times they can be boiled down to profit and greed. If you apply sufficient time and knowledge towards analyzing your product's macroeconomic environment then the odds of your getting timing on your side is much higher.

By the same token, based on my own experience it is somewhat possible to anticipate bad timing on a macro sense as well. In my case, oil price was the most challenging factor to manage. It was rational to assume that the seemingly insatiable thirst for oil from China's new manufacturing powerhouse and India's technological advances would continue to drive the oil price upwards for several years. The reality was that oil producer cartels had the power and did plenty of manipulation of the crude oil prices. The laws of supply and demand simply seemed to be tossed out of the window. Ultra greediness of the speculating traders made it a dynamic and purely volatile cocktail of uncertainty.

What was adding fuel to fire, sort of speak, was the emerging real estate crash from subprime loans and the subsequent financial meltdown from credit swap defaults. This too supposedly was also foreseeable since the Federal Reserve prime rate was so low for so long. Once again hindsight is always 20/20. Otherwise people would and could have anticipated this development and we would not have experienced the recession compounded by an oil crisis.

Taking a step back, however, shows that such macro economic forces did exhibit warning signs. I in fact took a sample report from an organization that forecasted oil supply and demand on a global basis with corresponding oil prices. My decision to walk away from the potentially lucrative Toys "R" Us opportunity in the spring of 2008 when the oil price was at about $108 bbl was correctly done in anticipating that the price would continue to rise at least during my production cycle. In fact by the summer of 2008 the price per barrel had spiked to a historical high of $147 bbl before it began its uneven descend. From that perspective I was able to make use of timing better with more experiences.

There is much to say about timing and little to do to control it. Nevertheless the lessons learned here is that knowledge is very powerful, the lack of which could subject you to operate at the whim of luck.

Luck, on the other hand, is similar to timing in the sense that you cannot control or dictate it. But if you consider that luck also requires readiness to seize the right opportunity when it presents itself, there is preparation work that can be done for the if and when it happens to cross your path. It would indeed be tragic if you had good timing and great opportunity but are not ready. In that case it is no longer timing and luck but yourself to blame.

These arch principles apply across the board to different business areas. The main point is that no matter how much you have learned about business or the art of invention, or even just about life in general, there is always the central theme of people.

It is people who you are serving with your product or service. It is people who created processes and systems. It is people you must interact with to get things done, and to achieve your vision and dream.

9.2   THE SEVEN CARDINAL RULES

Certain business management practices have more far-reaching implications than most others. They are not as broad-based as beliefs and principles but nevertheless set the tones on how to conduct businesses in the most effective and practical manner for particular business areas.

This superset of practices are gathered here as daily reminders for those who aspire to tackle the improbable path of entrepreneurial success from everyday ideas. They have been explained in detail throughout this book so we will just keep the highlights short and sweet. In no particular order of importance (they all are!):

THE COMMERCIALIZATION PROCESS IS BUILT FROM THE BOTTOM UP

The work associated with discovery and building a foundation for anything cannot be sidestepped; you will reap what you sow. It's okay to envision and dream big, but the commercialization process must be built from the bottom up, one step at a time. Skipping steps today may prove to be costly in the future.

IMPLEMENTATION IS DONE FROM THE OUTSIDE IN

In today's business environment, customer experience can spread like wildfire. Bad reviews travel faster than ever, and good reviews can become an integral part of the promotional strategy. It is now more crucial than ever to plan and build your entire company's infrastructure around the customer experience. What this also means is that all of your company's infrastructures and/or your planning process need to be a coherent whole; each component must be synchronized with one another. This concentric approach takes the view that experiences outside the wall of a company dictate the structure of the company. At the same time it puts the revenue source at the center of your company.

SALES IS EARNED $1 AT A TIME

You can be optimistic in your hope but must be realistic in your numbers. Sales projections and cost figures are measured in real dollars, not in wishful thinking. By that measure "hope" is a four-letter word in business as it has no practicality. Every financial calculation you make needs to be substantiated.

DISTRIBUTION IS YOUR BUSINESS'S LIFE LINE

Where your target customers will buy your product, and therefore who will distribute it needs to be a forethought, not an afterthought. With practice you will quickly evaluate a product's likelihood of market acceptance but you cannot achieve the same unless you have built up a distribution network already. Distribution network is about reaping the economies of scale. Once you've created the baseline work, there is no reason not to tap additional sales channels with incremental work.

MONEY IS BULL'S EYE, ALL ELSE SUBSIDES

This doesn't mean you should focus on making money constantly but it does mean that when you evaluate business proposals, opportunities, and even people's true motivations you should follow the money trail. In doing so you will develop an understanding of the opportunities and threats you face.

POWER LIES IN WHO YOU KNOW, NOT WHAT YOU KNOW

You don't have to know everything but you need to know other people who collectively know everything about what you are trying to accomplish. Building relationships by networking has a higher payback than spending all your time perfecting your product and skills.

ADAPTABILITY AND RESILIENCE ARE KEY TRAITS

When the rubber hits the road and starts to smoke, it's not so much determination and hard work that will get you through. To work smarter and not necessarily harder you need to become more adaptable to each new development, become resilient even as the circumstance become more challenging. These two traits are not something you simply wish for and appear; they require conscious discipline and practical optimism.

CHAPTER 9 ACTION ITEMS

1. Review these arch principles of business creation and management and determine how each affects your proposed commercialization path.

2. Be sure to use each rule to prioritize and align your activities over time.

Part V

MAKING THE RIGHT DECISION

"The roads we take are more important than the goals we announce.
Decisions determine destiny."

Frederick Speakman

Chapter 10

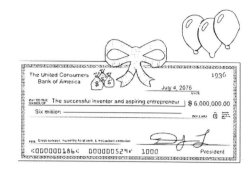

The United Consumers
Bank of America   1936
                                      July 4, 2076
                                           DATE
PAY TO THE
ORDER OF The successful inventor and aspiring entrepreneur | $ 6,000,000.00
Six million _____ DOLLARS
FOR Great concept, incredibly hard work, & meticulous execution
⑈000000186⑈ 000000529⑈ 1000   President

The Six Million Dollar Question... Is This For You?

"Youth is easily deceived because it is quick to hope."

Aristotle

In the entrepreneurial circle there is an ongoing debate about whether entrepreneurs are born or made. There seems to be ample evidence supporting claims from either camp.

The most famous example of an inventor turned entrepreneur is perhaps Thomas Edison. Recalling on Edison's lab display in Florida, I can't help but be amazed at the extent of his inventiveness. What is even more sobering is that he was not kidding when he said that genius is 1% inspiration and 99% perspiration. Taking into account of the vast amount of inspiration he had amassed, how much more perspiration was behind the scene to his eventual commercial success?

Yet you do not have to be Edison to become successful with your innovation; plenty of accidental entrepreneurs who never intended on starting a company became financially successful. Simply look around your kitchen, how many appliances were strategically rolled out as the next iterations of an existing product line and how many came about because someone wanted to find a better way of doing something?

Thomas Edison in his lab in 1888, with his phonograph

So what is the secret? Is there a set of prerequisites, formula, or recipe for success?

To answer this question we will start by looking at the most important piece of the equation – you. Metaphorically speaking, if there is a stream separating a tinkerer from an inventor, then a river runs between an inventor and an entrepreneur. But for an entrepreneur at heart to actually become one in practice, there is an entire ocean that he or she must cross.

The reality is that there is not a single profile or makeup that fits every entrepreneur. However there are common traits that they all share. One of them is creativity, another is unconventionality. Perhaps the most distinguishing trait is the eternal hopeful attitude that they can make it successfully.

First time entrepreneurs tend to be hopeful, excited even as they are cautious, and tinkerers at heart whose desire to continuously improve never ceases. Against such backdrop it is often difficult to administer doses of reality that include the financial risks that could consume them while their hearts are filled with possibilities.

The recipe (if there is one) to determine whether you have what it takes to be a full-fledge entrepreneur is like a 3-part cocktail. It makes most sense to organize the probing considerations into the following parts:

1. To thine own self be true[15]
2. It's not all or nothing
3. Making the right choice

PART 1. TO THINE OWN SELF BE TRUE

Let us assume for a second that your concept passed the difficult commercialization viability assessment with flying colors, now what will you do with it? Most people come to the conclusion of either licensing it to a company and get royalty or launching a business around it. Not so fast, please, for your own sake!

This decision is not as simple or objective as it seems. It is very much a life altering decision on multiple fronts. Under normal circumstances I can think of a few dimensions that you need to weigh carefully:

---

[15] William Shakespeare, Hamlet, Act 1, scene 3, 78–82

(1)   Personal characteristics (risk tolerance level, passion, and pride)

(2)   Quality of life preference

(3)   Capability (knowledge, physical energy and health, time horizon)

(4)   Financial resources

(1) Personal Characteristics

According to temperament theory we are all wired differently. What works for some may not work for others. There is no shame in admitting that doing the impossible isn't for most of us. Some people are simply exceptional. But the rest of us mortals, being exceptionally talented or lucky may just not be in the cards. Therefore, be true to yourself as you ponder the following questions.

Let us start with risk tolerance as the first mirror on the wall.

Risk Tolerance

Many weather disturbances in the Atlantic Ocean never get the right combination of elements to become a full-fledged category one hurricane. It takes various environmental factors such as water temperature, wind direction, atmospheric pressure, and continued equilibrium in air mass distribution for the disturbance to garner enough strength and momentum to become a formidable force of nature.

In a similar way, someone who has successfully launched a product/service to market and reaped financial rewards can be said to have had the right combination of factors that came together.

In other cases, a typical fishing trip could end up in a devastating disaster as in the case of the Andrea Gail, which sailed out of the Cape Ann, Massachusetts harbor straight into the infamous perfect storm, killing everyone onboard. This was a case where not one but three deadly forces came together. Despite the best efforts and skills of the crew the outcome was tragic.

The determining factors of success and failure are both external and internal. In the case of an accidental entrepreneur, the flash of genius often comes about as a consequence of trying to solve a particular problem. However, as good as the idea/innovation/solution might be, it is often insufficient to get to market successfully by its own merit.

External factors such as timing, luck (a.k.a. opportunities), availability of the right resources, and even the unforeseen demise of direct competition (with no relation to your own efforts), or changes in geopolitical factors can suddenly thrust your idea onto center stage. Unfortunately the reverse scenario is also just as likely, if not more common. Years of tumultuous hard work can vaporize overnight due to factors far beyond your control. Unfavorable changes in currency fluctuation, economic conditions, product regulation, or even natural disasters can ruin you overnight.

After the hastily executed CPSIA (consumer product safety information act of 2008) was signed into law (there were obvious spelling and grammatical mistakes in the bill), many children's products were declared illegal because they contained the plastic softener compound phthalate even as there was never any related human case to prove the harmful claims. This event created many untold stories of heartbreaking economic ruins that affected millions of lives when businesses were forced to shut down.

As for internal factors, most people who have gone through the entrepreneur experience tend to be more resilient, optimistic, and disciplined than the average person. Whether these traits were born or acquired through a necessity is entirely situation-dependent and individualized. Some people will cave under pressure whereas others become stronger.

Speaking of risk, I never saw myself as a daredevil who enjoys risk. Rather, I tend to rely on rational analysis before taking on anything risky.

The truth is, if I had known that I would have spent a few hundred thousand dollars of my own and investors' money only to face an eventual streak of uncontrollable rising costs and a big regulatory hammer, I probably would have never attempted the AeroBloks venture. Yet again I am glad for the life-changing experience that would otherwise not be possible. In the end (rather, beginning) you need to decide if you want to expand your life experiences and at what cost.

Passion and Motivation

Don't automatically assume that money is the first factor. Look deeper within. Sometimes you'll hear people say that they want to do good but the real reason is that they want to have a huge impact on society via a good force. Some people do good via humility while others use doing good to acquire influence. If you understand this difference then later on it will be easier to keep going when the going gets really tough.

Or say it another way, when the going gets really tough, is it financially tough or is it a loss of control kind of "tough"? Are you willing not to make as much money in order to achieve a significant task and getting your name down in history? Some people care more about significance than money. If so, then maybe you would continue even if it means sacrificing your portion of payout just to make it happen. This self-introspection, soul searching type of analysis needs to happen as early as possible.

These soul-searching questions require honesty, clarity of thoughts, and commitment. They are potentially life-changing questions to ponder.

Another motivator is passion. If you are absolutely passionate about your new business idea and/or invention, then taking the time and risk to pursue it may be more rewarding than the potential financial gain. Some people take on the challenges because they have a point to prove; whether that point is proving others wrong and themselves right about their own capabilities, or finding justification for their own actions. This second type of motivation is really emotion-based and will not sustain you through the real challenges. You must be true to your own motivation.

(2)   Quality of Life Preference

If you like or need to have the security of a steady paycheck, then launching a business is not for you. By the same token, if you prefer a routine, predictable lifestyle, then you would not enjoy the unpredictability and madness associated with running a startup. If you have hobbies or like to watch cable TV in the evenings, then you must decide whether you can give them up in order to pursue a larger objective. If you like to sleep and relax, then try this little story on for size...

One time I rushed to a dental cleaning and promptly fell asleep within minutes of being in a chair. My dentist was kind enough not to embarrass me about it, but did comment that if I in fact went for a cleaning to get a break from work (which was true), then I must have had a pathetic life. I was literally that tired and hustled that falling asleep in a dentist's chair was unavoidable. There was no TV watching, no weekends to speak of, no dinners out, and no reading for pleasure except for need-to-know knowledge. Indeed I had a pathetic quality-of-life, but I did not mind it because I kept my eyes on the prize. Of course by now you know that I almost grabbed the grand prize only to watch it evaporate in front of me, it was the risk I took.

In Shakespeare's *As You Like It* play he wrote "All the world's a stage, and all the men and women merely players."[16] Each of us wears many hats and plays different roles in our daily lives. We are children, parents, students, teachers, employees, employers, friends, neighbors, subordinates, and leaders. Some of us will play many roles throughout the day; for most of us our roles will stay in some relatively fixed pattern or routine and evolve through various stages of our lives.

---

[16] William Shakespeare, As You Like It, Act 2, scene 7, 139–143

Now imagine that you were to compress the timeframe and end up playing multiple roles not only throughout the day, but within the hours. In addition, you were performing not just one function at a time but instead were multitasking the different responsibilities simultaneously. This gives you a taste for what it feels like to be an entrepreneur in action.

If you are a functional specialist in a corporate setting, for instance a marketer, sales rep, or an engineer, you would now assume each and possibly all of the functional roles of a corporation. Quite possibly with the flick of a mental switch, you would have to deal with manufacturing issues of your product while talking with a prospective client as a salesperson, and figuring out what additional resources you would need to make it all happen, as the president of your own company.

This isn't fiction at all; this is real life in compression. A friend once asked me what it's like being an entrepreneur; I remember answering that it was an "expanding" experience, feeling literally drinking from several fire hydrants at the same time. It enlarged both my mental capacity and emotional reservoir, as if to stretch out my whole being multiple folds along with all the stresses and discomfort. Yet whenever I got a breather, I will feel so much "larger" in my understandings of the business world and human nature. It is certainly not an experience you can learn from reading or even buy with money.

(3) Capability

By capability I include several factors, namely the required knowledge, physical health, energy level, and time horizon. This is the easiest part to address because the answer is fairly straightforward. You either have or have not the capabilities.

We are all here on earth for just a short while. How would you like to spend your time? This depends on your age and obligations. As a student in college you have your entire future ahead of you. Not taking a calculated risk could lead to much regret later if that's your personality.

If you are middle-aged and have multiple responsibilities and obligations, then taking a reasonable risk requires more soul-searching and calculations. A major financial mistake made at this phase of life has far reaching consequences. For those who don't succeed (statistically most people), some will bounce back with a richer experience and perspective but financially poorer, and some never bounce back. The remaining productive years are also limited, so some caution needs to be exercised.

If you are at the later stage of your life, then you need to ask whether spending your remaining years toiling in hard labor is the right thing to do. Is the tradeoff worth it? Would it be better to minimize your risk level by considering something other than launching a company around your product?

This is a highly personal and individualized question that only you can answer.

(4)   Financial Resources

If your goal is to start a business with your concept, presumably the last section on the concept evaluation form in Appendix 4 has helped you determine that you can pull this venture off financially because you have, or know how to obtain, the financial resources necessary to operate and sustain a venture for at least five years. Then there's the question of whether this arrangement would require you to live on a shoestring budget, learn how to manage the venture's finances, or possibly even forgo salary for some time as most first-time entrepreneurs do, etc.

A related question is whether you are willing and able to take at least six months up to a year to find funding? By the way, this isn't a part-time task that you do after a day job. Not only do the people not sit around at night waiting to hear your pitch, often times you might need to knock on tens of doors to finally get the funding you need. Make no mistake about it, it is a full-time job getting funding. Can you afford it?

How do you know if you're making a sound and responsible decision? One objective measure is payback. How much money can you realistically make if you go all out setting up a venture versus getting a 5% to 7% royalty?

The financial analysis examples in Chapter 7 should give you a sense of what you could make if the business were successful in both generating the projected revenue and controlling the business operating expenses. Do not forget that you also have foregone a previous daytime income in order to do this full-time. Contrast your potential income from the new business to your previous income. Is it at least comparable or in multiples in order to compensate for the other sacrifices you will need to make?

PART 2. IT'S NOT ALL OR NOTHING

When contemplating on whether becoming an entrepreneur is the right path for you, don't automatically assume that "it" means launching a business from your idea. In fact "it" can be many things.

You do not have to eat the whole pie when it's in front of you. Inviting others to share the risks and rewards is often a better strategy than an all-or-nothing approach.

Let us look at the concept development, evaluation, and commercialization process as (mostly) linear like a timeline.

Because it is a linear process that requires many activities over time, different resources such as people and organizations can inject themselves at various points along the process. Think of it as a human chain. Some will enter it at a particular point, troubleshoot, and then get out (consultants). Some will provide prototyping and modeling service. Some will offer business plan writing service. Some will offer marketing service. Some will offer funding help. Rarely will you find one person who can do everything.

Recalling that in Chapter 2 - *Who's Who in the Commerce Loop?* we looked at the concept to commercialization ecosystem and its players. That ecosystem may now include other business service providers whom you may or may not hire depending on how much of the process you handle by yourself.

The key point is that regardless of who does the work, the process remains the same.

The Concept to Commercialization Process Components View

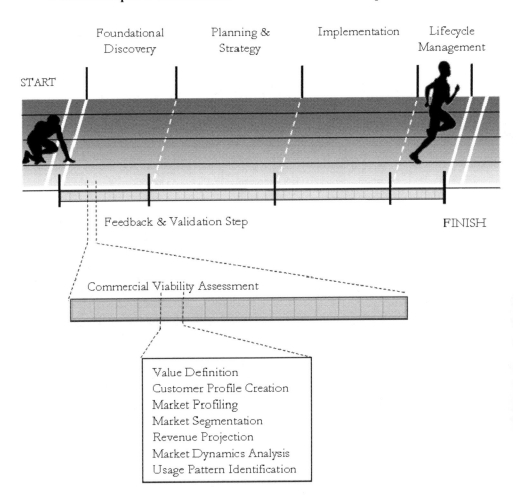

You may decide to tackle the entire venture but outsource only those components that require major infrastructures such as warehousing and shipping to other established companies. Or, you may decide to stop after you obtain legal protection for your intellectual property and let a product commercialization company take over. In some cases it makes most sense if you become intimately involved in the process but hire others and outsource major business functions. In other words, the race to the finish can be a relay and not necessarily an individual long distance race.

However you proceed, knowing the different resources available to entrepreneurs will help you decide which portions of the process to outsource.

The resources can generally be categorized as free or for-fee. We will begin by looking at the fee-based products and service you can obtain.

Appendix 6 shows a much larger chart that illustrates the different resources/service providers and where they can be of value in the concept commercialization process. You might want to refer to it when reading the following material.

The Resources section in the back of this book has a listing of the better known and established players in each category. Keep in mind that web links are dynamic and may become obsolete as soon as someone updates them. Regardless, keyword searches online using similar terms should yield similar results.

Let's look at some resources and what they can do for you.

Cost Based Resources

1. Business start up books

Books that provide value to an inventor or aspiring entrepreneur cover a wide variety of topics. This is not surprising; bringing an idea to market is a very involved process that touches upon many different business disciplines.

 You can be sure that there is not a single book that offers the proverbial magic bullet. Instead, if you treat this subject as a conglomerate of multiple business management expertise, then it should become obvious that some prioritization is required in terms of how you go about tackling this monumental task.

There will be books on niche marketing, intellectual property protection, financial analysis, someone's (one time) success story, how-to advice on getting sales, general business management, getting funding, etc. Such information is readily available, but takes time to digest and convert into knowledge. The best way to begin is to understand the entire process and become efficient at categorizing the different types of information which you can synthesize later on. This is why I stated in the Introduction that this book should be read as the first, but definitely not the only book that you will need.

Keep in mind, however, that books are static. That is, information in the real world is dynamic in that it is constantly changing and getting updated. Proven business management concepts and techniques have a much longer shelf life than most web-based articles and comments. For that matter, web links are put up and taken down on a daily basis. Your best bet is to rely on static information at a conceptual level as well as actively seek out others who have the expertise described in books to help you along.

2. Business service vendors that cater to inventors and entrepreneurs

Web portals of business listings are information exchange sites that cater to both the entrepreneur and the various service providers. You can expect to find short articles or blogs that dispense small doses of advice on anything from how to position your product to how to find the right fulfillment center. There is usually a networking section that links like-minds together, along with news and events that cater to entrepreneurs. Some are fee-based and others are free for browsing. The question you should be asking is how the portal makes money, how the advisers (consultants) make money, and whether any fee you pay is worth the advice you get.

Some portals are essentially online marketplaces where entrepreneurs can find different service providers. Entrepreneurs can find investors, service providers, or mentors. The "experts" range from someone who has experience in licensing, getting funding, to a professional accountant or IP attorney.

Some portals are set up as non-profit while others are set up by the very entrepreneur who is trying to sell you his formula for success and a system that worked in his particular venture. In cases like this, be sure to keep a wide-eye approach, cut through the marketing smoke and mirror, and follow the money trail to determine whether the information or system is in fact useful to your particular situation.

Another type of portal offers an exchange where people can swap ideas and how-to advices. These are essentially online communities of like-mindedness. They offer a specific type of information and do not include the entire spectrum of service providers.

Niche service providers are those people or entities that provide a specific expertise. For example, the WIN-I2 Innovation Evaluation Service offers invention evaluation and product assessment services to individuals and corporations. There are others who provide similar service but at a different scale and with a different approach.

Within the concept to commercialization process are areas where a specific expertise should be provided by professionals. Whereas concept evaluation may be done by a formal process or small focus groups, you would not want to create your own accounting system or write your own patent application without the help of a professional. Saving money here is not necessary the best idea; the difference between a few thousand dollars now may mean hundreds more in loss if the patent claims are not wide enough to cover your invention, for instance.

The types of service range from startup consulting, prototype making, financial management, marketing press release, advertising, to finding office spaces. These service providers address a slice of the entire spectrum. Whether and how you decide to hire them is entirely up to you, and is subject to your own capabilities.

Product development service is a particular niche service that deserves a separate description. Unlike other service providers who specialize in a particular business discipline, product development combines the early stage prototyping service with mechanical design, material testing, functional design and testing, and maybe even packaging design to develop a complete, presentable finished product.

To do this, the service provider needs a network of mechanical drafting, computer modeling, prototype workshops, factories, and testing facilities, etc. Some will even include advice on finding distribution channels or doing patent searches and licensing negotiations type of work that belong to other specialists. The more elaborate ones include video production, advertising, and branding services. There are also others that go beyond making a physical product. Basically you pay for what you pick from the menu. However you must remember that "expertise" needs verification.

Product coaches and consultants are people who offer their own "been there, done that" advice to aspiring entrepreneurs. Their service repertoires address piece parts of the concept to commercialization process described in this book although may not necessarily follow the particular order. There are

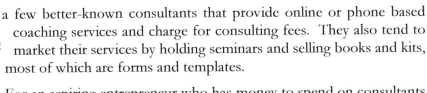

a few better-known consultants that provide online or phone based coaching services and charge for consulting fees. They also tend to market their services by holding seminars and selling books and kits, most of which are forms and templates.

For an aspiring entrepreneur who has money to spend on consultants, this is perhaps the best avenue to get the information across efficiently. However, as with any other type of consultation, the person giving the advice needs to have the expertise in the particular topic that needs answers. Additionally a consultant does not do the work of implementation. As a rule of thumb, that is not the real value of consultants.

You should be aware that too many people call themselves consultants especially in times when steady employment is difficult to secure. Be sure to ask for the credentials of any consultant you are considering hiring and match them to your specific needs. One way to substantiate the professional credentials of a consultant is by looking at his or her professional affiliations. Bona fide, full time consultants tend to belong to established organizations such as the United Inventors Association. Otherwise they should be able to readily provide evidence of their own relevant experiences.

Product commercialization company is a special breed that has raised many eyebrows and red flags amongst the inventor communities. The premise of these companies is that they have the expertise and resources that most inventors lack in bringing new products to market. The business model at a simplistic level gives these entities the rights to the intellectual product, with which they own and operate all commercialization activities once the inventor signs over the rights. The inventor in turn receives a royalty similar to that of licensing fee.

If the company does what is expected of a prudent business partner and implements all the necessary steps in the commercialization process, then the partnership would produce equitable returns for them and the inventor. The trouble is, there are plenty of ill-reputed companies that make money from other than doing the bona fide activities of commercialization. One typical red flag is when they charge an upfront fee from the inventor for whatever justification they come up with.

Knowing the entire process of bringing an idea to the shelf makes it reasonable to forego most of the potential revenue to the commercialization company. After all, the company needs to pay for all the business expenditures and make a profit just as if you had launched a business yourself. The problem comes when there is no way for an inventor to actively monitor the activities of such a company to ensure that due diligence is done at the same level. Because there is no direct management involvement, the inventor is left with almost no control over the fate of his product in the hands of the commercialization company. There is no telling if a product fails in the market because of its lack of consumer appeal or if the marketing job was botched, or if the product was doomed way back in the production line due to poor quality control. Once signed, the rights to manage belong to the company and the inventor simply hopes that he will receive a royalty paycheck.

Other horror stories tell of tales where excited inventors are invited for "product screenings" where their product was given the big green light. By then the inventor would have spent money on developing the prototype, getting it patented, and traveling, in addition to whatever required upfront fees are stipulated by such a company. There are many stories told on websites dedicated to exposing scams that target unsuspecting inventors who lose thousands of dollars. Even the Federal Trade Commission has set up a web page to alert people of these activities.

There are different business models within this type of entity. The so called invention submission companies fit the description above most closely. There are other legitimate companies who work with inventors without charging any upfront fees. They operate by commissions, whether from the inventor once the product is sold or obtain revenues from licensees of the inventions and in turn pay the inventor a royalty fee. They are able to do this because of their established network of retail stores, licensee companies of innovations, and even manufacturers and wholesalers, not to mention broad distribution channels. In essence their value-add to the commercialization equation is the combination of their networks and relationships.

Most of the services begin with concept evaluation, which includes market assessment. The work also includes licensing negotiation with potential licensees, which is sometimes known as technology transfer (especially from university research labs to commercial companies). Some of them charge an upfront fee for initial consultation, outsourced product evaluation, and/or market evaluation. Others have a reserve of capital that they can use to develop the concept to the point where licensing can take place. They in turn share the royalty or licensing fee with the inventor.

In most cases the companies will require exclusive manufacturing/distribution rights. The practices vary, but the key point is that if any money is spent upfront, you must ascertain on what the value is for you.

> Remember that an expert in name may not be an expert in deed; you must be diligent in assessing their services.

Free Resources

Regardless of what portions of the commercialization process you might outsource or hire help for, if any at all, you will benefit from having an arsenal of useful information available to you, especially if they are free.

The next set of inventor resources range from inventor associations, online networks, higher education institutes, other non-profit foundations, to government entities dedicated to helping the inventor and aspiring entrepreneur.

1. **Inventor clubs and associations** are just that. They are organizations of like-minded inventors and entrepreneurs who share knowledge and  resources. As an individual inventor who aspires to bring a concept to market, you will benefit much from joining these networks. There are the usual pool of talents that you can draw from, including IP protection, mechanical design help, evaluation and feedback, and even sales and marketing experiences from someone who has successfully brought an invention to market. The greatest asset is the combined knowledge pool which can shave off much time and misdirected efforts during the initial Foundational Discovery phase.

   Where inventor clubs may be inadequate is in the difference between inventors and entrepreneurs. The former tends to focus on creative inventing whereas the latter focuses on business creation activities. Inventor clubs provide much value from the concept feedback and validation of market and financial projection assessment but tend not to have much of a role in the planning and strategy phase and beyond.

2. **Educational entities and foundations** provide a wealth of information, and are not restricted to academic studies either. Both Stanford University and MIT are renowned for their entrepreneurial resources. They have well respected technology transfer offices that help aspiring entrepreneurs with finding information and data.

   The drawback of course, is that if you are not an attending student or alumni then you would not have as much access to the treasure. Secondarily, getting useful information still requires that one understands how to interpret and use them in the proper course. It is no substitute for consultation or outsourcing the venture where real people

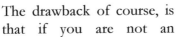

are working in real time to address issues. Similarly, the non-profit Kauffman Foundation is available to all entrepreneurs and provides a wealth of research data on entrepreneurs, network, and market trends. It is no substitute for a real person but is still an information gold mine for entrepreneurs.

3. **Free articles and interviews online** are another source of information.

Over the last decade the amount of entrepreneurial and commercialization related articles have exploded over the internet. This is both good and bad news. Keyword search returns yield much more information, yet the information quality has also been muddled. There are now blogs that contain short bursts of advice which scratch only the surface of any major issue. They serve the bloggers better in terms of getting eyeballs and therefore ranking and potential advertising revenue than the entrepreneur looking for in-depth answers. Misleading and outdated information are also popping up as a natural course of time, given that there is no "quality police" to ensure the accuracy and usefulness of information, minus any tint of commercial interest. When using such source, caution is in order. If possible, any data that sounds suspicious should be double-checked against other bona fide sources of data such as government agencies.

4. **Government and small business administration sites** offer government published statistics useful for making market assessments. The types of data consist of population and business census, sortable by location and other demographics. The U.S. Census Bureau, for instance, provides free statistics on demographics data you can use to define the size of your target market. The U.S. Patent and Trade Office (USPTO) allows for free patent searches and supplies information on how to copyright and trademark your intellectual property. The US International Trade Commission produces harmonized tariff schedule for use in products classification which is necessary for freight. For questions regarding incorporation and filing tax forms, there is always the IRS or the local state departments of revenue.

There are many other local (state level) resources that help with entrepreneurial and startup activities. The easiest way is to simply search online with keywords in your own state.

Each of these resources, whether free or fee-based, tackles a slice or a chunk of the commercialization process spectrum. If you are fully capable and have the resources, you could always handle the entire spectrum. However, for most aspiring entrepreneurs this is not an option. Instead, understanding the roles of each potential player in the grand scheme of things helps one to figure out different options. There is no fixed answer to the question of whether you should license or venture with your innovation; the options are based on which piece of the actions is most practically done by whom, in what order. Just as building a house is not an all or nothing effort for an individual; when you act as the general contractor of the building process you can dictate the level of outsourcing you will need in order to optimize your goal.

At the risk of repeating, no man or woman is an island onto himself or herself. Your own level of experience, knowledge, expertise, and amount of resources will dictate whether you farm out none, some, or the entire process to others. Likewise, even if you are fully able, sharing some risks and rewards may also be a very good thing.

PART 3. MAKING THE RIGHT CHOICE

Just like the concept evaluation process, answering the question of what you should do with a validated concept is not a simple go or no go decision. The concept evaluation process dissects the various aspects of commercializing an innovation by objectively measuring them against known criteria. Similarly, the decision about what to do with the concept that receives a "go" signal can also benefit from objective analysis. The difference is that one deals with a concept, the other a human being. That alone should tell you that the latter decision is even more complex.

Ask and ponder the following aspects if you will:

1. What outcome do I idealistically want? Is it money, freedom, experience, or something else?

2. Do I have the necessary resources (knowledge, experience, money, talents, and time) to accomplish my objective?

3. Do I have strong enough desire, the right attitudes, the willpower and resilience to overcome, and the confidence in my own idea to reach my goal? In other words, can I both sprint and run long distance?

4. Is my timing good? What does my market analysis tell me?

5. Would I be brave enough to keep going when things get rough, and disciplined enough to stop when it's no longer practical to go on?

I have a favorite Chinese proverb that says something like "even a sparrow has all major organs despite its tiny frame." This is a profoundly accurate depiction of the small business experience, especially if it is product related.

Despite its size, a small business must also perform similar functions as that of a larger corporation. From R&D to sales/marketing, to vendors/customer relationships, managing human/infrastructure resources, etc., size does not negate the processes and procedures required to meet all the necessary functions that make a business operation hum and keep it humming. The major difference is in the number of people performing the tasks.

In a corporation you might have hundreds or hundreds of thousands of people working all the functions. In a typical situation (at least initially) for a startup or small business, you might operate the entire venture with just one or two people. Imagine such one or two person team performing all the necessary tasks of a regular business entity and you would get an appreciation of the amount of work, the necessity to quickly "expand" one's knowledge, and the level of commitment and work-related stress that can be reasonably expected.

The transition to the entrepreneurial lifestyle may be especially hard for lifetime corporate warriors. Switching to an entrepreneur mode is almost like joining a guerrilla force to fight established armies for a piece of the Promised Land.

The same can be said for someone without exposure to the various business disciplines whether through formal business education, training, or simply related work experiences. In this latter case it would take an accelerated approach to quickly learn and apply new found knowledge, or at least be able to manage hired resources that would have such expertise.

> You may not be able to anticipate life-changing events but you should at least know if you are willing to accept the possibility.

IN SUMMARY

All said, I believe entrepreneurship is a state of mind, a belief system, a way of life that you endorse, admire, or disregard. It is a game of resilience. It is about overcoming obstacles in physical, financial, and logistical terms and objections in psychological terms.

To successfully commercialize something and make it profitable takes a huge amount of tenacity, drive, and optimism even in the midst of tremendous challenges.

To take on this path means to go into a long, drawn-out battle against formidable enemies who are much better prepared, experienced, and endowed with resources.

Chasing this dream requires more than inspiration and perspiration; it takes imagination, courage, will power, and sometimes a bit of naiveté, but definitely lots of good luck.

Whatever your goal is for wanting to commercialize your idea, it must be matched with a corresponding tolerance level for the risks associated with financial, lifestyle, and other potential impacts. For example, if you're looking for supplemental income, then don't launch a capital-intensive product-based venture which carries with it a financial risk far beyond the scope of just generating supplemental income.

On the other hand if you are extremely confident about your innovation's acceptance by the market as well as determined to reap substantiated financial rewards, then you must recognize that it takes more than just part-time effort to reach your goal.

In my experience, inventors and entrepreneurs tend to be two different breeds. They differ in their belief towards the amount of effort required to get to market. While entrepreneurs tend to believe they need to put in at least 12-hours per day, most inventors believe falsely that they can work a full-time job and tinker with their ideas on a part-time basis. They believe this level of effort is sufficient to get their product to market. Many of them looked at me incredulously when I told them that I quit the regular daytime job to work on my venture full-time.

In fact, many people have advised me to find one or two part-time jobs in addition to launching the product as a means of providing the income necessary for the venture. What these well-meaning folks didn't realize was the amount of time, effort, resources, and money it takes to launch and run a real company regardless of its size. Imagine wearing different hats and having to deal with every aspect of the business operations in real-time. It becomes apparent very quickly that the world does not revolve around your own schedule. In the business world, where time is definitely money, there is no other way than to be thoroughly immersed in the venture.

All these are real issues but they are not meant to discourage you from doing something entrepreneurial. They are meant to help you become more aware and realistic before you take that plunge.

A simple test for you to decide if you have what it takes is to weigh your concept against this set of realities. How strongly do you still feel about going to market after considering these risks?

If you are undeterred, then it is good because you are now more prepared than before. If you are deterred it is also good since walking away now costs very little but crashing later because you lacked the psychological elements to fight drawn-out guerrilla warfare could literally cost you everything you hold dear.

Every product or service that ends up being commercialized was driven by somebody (except those that came out of the corporate machinery). Someone else had done it. It is not impossible, just improbable. But you can improve your odds by being honest with yourself, being prepared with resources, and being the warrior that can defeat obstacles because of his or her drive and capabilities.

What will it be for you? The material in this book works like a compass, a map, a mirror, but not a crystal ball. Only you can assess your own situation and be accountable to your decisions. Re-read some of the material here and project your potential path. Let the work involved and the risks and rewards help you balance your decision.

What I hope is that the information contained in this book has at the very least given you a sense of the amount of work and the level of commitment in a relatively logical framework. There is enough noises and confusion surrounding the topic of marketing your product any way you turn. Without guidance and the proper set of expectations, you can reasonably expect to make costly mistakes and perform reworks that otherwise could have been prevented. Now armed with the blueprint and business insights contained here, you are already much more prepared than anyone else who would become an accidental entrepreneur. The most important takeaway lessons have been summarized for you to ponder and apply.

I sincerely believe that true failure is the failure to act especially if it's because of unfounded fear. Take the time to decide what will make you happiest on the last day of your life. Fulfilling your obligations and responsibilities by providing for those who depend on you without taking unnecessary financial risks is just as respectable as taking a calculated risk in either succeeding financially or succeeding in expanding your own being and thereby becoming a wiser and better person.

I wish you wisdom and success for whichever decision you make. No matter what, I would like to suggest that you contemplate the wisdom from one who has gone against all odds and accomplished great feats in his life...

"Success is to be measured not so much by the position that one has reached in life as by the obstacles which he has overcome while trying to succeed."

Booker T. Washington

CHAPTER 10 ACTION ITEMS

1. Identify your goals and measure them against your resources and lifestyle preferences.

2. Review and research resources that you will most likely need to use to commercialize your concept. Use the Entrepreneurial Resources section in the back of the book to gather data.

3. Weigh your options and make the most appropriate go-to-market decision for your situation. Do this with a soul-searching mental state.

Afterword

Just like a giant tsunami, the Great Recession of 2007 sent ripples of destruction along its path across the globe, impacting every sector of the daily life. Mine was no exception.

My decision to close down the AeroBloks venture was directly driven by an anticipated drastic reduction in toy sales. But even this thought brought little comfort in the face of reality. People were getting laid off left and right and factories in China were closing down by the thousands. This tremendous force of demolition coupled with the horrendous timing of the CPSIA act of 2008 spelled the annihilation of tons of small toy companies, many of which were launched from toy inventions. I was not alone, but that also made no difference.

As I gathered the remnants of my hard-earned business and began tearing down each infrastructure that took months to build, I couldn't help but reflect on what it all meant. While backing up five plus years of business data onto a 500GB hard drive, I was surprised that it took over 24 hours of continuous writing.

I realized that the amount of information represented only what had been kept on record, and not necessarily the knowledge, experience, and insights. Every bit of data was acquired with work, especially the photographs and video clips of product structures used in promotional materials. Each structure was built piece by piece, each picture was selected from many others, and each final image was edited time and again. In effect the hard drive captured only the end products and not the labor or thought processes behind them.

Was that all there was to it? Just a 500GB hard drive that says I was really there? It certainly seemed surreal. All the dreams and hopes, working 16-hour days, and overcoming incredibly difficult obstacles all came down to a black box. If it could only speak it would tell stories that no one would believe. But there it was, just a piece of hardware representing all the years of sweat and tears in silence. This was an injustice that we did nothing to deserve.

Was this it? It didn't make sense. But one thing was undeniable…it was the understanding that time heals all wounds by erasing or dulling memories. On one hand I couldn't wait for Father Time to wave his magic scythe and help me forget about all the traumatic endings, on the other hand I could not bear the thought of having worked so hard with nothing to show. Something was amiss.

Then I received a phone call from a friend. She wanted to know if I could help her with some small business issues for she too had been laid off and was trying to start a service business on her own. And it dawned on me, just like that; that perhaps the real fruit of our hard labor was not the amount of money we earned during the venture's course but something much larger and longer lasting.

What I have gained is a mind filled with experiences and insights that budding entrepreneurs can only wish they had, just as I did when I first started. It is this "know-how" that holds value for others, be it an employer or a consulting client.

The best time to reflect and learn is when you have been shot down and are licking your wounds. Otherwise high achievers will continue to push forward and never look back. This was an opportunity for me to summon what I have learned and produce a living record so that others can reap the benefits. My proverbial "fruit tree" may have been cut down but the soil I tilled and the lessons I learned can now be applied towards vineyards of fruit trees. We definitely have suffered great injustice, but a greater injustice is to allow such knowledge to expire over time. It was time to make lemonades out of life's lemons.

This writing represents a cumulative compilation of business and life experiences. It encompasses ergonomic design principles from my education, professional product management and marketing experiences working in the corporate setting, business infrastructure and process design experiences from two startups, and bare-hand combat experiences in the sales trenches in retail. I once saw a bumper sticker that said "I've been to Hell; I'm in retail." This was at once too funny and too true to ignore.

So now I have written this huge volume of knowledge to help my fellow inventors and aspiring entrepreneurs. The information is by no means comprehensive as it is impossible to write everything about starting up with an invention or business idea in a single volume, lest the book contains several thousand pages. I somehow don't think anyone is crazy enough to write one or read one.

In any case, clearly my path isn't the only or a typical one for an entrepreneur. There really isn't a standard path because the circumstances surrounding each venture are as varied as the seashells on the beach.

I know other entrepreneurs who started out as the inventor of a single idea. Some of them encountered much success while others met demise. The successful ones often tell of luck as being the single most important factor. They were at the right place at the right time, talked to the right person with the right connections, etc. The not so lucky ones often worked just as hard, if not harder, at trying to succeed at their ventures. One thing everyone had in common was that each person was extremely driven by their vision and stayed focused. Some took a big loop getting to their goals while others had guidance.

Luck is not within control, but having the knowledge, the determination, and the resources can help you overcome many difficulties and bring you closer to your heart's desire. Short of wishing you good luck alone I hope the insights and knowhow contained here will have made a positive contribution to achieving your dreams of becoming a successful entrepreneur.

Appendix

Appendix 1. An Evaluation List "On the Go"

When you come in contact with a new idea, product, or service, chances are you will have lots of questions or know that you should have lots of questions but can't think of any at that moment. Use this list to quickly sort out the potential of an idea, whether it's your own or someone else's.

#	Category	Questioning Sequence
1	Product	**What is it?** (purpose, is it obvious)
2	Product	**What does it do?** (function)
3	Product	**How does it work?** (technology, material, design)
4	Product	**Does the solution already exist in some other form** (comparative)
5	Product	**How is this solution superior to others** (comparative)
6	Profit	**How is it produced?** (skills, machinery, facilities required)
7	People	**Who is it for?** (target market)
8	People	**Why would they like it?** (value proposition, ergonomics)
9	People	**How easy is it to adopt?** (newness, adoption curve, disruptive innovation issues)
10	Prospect	**How big is the market?** (revenue potential, mass/niche markets)
11	Prospect	**How else can it be used?** (secondary markets, alternative usage, cross industry transferability)
12	Prospect	**How much does it cost?** (price to value comparison)
13	People	**Will people pay for it?** (from value, price, need vs. want perspective)
14	Prospect	**Who will distribute it?** (distributors, resellers, primary/secondary channels)
15	Prospect	**How difficult is distribution?** (tradeshows, social networks, direct mail)
16	Prospect	**Can it be easily knocked off?** (barrier to entry, IP protection)
17	People	**Is the operation's frontend user friendly?** (user experience)
18	Profit	**Is it a capital intensive venture?** (production costs and infrastructures required)
19	Profit	**How is it funded?** (self, angels, VCs, public)
20	Prospect	**Is it a sustainable business?** (cost, trend, value, market size, macroeconomics)
21	Profit	**Is it profitable?** (gross margin, units sold, ROI, breakeven analysis)
22	People	**Does the company have right management skills?** (technical, business, maturity)
23	Profit	**Will I invest in it?** (confidence level of innovation & people, as a stockholder, employee)

Appendix 2. The Concept to Commercialization Blueprint

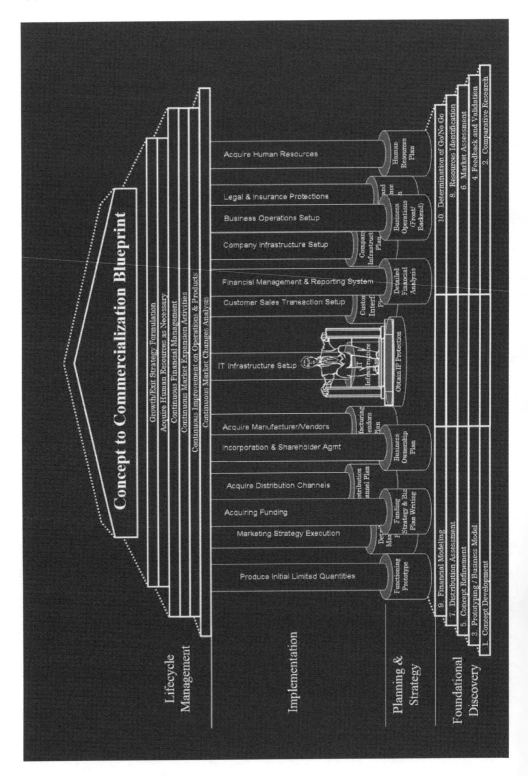

Appendix 3. The Commercialization Phases Quadrant (clockwise)

Ongoing Management Phase	**IV.**	**I.**	**Foundation Building Phase**

Market Changes Analysis	Concept Development
Operations & Product Improvements	Comparative Research
Market Expansion Activities	Prototyping/Biz Modeling
Financial Management	Feedback and Validation
HR Resources Management	Concept Refinement
Growth/Exit Strategy	Market Assessment
	Distribution Assessment
	Resources Identification
	Financial Modeling
	Determine Go/No Go

Implementation Phase	**III.**	**II.**	**Planning & Strategy Phase**

Obtain IP Protection

Acquire Funding	Functional Prototyping
Incorporate Business	Detailed Marketing Plan
Setup Financial System	Distribution Channel Plan
Setup Business Operations	Manufacture & Vendors Plan
Acquire Human Resources	IT Infrastructure Plan
Legal & Insurance Protections	Customer Interface Plan
Setup Company Infrastructure	Company Infrastructure
Setup Customer Transaction	Legal and Insurance Plan
Setup IT Infrastructure	Human Resources Plan
Acquire Manufacturer/Vendors	Business Operations Plan
Acquire Distribution Channels	Detailed Financial Analysis
Execute Marketing Strategy	Business Ownership Plan
Produce Limited Quantity	Funding & Business Plan

Appendix 4. Commercial Viability Assessment Questions

The Purpose of This Evaluation Form

From everyday household products to medical nano robots and superfast grapheme conductors, a concept is only as useful as if and when it has materialized. Similarly, it provides value only if it produces commercial payback for the aspiring entrepreneurs and their financial backers.

This form has been designed to follow the intuitive thinking pattern of someone who is trying to determine whether an idea should be pursued by looking at many of the factors that impact its potential profitability.

How to Use This Form

These questions have been categorized into five major **junctions** that work like traffic intersections. Each has **sections** that address similar sets of business concerns.

There may be more than one topic within each section. Each topic may have more than one **question** to be rated. To thoroughly understand and answer the questions you need to refer to the corresponding material covered from Chapter 4 through Chapter 7.

To make the most of this exercise you should read the clarifications, insights, and examples in the corresponding chapters first before answering each question. You will rate each question with a numerical value between 1 and 10. A rating of 1 is the lowest score and 10 represents that your answer completely satisfies the ideal requirements of the criteria.

You will also calculate an **average rating** for each section, bypassing any question that is not applicable in your particular situation. Similarly you will calculate the average junction rating.

Making Sense of the Rating Score

Imagine the five junctions as city limits with traffic lights leading up to them. If your averaged rating for a "traffic junction" is less than 7 then you should not proceed to the next area with confidence. This may seem harsh but considering the astronomical failure rate of new ventures, it is better safe than sorry. Any question that produces a very low rating should be treated as an automatic red light that stops you from moving forward until at least the issue is resolved satisfactorily or that you have decided to abandon the project/idea.

Next, add up all the averaged ratings from the five junctions. Multiple this sum by 2 and divide by 100. The resulting percentage represents the confidence level of your concept's having a high likelihood of being commercialized successfully and even profitably. For example, if the sum of the junction average ratings is 38, then the confidence level would be 38x2 divided by 100 which equals 76%.

The minimum passing score is recommended at 70%. This means that if your net evaluation score did not produce at least a 70% confidence level then you should either return to the low ratings and try to improve your readiness or consider abandoning your concept (at least for now) and move on to the next big idea.

A score between 70 and 100 should be considered a positive indicator that the concept should move forward (a GO decision) towards the planning and implementation stages.

There is of course no guarantee from interpreting the numerical result alone. However, if all the criteria have been met, then the concept's readiness to be commercialized is virtually 100% (not counting the uncontrollable factors such as timing and luck). In the absence of certainty, it is a substantiated measurement.

You will notice that such a decision is not taken lightly, superficially, or single-mindedly without considering every aspect of the business experience. It's a much more prudent alternative than jumping in head first.

Table of Contents

Traffic Junction 1 – Testing the Water

Section 1-1 Concept Exploration: What is it?

Concept evaluation begins with rating the innovator's presentation preparedness. The question here forces the innovator to think through the innovation and make self-determination of exactly what the concept's attributes and impacts are. Next, others will either be interested in or move on after hearing the initial description.

Your objective is to communicate your idea into something that others can clearly understand. The more well defined and fleshed out your idea is, the easier it will be for you to move on to the next steps. This is equivalent to the "elevator speech" pitched to potential investors. The types of activities you will do include a quick description of the product function and feature, usage and user identification, and why you think it's a good idea.

Reference:	**Chapter 4.1**	
Topics and Questions		Rating
1.	How well can you describe the essence of your innovation in one minute or less? Measure your delivery against the ABC rule (Accuracy, Brevity, and Clarity) of communications.	
	SECTION 1-1 RATING	

Section 1-2 Designing and Prototyping: Will it work?

Your objective is to transform your idea into something tangible. At this point the goal is to make something that is good enough to represent and perhaps simulate how your idea works. There is no need to spend thousands of dollars. Nevertheless key design considerations and features need to be demonstrated and evaluated here.

The types of activities you will do may include going to craft stores or hardware stores for some raw material. This is the time to experiment with different types of material that will perform the functions your product promises. Sometimes a non-functional mock-up will do as well at this point as long as you are able to effectively describe how it would have worked if actual materials were used.

Reference:	**Chapter 5.1.1-5.1.2**	
Topics and Questions		Rating
RESEARCH AND DEVELOPMENT (5.1.1)		
2.	Do you see challenges or difficulties in developing your concept into a physical product or a business process?	
3.	What is the total cost on expected research and developmental expenditures?	
4.	Does your concept require continuous R&D expenditure to keep up	

with competition or updates in technology? If so, what percentage of budget will it be?	
5. Are you possibly infringing on someone else's patent?	

PRODUCT DESIGN (5.1.1)

6. How well did you apply the K.I.S.S. design principle?	
7. Is your design based on a user-centric approach that incorporates what the market's needs and wants are?	
8. Do you have a clear formulation of the design's function, form, material, quality, safety, and liability requirements?	

PROTOTYPING (5.1.1)

9. Do you have a prototype making strategy that maps to your presentation objective, including where and how to source the materials and skills?	
10. Do you know the type of material and costs associated with the various forms of prototypes you will need?	
SECTION 1-2 RATING	

Section 1-3 Comparative Landscape: Does it already exist?

Your objective is to find out if someone else already developed this idea into a commercialized product or service. If someone has beaten you to it, you still might be able to commercialize it if your idea is better or has superior features in some way.

The types of activities you will do include looking around online by doing keyword and patent searches and/or by asking someone familiar with the particular industry. Keep in mind that sometimes a patented design by someone else may not surface in the marketplace for years.

Reference: **Chapter 4.3.1-4.3.4**	
Topics and Questions	Rating

COMPETITOR PROFILING (4.3.1)

11. Do you know your competitive landscape and can you identify their strengths and weaknesses?	
12. How do you compete in terms of price, performance, service, and warranties?	
13. Do you have significant resource constraints, such as lacking in branding, established customer base, cash reserves, favorable location, and experiences?	
14. If you plan to take market share, will you become a me-too, best in class, or just picking off the table crumbs?	

BARRIER TO ENTRY (4.3.2)

15.	Do you have a strategy to overcome any existing barriers to entry into the market your concept is geared for?
16.	How easy is it to create a knockoff replicating your innovation's function with lower cost material and design?
17.	What barriers of entry can you erect to prevent future competition from eroding your market place?

DIFFERENTIATION (4.3.3)

18.	In what ways is your concept better than the competition? Is it function, design, style, user experience, convenience, safety, cost, or overall value?
19.	Is there sufficient differentiation between your proposed concept and an existing product to justify developing yours, or are people already happy with the existing?

SUBSTITUTION (4.3.4)

20.	Are there any obvious substitutes for your product/service?
21.	What are other substitute products or advances in technology that can affect your product?
22.	Do you have a strategy to prevent substitute products from taking away your market share?

SECTION 1-3 RATING	

Section 1-4 Market Identification: Who might want it?

Your objective is to understand who will buy your product and why.

The types of activities you will do are to identify the market size, user profile, how similar products are priced, sold, and used. You will need to understand the basics of the conventional 4Ps of Marketing to do a good job here.

Reference:	**Chapter 4.2.1-4.2.4, 4.4.1-4.4.5**

Topics and Questions	Rating

MARKET AND REVENUE SIZE (4.2.1)

23.	How did you determine total sales of the industry and its growth rate? Is it expected to grow in size, remain constant, or decline?	
24.	How large is your market size/potential revenue? Can it support your operational costs, production costs, marketing costs, management costs, etc. and absorb new market entrants without causing major shifts?	

MARKET CHARACTERISTICS (4.2.2)

25. Do you know the key drivers of success in your market?	
26. Are there market factors that can dramatically impact your profits?	
27. Are there seasonal effects or cyclical natures that exist in your industry?	
28. How does your company and product fit into the industry?	

MARKET DYNAMICS (4.2.3)

29. What are the current market trends? Are there windows of opportunity or special circumstances that make your product or service concept especially favorable now or in the projected timeframe of your product launch?	
30. Are there foreseeable potential threats for your type of product or service?	

MARKET SEGMENTATION (4.2.4)

31. Does this product have mass market appeal or is it better suited for specialty, niche markets?	
32. Are you able to identify market segments and their characteristics?	

RESEARCH (4.4.1)

33. What is the degree of difficulty in getting accurate and up-to-date data that is specific to your research needs at a cost you can afford?	
34. What is the quality of your market research? Does it cover industry size, trend, competitive analysis, cyclical behaviors, windows of opportunity, cost of marketing, and approaches to promotion?	

DEMOGRAPHICS (4.4.2)

35. Have you defined who would be most interested in your innovation?	
36. Have you identified who will actually pay for this product or service? Who are the primary user and the primary buyer? Who has greater influence?	
37. What are the demographics of your targeted customer base? Are the demographics of your target customer reachable?	

USAGE PATTERN (4.4.3)

38. How well can you clearly identify how someone would use your proposed product or service, including when and where they are most likely to use it?	
39. Is the proposed product usage intuitive for the intended end-user and not just for the designer? If learning is required, how easy is it for the user to learn to use your product?	

SOURCES OF INFLUENCE (4.4.4)

40. Is your concept one that is heavily influenced by peer reviews or is it one that can be sold independently of market influences?	
41. How well can you identify the sources of influence and channels of information that your target segment relies on to make product or service purchase decisions?	

IDENTIFYING CUSTOMER VALUES (4.4.5)

42. Are you able to identify and prioritize a list of features and benefits your intended customers care most about?	
SECTION 1-4 RATING	

Section 1-5 Feedback & Refinement: What do others think?

Your objective is to be objective. If you want broad acceptance, then getting someone else's honest opinion (preferably from the targeted user and buyer groups) is essential. Get as many diverse feedbacks as possible to validate your own assumptions.

The types of activities you will do may include going to friends and families first, but definitely ask people further removed from you for honest feedback. You might also attend small groups and use them as focus groups to tell you how people perceive your idea and whether they would buy it and at what price. Refine the concept as appropriate.

Reference:	**Chapter 5.1.3**

Topics and Questions	Rating

FEEDBACK AND VALIDATION (5.1.3)

43. Is your source of feedback qualified to give you substantiated comments and concept validation?	
44. Did your concept receive positive feedback on its form, function, material, safety, marketing positioning, production cost, retail price, and financial projection, etc.?	
45. Are you able to validate the feedback and implement them onto your prototype or business modeling?	
SECTION 1-5 RATING	
Junction One AVERAGED Rating	
GO/STOP DECISION	

Traffic Junction 2 – Out In the Real World

Section 2-1 Marketing Strategy: 6Ps of Marketing meet the 5Ws

Your objective is to clearly communicate your product's value propositions to the target user group. The marketing work should be integrated to generate a comprehensive strategy on how to tackle the market including the product's proposition, positioning, placement, pricing, promotion, and packaging statements. The goal here is not to implement but to understand and ultimately be able to justify your value and pricing.

The types of activities you will do include competitive research, user profile research, distribution channel research, pricing research, and packaging research. Expect to do lots of online research, reading industry magazines and articles, join associations, go window shopping for the actual feel of competitive products and how they are presented, etc.

Reference:	**Chapter 5.2-5.5, 5.7**	
Topics and Questions		Rating

POSITIONING (5.2)

46.	What is the degree of relevance in the consumer's mind for your product or service, in terms of what they look for?	
47.	Can you specifically identify the primary and secondary values and benefits your idea brings to the target audience?	
48.	What is the level of familiarity your target market has towards your invention's function and usage. In other words, what is the effort required to become familiar with your invention?	
49.	How well does your positioning statement entice your target market to buy your product/service?	
50.	Do you have a branding strategy that is in alignment with your positioning strategy?	
51.	Does the concept have a name and a logo (identifiers) that are highly relevant and easy to recall by the target customers?	
52.	Are you able to easily differentiate your creation from those of the competition?	

PRICING (5.3)

53.	Do you have a pricing strategy that takes into consideration your product's intrinsic value, the perception your positioning statement creates, your cost, competitive price ranges, and your profit margin?	
54.	Will you be able to execute your pricing strategy in concert with the rest of your business activities such as marketing, finance, and operations support?	

PACKAGING (5.4)

55. Is your packaging strategy coherent with your positioning and pricing strategies?	
56. Does your package design effectively communicate the product's value propositions at a glance?	
57. Does your package entice the customers to interact with it so they can experience it before buying?	

PROMOTION (5.5)

58. What is the primary purpose of your promotion?	
59. What promotional channels will be most effective for this type of product or service?	
60. What are the promotional media and their associated costs?	
61. What is the marketing budget percentage relative to your revenue?	
62. How important is advertising in your promotional plan?	
63. Is your promotional strategy in synch with the other marketing components?	

PRODUCT LIFECYCLE MANAGEMENT (5.7.1)

64. Is the projected product lifecycle in alignment with the profit expectation? In other words, will the product generate enough investment payback during its life time to justify setting up a company?	
65. How will your marketing strategy change as the product progresses through its lifecycle?	
66. Are there foreseeable market forces such as shifting trends, regulatory, testing requirements, and substitution technology that might impact the rollout or acceptance of your product?	

GO-TO-MARKET STRATEGY (5.7.2)

67. Do you have a go-to-market strategy that covers the entire spectrum of marketing activities and coordinates with the business operations and financial activities?	
68. What will be the cost of marketing relative to your revenue? Does this product need a lot of promotion to the distribution channels?	
SECTION 2-1 RATING	

Section 2-2 Distribution & Sales: How does it get to the customers?

Your objective is to identify the industry structure and distribution network for your product. You need to acquire some understanding of who's who in the industry and how the industry operates, such as any specific windows of opportunity, cycles that insiders adhere to which if you miss could cost you an entire season or year.

The types of activities you will do is to identify where similar products are sold and by whom. You may need to contact potential distributors and resellers and see if they have any stated requirements for new vendors. You will also need to know the margin requirements of resellers and typical quantities that they wholesale.

Reference: **Chapter 5.6**

Topics and Questions	Rating
69. How well developed is your distribution strategy which identifies the distributors, manufacturer rep, and sales channels for your concept?	
70. What is the extent of your sales strategy which incorporates buyer motivation, buying process, and sales management technique?	
SECTION 2-2 RATING	
Junction Two AVERAGED Rating	
GO/STOP DECISION	

Traffic Junction 3 – Protecting Your Assets

Section 3-1 Intellectual Properties: Protecting your brainchild

Your objective is to be able to shop your intellectual creation beyond the trusted groups without fear of someone stealing your hard work.

The types of activities you will do include patent, trademark, and copyright research.

Reference: **Chapter 6.1.1**

Topics and Questions	Rating
71. Is your innovation truly unique to warrant applying for a patent?	
72. Can your trade name and other intellectual creations be trademarked or copyrighted?	
73. Have you determined whether it makes strategic sense, not just legal sense, to patent your innovation?	

74.	How effective are the legal claims on your patent application; how easily can someone bypass your legal protection?	
75.	Will your innovation infringe on someone else's protected work?	
76.	Do licensing arrangements exist for products similar to your concept?	
	SECTION 3-1 RATING	

Section 3-2 Legal and Insurance: Protecting you and your investment

Your objective is protection. Protect your company, your product, and especially yourself against frivolous lawsuits or legitimate damage claims.

The types of activities you will do include finding a business attorney who can draft business agreements for you. The business agreement may extend from confidential agreement to sales, licensing, incorporation, shareholder, and employment agreement. You will also need to research insurance agents and companies willing to issue insurance for your type of product. The amount of insurance will depend largely on your distribution channel's liability coverage requirement.

Reference:	**Chapter 6.1**

Topics and Questions	Rating
Legal Protection (6.1.2)	
77. Have you determined the appropriate type of business entity if you are to commercialize your concept?	
78. Are your personal assets protected in case of business related lawsuits?	
79. If you require legal documents are you able to obtain them at a reasonable cost?	
Liability and Insurance Protection (6.1.3)	
80. Does your concept design lead to potential bodily injury or property damage?	
81. What is the minimum amount of business liability insurance coverage required by your potential distribution channel?	
82. Will you be able to obtain business liability insurance for your type of product?	
83. Is the insurance premium justifiable from a profitability standpoint?	
SECTION 3-2 RATING	
Junction Three AVERAGED Rating	
GO/STOP DECISION	

Traffic Junction 4 – Looking Under the Hood

Section 4-1 Factories & Suppliers: Working with suppliers

Your objective is to find factories and suppliers who can cater to you at the minimum production quantity with the lowest cost and highest quality possible.

The types of activities you will do include online keyword search for manufacturers and suppliers. It may include talking to professional trade associations or go to tradeshows where such service providers solicit their business. You will need to assess samples they send for quality and price. You will also need to ensure cost control, delivery arrangement, and compliance testing. If doing business overseas, you will have the extra duties of understanding export control laws, custom inspection process, warehousing, freight schedules, etc.

Reference:	**Chapter 6.2.1**	
Topics and Questions		Rating
84. Do you have a clear idea on what capabilities are needed to commercialize your concept?		
85. Do you have the means to evaluate providers of such capabilities including how to acquire their services?		
86. Is there a plan on how to communicate and manage factories and suppliers?		
	SECTION 4-1 RATING	

Section 4-2 Vendors & Service Providers: Assembling the A-team

Your objective is to be able to handle every requirement and interaction at a professional level.

The types of activities you will do include identifying the types of talent you will need and what each person's responsibilities are. You will need to determine whether to hire permanent or temporary employees and how to compensate them. You will also need to find the expertise associated with employment law and benefits and tax reporting. You should research extensively on service providers and have a hiring strategy as business grows.

Reference:	**Chapter 6.2.2**	
Topics and Questions		Rating
87. How well can you identify the skill sets and experiences needed to manage the company behind your concept?		
88. How prepared are you to evaluate potential vendors and suppliers?		
89. Do you have the resources to hire and manage contractors and employees, including meeting employment law compliance?		
	SECTION 4-2 RATING	

Section 4-3 Business Systems: Operations and support systems

Your objective is to be able to conduct business activities professionally. The goal is to be able to handle and manage every process of your business operation from communications, order processing, customer interfacing, financial management, warehousing and inventory control, and any other frontend and backend operational systems your business needs.

The types of activities you will do include determining the type of office facility and space required. It also includes researching systems for telecommunications, data warehousing, web hosting, and eCommerce modules if you choose to sell direct.

Reference:	**Chapter 6.3.1**

Topics and Questions	Rating
90. Do you or a licensee have a business infrastructure strategy that incorporates customer-centric systems, processes, and methods and procedures?	
91. Will you or a licensee be able to identify and implement all the necessary infrastructures and systems based on their costs?	
SECTION 4-3 RATING	

Section 4-4 Business Processes: Methods and procedures

Your objective is to be able to walk away and yet the business continues to operate smoothly as designed. You need to understand and design how the business operates at every level and what processes and procedures are required. It includes establishing the necessary methods and procedures that allow all customer friendly interactions.

The types of activities you will do include tracing through each aspect of the business by functional areas. You need to visualize or simulate data and physical product movements and transactions. You will probably use a flowchart or similar to depict the steps involved in the transfer of goods from warehouse to consumer via several layers of middlemen. You need to understand the interfaces from each party's perspective. The interface design needs to include both frontend and backend systems including inventory control considerations.

Reference:	**Chapter 6.3.2**

Topics and Questions	Rating
92. Will a licensee's or your systems and processes align to the current company size and business scope while being scalable for potential growth scenarios?	
93. Is there a process map that captures the entire customer experience, including both frontend and backend processes and procedures?	
SECTION 4-4 RATING	
Junction Four AVERAGED Rating	
GO/STOP DECISION	

Traffic Junction 5 – Money Talks...

Section 5-1 Detailed Financial Assessment: Will it be profitable?

Your objective is to think critically about why this idea will or will not ever be profitable. If profitable, is it sufficient to meet your own financial goals?

The types of activities you will do at this point are at a rudimentary level from a financial analysis perspective. You want to do a high level assessment of the cost of goods, potential price ranges, and your profit margin. You need to build a financial spreadsheet to run different scenarios by manipulating cost, units, price, and required margin. You will determine how much financial investment you will need based on growth and cash flow scenarios. You might also consider how to identify potential investors who are most likely to fund your type of product.

Reference: **Chapter 7.1-7.9**

Topics and Questions	Rating
COST (7.1)	
94. Do you have sufficient data to identify the total cost per unit for your product or service?	
95. Are the cost elements for the product likely to remain stable or will they fluctuate/increase?	
REVENUE GENERATION (7.2)	
96. Can you determine the retail price range and the product's/service's revenue?	
97. If your product is seasonal, can the business be maintained year round?	
98. Does the product generate repeat sales or revenue from accessories?	
PROFITABILITY (7.3)	
99. Do you have enough information to do a profit analysis for your concept?	
100. Is your concept's projected profit margin in alignment with the industry's norm?	
101. At a very high level, will your concept have the potential to be profitable?	
FINANCIAL PROJECTIONS (7.4)	
102. Do you have enough information to run financial projections on three scenarios for your concept?	
103. Are your projection assumptions backed with solid research?	
104. Does your projection allow for unforeseen developments or significant changes in the data values?	
105. Do you know the typical expenses allocation scheme for your type of	

product based business?	

BREAKEVEN (7.5)

106. How many units do you have to sell to breakeven?	
107. When will you breakeven, and is the timeframe within the product's expected shelf life?	

CASH FLOW (7.6)

108. Are you able to perform a cash flow analysis with accurate revenue for a venture based on your concept?	
109. Is your type of product/service more susceptible to cash flow issues?	

CAPITAL REQUIREMENTS (7.7)

110. How much capital do you need to run the business until it becomes self-financing?	
111. How long is the payback period for the capital investment?	
112. What is the cost of capital for the project?	
113. What is the Net Present Value for the project?	
114. Is the venture worth doing from a quantitative perspective?	

FUNDING STRATEGY (7.8)

115. Have you determined the most appropriate types of funding for commercializing your concept?	
116. Can your concept attract the amount of investment money required to launch a business?	
117. Do you have a funding strategy (5Ws + H)?	
118. Will you have a business plan ready for funding purposes?	

LICENSING AND ROYALTY (7.9)

119. Is it worthwhile to pursue a venture or is royalty payment a more practical approach for you?	

IT'S ABOUT YOU (CHAPTER 10)

120. Are you ready to take on this challenge?	

SECTION 5 RATING	
Junction Five AVERAGED Rating	
GO/STOP DECISION	

THE CONCEPT'S GO/NO-GO DECISION	

Appendix 5. SnapIt! Sample Income Statements (1 of 3)

Income Statement

Period Ending	31-Dec-10	31-Dec-09	31-Dec-08
Total Revenue	**568,512**	**501,032**	**574,724**
Cost of Goods Sold	312,681	235,485	252,878
Gross Profit	**255,831**	**265,547**	**321,846**
GM	45%	53%	56%
Operating Expenses			
Research Development		925	
Selling General and Administrative	220,413	243,111	284,256
Non Recurring	11,566	3,422	8,527
Operating Income or Loss	**23,852**	**18,089**	**29,063**
Income from Continuing Operations	-1957	-728	
Total Other Income/Expenses Net	-184	-2,177	-226
Earnings Before Interest And Taxes	**21,711**	**15,184**	**28,837**
Interest Expense			2,846
Income Before Tax	21,711	15,184	25,991
Income Tax Expense	8,207	5,924	9,669
Net Income From Continuing Ops	13,504	9,260	16,322
Net Income	**13,504**	**9,260**	**16,322**

Appendix 5. SnapIt! Sample Cash Flow Statement (2 of 3)

Cash Flow Statement

Period Ending	31-Dec-10	31-Dec-09	31-Dec-08
Net Income	**13,504**	**9,260**	**16,322**
Operating Activities			
Depreciation	10,268	6,960	6,882
Adjustments To Net Income	5,596	3,319	2,384
Changes In Accounts Receivables	1,304	13,295	-5,103
Changes In Liabilities	3,336	-14,873	14,410
Changes In Inventories	2,532	10,854	-4,653
Changes In Other Operating Activities	-2,517	1,623	-3,807
Total Cash Flow From Operating Activities	**34,023**	**30,438**	**26,435**
Investing Activities			
Capital Expenditures	-9,776	-7,517	-9,176
Investments	-	-	-
Other Cash flows from Investing Activities	-63,736	-	124
Total Cash Flows From Investing Activities	**-73,512**	**-7,517**	**-9,052**
Financing Activities			
Dividends Paid	-3,513	-3,463	-2,596
Sale Purchase of Stock	521	709	381
Net Borrowings	51,500	-18,500	46,650
Other Cash Flows from Financing Activities	-	758	-56,847
Total Cash Flows From Financing Activities	**48,874**	**-20,496**	**-12,412**
Effect Of Exchange Rate Changes	-779	-302	415
Change In Cash and Cash Equivalents	**8,606**	**2,123**	**5,386**

Appendix 5. SnapIt! Sample Balance Sheet (3 of 3)

Balance Sheet

Period Ending	31-Dec-10	31-Dec-09	31-Dec-08
Assets			
Current Assets			
Cash and Cash Equivalents	25,257	16,651	14,528
Net Receivables	99,015	92,919	105,715
Inventory	53,192	39,618	50,782
Other Current Assets	9,779	6,772	7,300
Total Current Assets	187,243	155,960	178,325
Long Term Investments			
Property Plant and Equipment	66,874	54,475	54,612
Intangible Assets	88,731	39183	41134
Total Assets	**342,848**	**249,618**	**274,071**
Liabilities			
Current Liabilities			
Accounts Payable	101,836	81,524	94,719
Short/Current Long Term Debt	15,000	12,000	12,000
Total Current Liabilities	116,836	93,524	106,719
Long Term Debt	77,150	28,650	47,150
Other Liabilities	26,689	18,179	20,485
Total Liabilities	**220,675**	**140,353**	**174,354**
Owner's Equity			
Preferred Stock	213	212	210
Retained Earnings	121,960	109,053	99,507
Total Stockholder Equity	122,173	109,265	99,717
Total Liabilities and Owners Equity	**342,848**	**249,618**	**274,071**

Appendix 6. C2C Activities & Resources Mapping (1 of 4)

Phase: **FOUNDATIONAL DISCOVERY PHASE**

Activities:

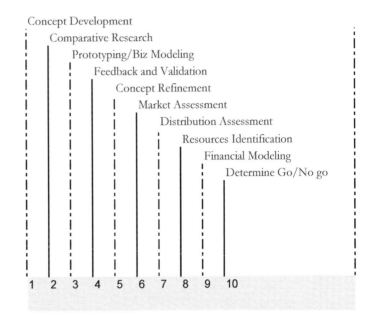

Concept Development
Comparative Research
Prototyping/Biz Modeling
Feedback and Validation
Concept Refinement
Market Assessment
Distribution Assessment
Resources Identification
Financial Modeling
Determine Go/No go

1   2   3   4   5   6   7   8   9   10

Players: **Where They Tend to (But Not Always) Provide Value:**

Inventor
Inventor Associations
Product Development Coaches
Concept Evaluation Service
Commercialization Consultants
Entrepreneur Associations
Product Commercialization Co.
Startup Web Portals
Business Directories
Educational Entities
Business Service Providers
Professional Managers
Venture Capitalists
Employees
Product Launch Companies
Books and Articles
Government Resources
Inventor turned Entrepreneur

Appendix 6. C2C Activities & Resources Mapping (2 of 4)

Phase: **PLANNING & STRATEGY PHASE**

Activities:

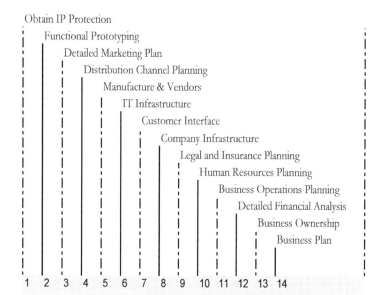

Obtain IP Protection
Functional Prototyping
Detailed Marketing Plan
Distribution Channel Planning
Manufacture & Vendors
IT Infrastructure
Customer Interface
Company Infrastructure
Legal and Insurance Planning
Human Resources Planning
Business Operations Planning
Detailed Financial Analysis
Business Ownership
Business Plan

1 2 3 4 5 6 7 8 9 10 11 12 13 14

Players:

Inventor
Inventor Associations
Product Development Coaches
Concept Evaluation Service
Commercialization Consultants
Entrepreneur Associations
Product Commercialization Co.
Startup Web Portals
Business Directories
Educational Entities
Business Service Providers
Professional Managers
Venture Capitalists
Employees
Product Launch Companies
Books and Articles
Government Resources
Inventor turned Entrepreneur

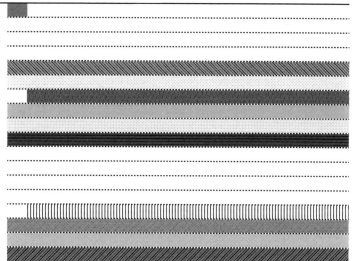

Appendix 6. C2C Activities & Resources Mapping (3 of 4)

Phase: **IMPLEMENTATION PHASE**

Activities:

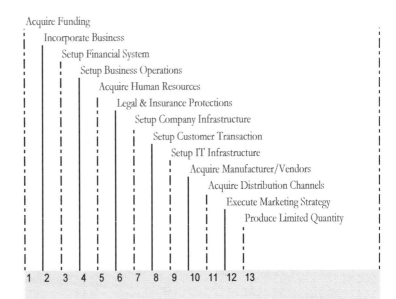

Players:

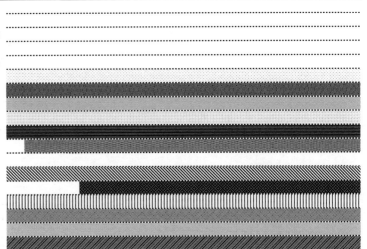

Inventor
Inventor Associations
Product Development Coaches
Concept Evaluation Service
Commercialization Consultants
Entrepreneur Associations
Product Commercialization Co.
Startup Web Portals
Business Directories
Educational Entities
Business Service Providers
Professional Managers
Venture Capitalists
Employees
Product Launch Companies
Books and Articles
Government Resources
Inventor turned Entrepreneur

Appendix 6. C2C Activities & Resources Mapping (4 of 4)

Phase: **LIFECYCLE MANAGEMENT PHASE**

Market Changes Analysis
Operations & Product Improvements
Market Expansion Activities
Financial Management
HR Resources Management
Growth/Exit Strategy

Activities:

1 2 3 4 5 6

Players:

Inventor
Inventor Associations
Product Development Coaches
Concept Evaluation Service
Commercialization Consultants
Entrepreneur Associations
Product Commercialization Co.
Startup Web Portals
Business Directories
Educational Entities
Business Service Providers
Professional Managers
Venture Capitalists
Employees
Product Launch Companies
Books and Articles
Government Resources
Inventor turned Entrepreneur

Entrepreneurial Resources

FEE-BASED

Books - The list of books below represent what I believe would be helpful to aspiring entrepreneurs. I have not read all of them but wanted to provide a sample reference list as a starting point for book readings. You should find them easily using online searches.

Mastering the VC Game by Jeffrey Bussgang

This is a very well written book that shares inside perspectives from several venture capitalists. It explains the dynamics between VCs and entrepreneurs seeking funding and also provides relevant advice on the strategy of approaching VCs including finding the right match.

Inbound Marketing by Brian Halligan and Dharmesh Shah

The art of promotion has dramatically changed with the advent of the internet technology and culture. This book explains the necessity to use inbound marketing techniques instead of the traditional outbound techniques. It contains many concrete and easy to follow implementation steps.

Mommy Millionaire: How I Turned My Kitchen Table Idea into a Million Dollars and How You Can, Too! By Kim Lavine

Beyond understanding the overall concept commercialization process, an aspiring entrepreneur can learn much from reading another's success story. Although, one must keep in mind that success duplication is not guaranteed. This book provides one such example for aspiring entrepreneurs who has developed a potential consumer product.

Business Service Vendors – This list contains dynamic web addresses which may or may not be current, depending on how frequently the contents are updated. Nevertheless, it gives a flavor of what type of service providers may be of value to aspiring entrepreneurs. **You should exercise the same amount of caution when dealing with any of the service providers listed here just as if you were to have found them on the web by yourself. This list is provided as a sampling to increase your awareness of available resources and is not an endorsement of any kind.**

Idea Crossing https://www.ideacrossing.org/

This is a portal where entrepreneurs, investors, and service providers list their services and find corresponding clients or service providers. It is one of several of its type.

I2 Innovation Institute http://www.wini2.com/

This company provides invention evaluation and product assessment for inventors and corporations alike. It has a well-developed concept evaluation process as the original WIN program which I have used and can recommend.

IPWatchdog.com http://ipwatchdog.com/

Founded by Gene Quinn, a well respected U.S. patent attorney in the inventor's circle. This site provides updated and relevant news and developments on the intellectual property front. For anyone interested in learning more about intellectual property protection this is a great site to start with.

NOLO http://www.nolo.com/

Another great place for legal issues and more for the aspiring entrepreneur who needs to quickly catch up on knowledge and information. This site provides legal forms and books for sale.

Inventnet.com http://www.inventnet.com/info.html

The Inventors Network is an online inventors' organization that provides free articles, sells inventor books, allows for patent searches, and has a reader forum.

Patent Buddy http://www.patentbuddy.com/

A business directory for online search of patent attorneys in your area.

OwnYourVenture http://www.ownyourventure.com/

This site provides a free equity simulator used to calculate owner shares.

Envision Sales & Marketing http://www.entrepreneursales.com/

An example of a marketing and sales company targeting entrepreneurs. Services include marketing research, strategy, branding, etc. as well as sales program and strategy development.

Office.net http://www.offices.net/

An online office rental service provider. It is also a good research site to determine your office requirements and associated costs.

Lambert & Lambert http://www.lambertinvent.com/home.php

An example of a firm that provides invention evaluation (for a fee), marketing, and licensing services.

Enventys http://www.enventys.com/

Provides services to inventors in industrial design, engineering, prototyping, web and interactive, branding and advertising, public relations and video production.

Productcoach.com http://www.productcoach.com/

Matthew Yubas is an established product coach/consultant for the aspiring entrepreneurs. You can find various free tips and articles on his site as well as books and kits, and consultations for a fee.

Jim DeBetta.com http://www.jimdebetta.com/

Jim DeBetta is also an established product coach and consultant. His website contains similarly useful information in the form of links, advice, blogs where entrepreneurs can pay for advice from other consultants.

Product Commercialization Companies – There are many ill-reputed companies involved in scamming inventors. This list below is very limited as it contains only well-known "good guys" within the inventor's communities. The list is not meant to be exclusive however it is highly advisable that anyone interested in soliciting the involvement of a product commercialization company thoroughly understand the terms and conditions of the business relationship before taking steps forward.

Edison Nation http://www.edisonnation.com/

This is the sister site for the TV series Everyday Edisons known for portraying inventors and entrepreneurs. It is one of the most reputable companies for inventors to work with.

EverGreen IP http://www.evergreenip.com/

The company evaluates products to commercialize. Their unique process invests their own capital in procuring an invention and takes compensation only when a licensing agreement has been reached.

BigIdeaGroup http://bigideagroup.net/inventors/index.htm

This company evaluates ideas and product for potential licensing deals. They serve as an agent for the inventor/entrepreneur and provide help in developing, designing, and presenting to target audiences.

FREE RESOURCES

Inventor Clubs and Associations (a sampling)

United Inventors Association http://www.uiausa.com/

Inventors Association of New England http://www.inventne.org/

Inventors Association of South Florida http://www.inventorssociety.net

Mom Invented® http://www.mominventors.com/

TV Shows

Innovation Nation http://www.innovationnation.tv/

Everyday Edisons http://www.everydayedisons.com/

Educational Institutions and Foundations

Stanford University Office of Technology Licensing
http://www.stanford.edu/group/OTL/inventors/inventors_process.html

MIT Technology Licensing Office http://web.mit.edu/tlo/www/

The Kauffman Foundation http://www.entrepreneurship.org/

The National Congress of Inventors Association
http://www.inventionconvention.com/ncio/index.html

Magazines and Articles

Inventors Digest http://www.inventorsdigest.com/

Entrepreneur Magazine http://www.entrepreneur.com/

Inc. Magazine http://www.inc.com/

Business Week http://bx.businessweek.com/entrepreneurship/

Other Online Resources

Small Business Television.com http://www.sbtv.com/

Google Patent Search http://www.google.com/patents

Business Owner's Toolkit http://www.toolkit.com/

Invention statistics www.inventionstatistics.com/index.html

National Venture Capital Association http://www.nvca.org/

Government and Small Business Associations

US Bureau of Labor statistics http://www.bls.gov/

SBA, Small Business Administration http://www.sba.gov/

USPTO http://www.uspto.gov/

US Internal Trade Commission
http://www.usitc.gov/tata/hts/bychapter/index.htm

US Census Bureau https://ask.census.gov/cgi-bin/askcensus.cfg/php/enduser/std_alp.php?p_sid=29bCmbjk

FedStats www.fedstats.gov/

Business.Gov http://www.business.gov/

SCORE http://www.score.org/index.html

Intellectual Property Resources

Federal Trade Commission (on Invention Promotion Firms and Scams)
http://www.ftc.gov/bcp/index.shtml

National Inventor Fraud Center http://www.inventorfraud.com/

Stopfakes.gov http://stopfakes.gov/

Inventors Assistance League, Inc. http://www.inventions.org/

Copyright Clearance Center http://www.copyright.com/

Index

About The Author

Dick J. Liou began his latest venture as an accidental inventor turned entrepreneur, although it might appear otherwise from his career track.

His professional experiences cover a wide range of business specialties including consulting, engineering, operations, strategic planning, marketing, sales, and particularly product management. To date he has launched two startup businesses from scratch and played a pivotal role in a startup team within a large corporation. His industry experiences include banking, telecommunications, information technology, and consumer products. His greatest asset remains the ability to integrate different aspects of business and life experiences into a coherent whole.

Intrinsically a high achiever, he earned his high tech MBA program from one of the nation's first two-year accelerated programs while working full time professionally. With his proven track records of noteworthy accomplishments, it is only logical, though in hindsight, that he's now well-qualified to bring this exceptionally insightful and practical approach to share with all who aspire to bring a better product or service to market and in the process achieve their personal dreams.

Made in the USA
Charleston, SC
05 December 2015